D0900145

Ernest W. Burgess

ON COMMUNITY, FAMILY,

AND DELINQUENCY

THE HERITAGE OF SOCIOLOGY
A Series Edited by Morris Janowitz

Ernest W. Burgess

ON COMMUNITY, FAMILY,

AND DELINQUENCY

Selected Writings

Edited by

LEONARD S. COTTRELL, JR.
ALBERT HUNTER
JAMES F. SHORT, JR.

THE UNIVERSITY OF CHICAGO PRESS

CHICAGO AND LONDON

THE UNIVERSITY OF CHICAGO PRESS, CHICAGO 60637
The University of Chicago Press, Ltd., London

© 1973 by The University of Chicago
All rights reserved. Published 1973
Printed in the United States of America
International Standard Book Number: 0–226–08057–9 (clothbound)
Library of Congress Catalog Card Number: 73–83572

Contents

PREFACE *by Morris Janowitz*   vii

I. COMMUNITY   1

INTRODUCTION *by Albert Hunter, with the assistance of Nancy Goldman*   3

1. Society, the Community, and the Group   16
2. The Growth of the City   23
3. Can Neighborhood Work Have a Scientific Basis?   37
4. Residential Segregation in American Cities   50

II. THE FAMILY   65

INTRODUCTION *by Leonard S. Cottrell, Jr.*   67

5. The Family as a Unity of Interacting Personalities   81
6. The Family and the Person   95
7. The Prediction of Adjustment in Marriage   107
8. Adjustment in Marriage   124
9. Family Living in the Later Decades   138
10. Economic, Cultural, and Social Factors in Family Breakdown   152

III. CRIME AND DELINQUENCY   165

INTRODUCTION *by James F. Short, Jr.*   167

11. The Delinquent as a Person   176
12. Factors Making for Success or Failure on Parole   201

65384

13.   Protecting the Public by Parole and by Parole
        Prediction   220
14.   Can Potential Delinquents be Identified
        Scientifically?   233
15.   Discussion of *The Jack-Roller*   244

IV. METHODOLOGY AND
SOCIAL VALUES   259

INTRODUCTION *by Morris Janowitz*   261
16.   The Social Survey: A Field for Constructive Service
        by Departments of Sociology   264
17.   Statistics and Case Studies as Methods of
        Sociological Research   273
18.   Social Planning and the Mores   288
19.   Values and Sociological Research   307

NOTES   315

BIOGRAPHICAL SKETCH *by Nancy Goldman*   325

BIBLIOGRAPHY   331

Preface

THE PUBLICATION of a volume on Ernest W. Burgess in the *Heritage of Sociology Series* is long overdue. Burgess was a sociologist of many interests and a human being of endless energy and diligence. Alternative plans had to be explored before this book could be launched and completed. Thus, I am pleased that Leonard Cottrell, Jr., Albert Hunter, and James F. Short, Jr., were able to devote the time and effort required to prepare this assessment of Ernest W. Burgess and his contributions.

Each of these three sociologists brings a different perspective and interest to bear on Burgess. They also represent a wide range of generational contact with him. Leonard Cottrell, Jr., who has focused on Burgess's work on courtship and the family, studied under him at the University of Chicago in the 1920s and worked closely with him through the period of the 1930s. James F. Short, Jr., concerned with the themes of crime and delinquency, entered the Department of Sociology after World War II. He had extensive contact with Burgess and with the cohorts of sociologists who had been trained earlier by Burgess. Hunter, a student of Burgess's work on urbanism and the community, had only fleeting contact with him just before his death. He came to be acquainted both with the intellectual and personal outlook of Burgess through his writings and contacts with teachers who had been taught by him. Hunter also had the opportunity to examine the extensive archival files which Burgess left behind and which have survived. All of these men have a sense of devotion and respect for the man, but they are scholars of strong detached and balanced judgment so that they have been able to present a critical overview of his contributions. In assembling the necessary documentation on his rich and varied professional life, they have been assisted by Nancy Goldman, Research Associate, Center for Social Organization Studies, University of Chicago.

As a graduate student at the University of Chicago from 1946 to 1948, I had limited contact with Ernest Burgess, but I strongly felt his presence. These were the years after World War II, which produced an influx of strong-minded and outstanding graduate students—both men and women—who were to become outstanding sociologists and were to leave their mark on the discipline. Their presence and their personal outlook helped fasten me to a teaching career in sociology.

The atmosphere at the university was exciting, self critical and probing. The faculty, although extremely busy, still had its main skill in conveying long standing traditions toward the sociological endeavor. A strong sense of social distance existed between instructor and student, as an essential element in the tutorial system of instruction. But in the division of labor among the faculty, Burgess spoke for the students and reached out to make and maintain contact with them. We are all aware and appreciate the role he played, both organizationally and intellectually.

It was refreshing to be exposed in his seminar to a critical but sympathetic evaluation of Freud from a sociological standpoint, in contrast to the fanatical and fierce opposition to psychoanalysis which pervaded many quarters in the department. As all three contributors to this collective volume underline, while Burgess had little taste for excessively complicated and formalistic theoretical formulations, he understood the power of effective theory on empirical research. His lectures and writings on the family, for example, represented him as a "functionalist" even though he would hardly use the term to describe himself. While the theorists spoke of the "breakdown" of the family system, he penetrated more deeply into its systematic transformation. He also resisted the naïve logical positivism and operationalism which still haunted sociology. He presented the image of a man of broad interests but who avoided the excesses of eclectic formulations. He attacked important problems and had real ability to pose sociological research problems in sharp and penetrating terms. I deeply appreciated him personally since his daily life demonstrated that a sociologist could be an active and resourceful, public-spirited citizen while vigorously pursuing effective teaching and sound research.

Morris Janowitz

I. Community

Introduction

BY ALBERT HUNTER
WITH THE ASSISTANCE OF NANCY GOLDMAN

ERNEST W. BURGESS's research interests were wide and varied, but his concern with the urban community—the metropolis, the local residential community, and the neighborhood—was a major and persistent theme. First, for Burgess the urban community was an object of analysis in and of itself. The community—and in particular the local community—was a laboratory for the study of social change. His theoretical approach began from an ecological perspective; the local community as a natural area. The notion of territoriality which he used was rooted in physical contours and barriers, transportation systems and the impact of economic variables. But the local community, like any other social phenomenon, requires analysis in terms of the interplay of the ecological, the social, and the cultural dimensions.

Because he was influenced by W. I. Thomas and Robert E. Park, Burgess did not see the community as a residual category, a social network which would be eliminated with the growth of industrialization and urbanization. In 1925, while deeply involved in research in urban sociology, he wrote: "There are those who are convinced that the function of the neighborhood center is passing with the decay of the neighborhood in the city. For myself, I am not so certain. Surely the work of the neighborhood center must now be conceived and planned in terms of its relationship to the entire life of the city" (*The City*, p. 154). One half-century later, the sociological debate still continues in precisely similar terms. Burgess's formulations in the 1920s were at variance with those of his close personal colleague Louis Wirth, another member

3

of the Chicago School of Sociology. Wirth, in "Urbanism as a Way of Life" (*American Journal of Sociology* 44 [1938]:1–24) emphasized the overriding emergence of impersonality, the decline of the neighborhood, and the rise of bureaucratic forms in the modern metropolis.

Burgess was extensively engaged in writing and research on urban sociology from the time of his entrance into graduate school, until the publication in 1933, with Charles Newcomb, of the second volume on *Census Data of the City of Chicago*, which was based on the 1930 census. His interest had already begun to broaden to include the study of family, personality, and crime and delinquency. But during the remainder of his research career, his second approach to the community was ever present, namely, his use of the urban community as the context for the analysis of the particular social problems of his interest. Nor did he conceptualize or design research without reference to the community context. Likewise, he saw the problems of social control and social policy in terms of the surrounding urban environment.

When Burgess arrived on the campus of the University of Chicago in 1908, urban sociology had already been organized. In fact, the empirical study of the local community was launched with the very founding of the Department of Sociology in 1892. Thus, Charles Worthen Spencer, a graduate student, wrote in the *University of Chicago Weekly*, 18 February 1893, that Chicago was an excellent laboratory for the study of the city because it lacked "natural obstacles" to territorial expansion, and that the study of Chicago could "throw light on one of the great problems of American civilization—the assimilation of foreign elements."

The intellectual ingredients of urban sociology were varied. The Department of Sociology at the University of Chicago drew on the social survey which had been undertaken by cities both in Western Europe and the United States; on the perspectives of Herbert Spencer on conflict and social order; and on the strong interest in the study of the city and its social problems as a basis for scientific social reform. But it was the impact of W. I. Thomas first and of Robert E. Park later that produced a framework and an intellectual legitimacy for the analysis of the city. Clearly the writings of Georg Simmel and Max Weber on the city were indispensable elements in the intellectual ferment that developed.

In the Department of Sociology Charles R. Henderson gave the first course on urban sociology under the elegant and descriptive title "Modern Cities and Cooperation of their Beneficent Forces." In the Chicago school there was no question but that scientific knowledge had social improvements as its objective. In 1900, Henderson changed the course title to "Modern Communities"—a label which in one variant or another has persisted in the offerings of the University of Chicago. Since he taught the course regularly until 1914–15, Burgess had the opportunity to attend it as a graduate student. Henderson was active in the settlement house movement and the then current issues of welfare reform, but he approached sociology in the grand manner, concerned both with theoretical formulations and with training students in research and fieldwork.

In addition to Henderson's efforts, Charles Zueblin, a figure who has commanded little attention, organized a course during this early period entitled "Municipal Sociology." It focused on population movements and ecological dimensions and involved students in preparing statistical and map materials about the city of Chicago and its changing character. By 1910 the U.S. Bureau of the Census was taking its first steps toward small-unit reporting and thereby supplied urban sociologists with essential raw materials.

When Burgess returned to the campus as assistant professor in 1916, he took over Henderson's course on the human communities and included some of the materials covered by Charles Zueblin. Burgess had completed his doctoral dissertation on a social-psychological topic, "The Function of Socialization in Social Evolution," which bore the impact of aspects of W. I. Thomas's thinking. In his years away from Chicago, however, Burgess had been involved in "the social survey movement," and while at Kansas he had participated in community surveys of Lawrence, Belleville, and Topeka. At Chicago he saw his intellectual task as fusing the ecological perspective of the city with his interest in the normative aspects of social structure. Likewise, he defined his role as that of imposing a theoretical perspective on the energetic empirical efforts of students in the department who were engaged in studying Chicago.

Burgess worked closely with Robert Park. He wrote the section in the *Introduction to the Science of Sociology* (1921) entitled "Society, the Community and the Group" (this volume, chap. 1), which in effect sets forth the elements of his ecological-normative approach. In retrospect, this formulation appears primitive and diffuse in comparison with the writings which appeared only a few years later in 1925. The years 1920 to 1925 were those of the real advances in this field. The focus was initially on the territorial basis of the community, and on the mechanisms by which the ecological and normative order were engaged in mutual influence.

The excitement of life in Chicago in the period after World War I, as well as the intellectual currents in the Department of Sociology, were reflected in *The City*, published in 1925. This volume contained Robert E. Park's powerful essay "The City: Suggestions for the Investigation of Human Behavior in the Urban Environment." It also included Burgess's "The Growth of the City" (this volume, chap. 2). Presenting his zonal hypothesis, the essay was his most ambitious effort at generalization. By means of an "ideal type" model, Burgess sought to identify the regularities in urban growth in a period of unplanned urban expansion in the United States. His essay commanded extensive attention, both positive and negative.

Burgess saw the growth of the city as a product of both centripetal and centrifugal forces. The general process of urbanization, the centripetal flow of population and institutions, resulted from the magnetic ecological, economic, and administrative attractions of major urban centers such as Chicago. As competition and demand for location at a city's core increased, the centrifugal expansion would begin from the center and progress successively through the five concentric zones to the eventual expansion of the city's suburbs into rural areas at the fringe. The model was a synthesis of the many empirical efforts of Burgess and his students—the spot maps, the compilation of census data, the "natural histories" of local communities—and of the dominant theoretical forces of competition and symbiosis earlier advanced by Park and Burgess.

Criticisms of the specificity of the model to Chicago led to the development of alternative models, which attempted to interrelate spatial and functional utilization of the city. These are exemplified by Homer Hoyt's "sector" theory, the "multiple nuclei" theory of Harris and Ullman, and more recent syntheses of all three. The most extensive critique of the model, and of the Chicago School of human ecology generally, came in Milla Alihan's *Social Ecology: A Critical Analysis* (New York: Columbia University Press, 1938). The response of Burgess to many of his critics was to emphasize that his model was but an "ideal type." "If radial extension were the only factor affecting the growth of American cities, every city in this country would exhibit a perfect exemplification of these five urban zones. But since other factors affect urban development as situation, site, natural and artificial barriers, survival of an earlier use of a district, prevailing city plan, and its system of local transportation, many distortions and modifications of this pattern are actually found." ("Residential Segregation in American Cities," this volume, chap. 4). More than a quarter of a century after its first formulation, Burgess was still adapting his zonal model in the light of new observations and changing forces. In the Introduction to *Contributions to Urban Sociology* (University of Chicago Press, 1964), which he edited with Donald Bogue, he wrote: "We are now witnessing a new zonal phenomenon, as urban renewal begins at the core and gradually encroaches on slums as they develop in an ever widening arc." (p. 11).

In spite of its limitations the concentric zone model has continued to be the basis of two distinct approaches in urban sociology and human ecology. The first is a concern with urban "distance gradients" and the relation between social and physical space, whether in the form of the sociologist's occupational status, the economist's land values, the political scientist's election returns, or the geographer's transportation curves. The second approach is a continuing concern with the dynamics of community change, or "natural histories," as the processes of invasion, competition, and succession sweep outward across the urban landscape.

Also in *The City* was Burgess's essay "Can Neighborhood Work Have a Scientific Basis?" (this volume, chap. 3). This essay reflected Burgess's experiences with governmental agencies and private groups which were seeking more and more explicitly to fashion and refashion the urban environment. He was one of the early observers of the administrative and political fragmentation of the urban metropolis, with its resulting negative consequences on social control and social change. His strong preoccupation with "natural areas" led him to pose the question whether a more effective and more rational basis for communal life could not be constructed. Political, administrative and voluntary agencies should have boundaries which would take into account the structure of the real community and its neighborhood boundaries. There should be a convergence in the boundaries of the various social and cultural institutions in order to enhance their vitality. Burgess posed the question: "How far are the deficiencies in political action through our governmental bodies and in welfare action through our social agencies the result of the failure to base administrative districts upon ecological or cultural communities?" (p. 42).

The need for research as a basis for neighborhood work—community development as it has come to be called—was to enable the processes of social control to work more effectively. However, Burgess did not view the construction and reconstruction of communal life as merely a matter of formal authority and bureaucratic structures: "Especially are studies desired of the actual effect and role of intimate contacts in personal development and social control" (p. 49), he stressed.

For this objective his two alternative and theoretically related conceptions of the local community were relevant. "First of all, there is the community viewed almost exclusively in terms of location and movement"—the ecological perspective. "How far has the area itself, by its very topography and by all its other external and physical characteristics, such as railroads, parks, types of housing, conditioned community formation and exerted a determining influence upon the distribution of its inhabitants and upon their movements and life?" (p. 39). "In the second place, the community may be conceived in terms of the effects of communal life in a given area upon the formation or the maintenance of a local culture. Local culture includes those sentiments, forms of conduct, attachments, and ceremonies which are characteristic of a locality, which have either originated in the area or have become identified with it. This aspect of local life may be called the 'cultural community' " (p. 40).

Burgess underlined that the relation between cultural patterns and territorial areas had not yet been adequately studied. Such study was required for the sociology of the city and as a basis of more rational social change. The immediate task for the sociologists was to write the natural history of the local communities of the metropolis, to identify their boundaries, and to analyze the underlying social processes.

Burgess labored industriously to fashion a research effort, a collective enterprise to undertake the required historical and sociological study of the metropolis in terms of its local communities. In March 1923, the social science faculties of the University of Chicago founded the Local Community Research Committee—an interdisciplinary group to make use of the "local community of Chicago as a case for study." The funds were based on a grant of $25,000 from the Laura Spelman Rockefeller grant to be matched by local contributions. These resources made possible an undertaking of extensive scope by the standards of that day. From 1924 to 1934, Burgess, together with Vivien Palmer and a group of assistants and graduate students, created social base maps and statistical analyses of the natural areas of the city of Chicago. Initially they identified eighty areas which they called community areas; later they reduced the number to seventy-five. The strategy of research was to interview local citizens and to examine newspapers and archives on the historical and contemporary organization of the community in order to prepare local community histories. Twenty-one of these social histories have survived in the absence of an effective department archive and are housed in the Chicago Historical Society. They constitute an extraordinary documentation of the development of local urban institutions in the United States. Special emphasis was placed on the residents' social definitions of the local community, how they designated its name and its boundaries.

Burgess and Palmer related their social histories and social definitions of the local residents to the physical boundaries and barriers they observed in the city of Chicago. The seventy-five community areas they identified were primarily delimited in ecological terms, and amplified by the normative definitions they encountered.

Their research thrust led to the development and periodic publication of the *Local Community Fact Book* covering periods between 1920 and 1960. The first precursor to the *Local Community Fact Book* was the volume, *Census Data of the City of Chicago, 1920* (University of Chicago Press, 1931), edited by Burgess and Charles Newcomb.[1] This volume presented data from the 1920 census compiled by census tracts which were delimited largely from the research efforts of Burgess and his students. The seventy-five community areas made their first appearance as a larger grid for aggregating census tract data in Burgess and Newcomb's subsequent volume, *Census Data of the City of Chicago, 1930* (ibid., 1933). During the thirties a number of volumes appeared based upon statistics from the special 1934 census of Chicago. This census was initiated in large measure by Burgess and carried out as a project of the Civil Works Administration. These volumes included *Census Data of the City of Chicago, 1934* (edited by Charles Newcomb and Richard O. Lang, ibid., 1934), the *District Fact Book* (edited by Edward L. Burchard and Martin J. Arvin, Chicago Board of Education, Chicago Recreation Commission, and Illinois Emergency Relief Commission, 1935), and the first *Local Community Fact Book* (edited by Louis Wirth and Margaret Furez, Chicago Recreation Commission, 1938).

The second *Local Community Fact Book of Chicago, 1940*, based on the 1940 census, was not published until 1949. It was edited by Louis Wirth and Eleanor H. Bernert under the auspices of the Chicago Community Inventory. The CCI, started by Burgess and Wirth in 1946, became the heir of the older urban studies program at the university. Also published under the auspices of the CCI were the *Local Community Fact Book for Chicago, 1950* (edited by Philip M. Hauser and Evelyn M. Kitagawa) and the *Local Community Fact Book, Chicago Metropolitan Area, 1960* (edited by Evelyn M. Kitagawa and Karl E. Taeuber)—the latter being the first to include detailed data for the entire Chicago-North-western Indiana Standard Consolidated Area.

Burgess was pleased that he could organize local citizens' advisory groups to take an interest in, to assist, and to help finance the research. He believed that the boundaries defined by the research reflected social reality. At the same time, he worked closely with the Bureau of the Census to improve its reporting. In time the local communities and the agencies of the wider metropolis came to accept these boundaries as having an element of validity and of usefulness. From time to time, social welfare agencies as well as other public and private agencies attempted to organize their activities in terms of these boundaries. After World War II, a plan to organize election wards on the basis of community areas was developed, but not implemented. The definitions were used in de-limiting various federal programs and in a variety of social plan-ning efforts. Perhaps more effective than as a basis for administra-tion, the names of the community areas entered into the symbolic life of Chicago; the mass media, the local community press, and local community organizations made use of them, and in turn they came to have a meaning for the local residents.

Under the stimulus of the Park-Burgess intellectual leadership, generation after generation of undergraduate and graduate stu-dents were used as unpaid research workers. They were required to write extensive biographies and autobiographies and to help Burgess collect basic documentation. They carried out research on particular census tracts, prepared spot maps incorporating various ecological measures and social indicators from crime and de-linquency to ethnic concentrations. A vast mass of materials was assembled, and important segments are still housed in the Univer-sity of Chicago library and serve as a basic source. The extensive content of the education of these students is in part reflected in the outline of the course in field studies which Ernest Burgess began teaching jointly with Robert Park in 1918. Upon Park's retirement in 1933 the course continued to be taught jointly by Burgess and Louis Wirth.

The most promising students were encouraged to pursue doc-toral work and to prepare their theses for publication as monographs of the University of Chicago Press. The resulting volumes, generally the outcome of years of individual scholarship and research, were distinctive for their literary style, and they served to bridge the interests and aspirations of sociologists with those of the literary figures of the Chicago scene of the 1920s and 1930s. Some of the more widely known books in this series include Nels Anderson's *The Hobo* (1923); Ernest R. Mowrer's *Family Disorganization* (1927); Frederic M. Thrasher's *The Gang* (1927); Ruth S. Cavan's *Suicide* (1928); Louis Wirth's *The Ghetto* (1928); Harvey W. Zorbaugh's *The Gold Coast and the Slum* (1929); Clifford R. Shaw's *The Jack-Roller* (1930); E. Franklin Frazier's *The Negro Family in Chicago* (1932); Walter C. Reckless's *Vice in Chicago* (1933); Edwin H. Sutherland's *The Professional Thief* (1937); and Robert E. L. Faris and H. Warren Dunham's *Mental Disorders in Urban Areas* (1939).

In addition to sharing Park's emphasis on field methods, Burgess was directly concerned with the analysis of census data and developments in quantitative methods. He became interested in the quantitative and statistical basis of human ecology and urban sociology. His article "Residential Segregation in American Cities" (this volume, chap. 4), helped launch the analysis of patterns and measure of residential segregation, especially of blacks. This type of analysis was taken up subsequently by Otis Dudley Duncan and his disciples; by Ruth S. Cavan in her work on the ecological correlates of suicide; and, even more powerfully, by Robert E. L. Faris and H. Warren Dunham, in their work on mental illness. While in these ecological analyses important questions of causal relations were left unanswered, they established a prototype of research of importance not only to sociology but to related disciplines as well. The continuing interplay of field methods and quantitative methods which characterized Burgess's career is demonstrated in a discussion he had with Nels Anderson:

I recall Nels Anderson telling me he was greatly bored by his landlady, in the roominghouse district where he was studying the homeless man, telling him her life history. I told him, "Why, this is valuable, you must get it down on paper." . . . Out of this one document you get more insight into how life moves in the roominghouse area, and especially from the standpoint of the roominghouse keeper, than you do from a mountain of statistics that might be gathered. So what we get from the life history, of course, also enables us to pose more questions to the statistician, to get to the other answers. [*Contributions to Urban Sociology*, p. 9.]

In the mid-1930s, Burgess shifted his interest from the analysis of the urban community to specific social problems. Even as his efforts and his students' efforts in the field of delinquency research and the social control of crime increased, his interest in the community setting persisted. Burgess was a key figure in the Chicago Area Project, a comprehensive experimental program in delinquency control which involved extensive local participation and an effort at restructuring of community organization. In essence, this project was a forerunner of the community action programs and community self-development work of the 1960s.

When Robert E. Park retired, his influence weakened, and among the faculty there was no one to modernize the tradition and supply the necessary leadership. Institutional and department factors alone do not explain the temporary decline in research interest on urban communities. Intellectually, Louis Wirth's formulations in "Urbanism as a Way of Life," rather than the outlook of Park and Burgess, came to represent the immediate residues of the Chicago pioneer work in community and urban sociology. With the emergence of a highly urbanized society, the rubric "urban sociology" and, more recently "urban problems" became misleading, as they designate much more than the communal aspect of social organization.

In the immediate post–World War II period, new forms of theorizing diverted concern with the local community, and new methodologies, especially the sample survey, were only slowly adapted to the needs and requirements of community research. By the mid-1960s urban sociology and research on community organization had once more moved into the center of the sociological stage. The political imperatives of the inner city black and ethnic group and the social strains of the suburban communities forced a refocusing of interest. But it is essential to point out that, since the end of the war, despite the changing focus, the lines of development laid out by Park and Burgess have continued to be followed with profit. Community studies based on participant observation have been limited in number and often without strong theoretical rigor. But work of high quality has been and continues to be written, reflecting the institutionalization of this genre of research. More important have been the empirically based efforts to give greater theoretical precision and clarity to the local community as an object of analysis. One line of research work has clearly built on, but strived for reformulation of, the Park-Burgess ecological-normative tradition.

William Foote Whyte's *Street Corner Society* (University of Chicago Press, 1943) highlighted the social organization that exists in what many considered the disorganized slums. Walter Firey's *Land Use in Central Boston* (Harvard University Press, 1947), corrected an overemphasis upon "natural" ecological forces by pointing to the significance of symbols in urban land usage. In the fifties, Morris Janowitz offered a new orientation— the community of limited liability—in his study *The Community Press in an Urban Setting* (University of Chicago Press, 1952). This theory, drawing on the formulations of Thomas, Park, and Burgess, and focusing upon the voluntaristic element in communal attachments, was further expanded in Scott Greer's *The Emerging City* (Free Press, 1962). More recently the work of Gerald Suttles, in *The Social Order of the Slum* (University of Chicago Press, 1968) and *The Social Construction of Communities* (ibid., 1972) is an effort to redefine and elaborate the climate of community life in both territorial and social terms. And still another generation of researchers is exploring the themes and updating the traditions of the Chicago School: Richard Albares in a study of Germans in Chicago, William Kornblum in a study of the significance of neighborhood and ethnicity in the politics of local unions in South Chicago, and Albert Hunter in a study of change in the Burgess natural areas and emerging forms of ecological, social, and symbolic local communities.

Everett C. Hughes said of Ernest Burgess in a memorial address that he was the first "young" sociologist. Having received his degree in sociology at the age of twenty-seven in 1916, and retiring in 1957 from the same institution where he began, Ernest Burgess in his working career spanned the major part of the era of development in American sociology. Throughout his life he was continuously adding new research interests and strategies while seldom slighting those that preceded. As a result, much of his work assumes an eclectic nature reflecting the growth of the discipline, and in a benign sense it is devoid of theoretical dogma and empirical partisanship. His early concern with urban sociology led to his subsequent concern with the family, crime, and aging; his early emphasis upon field methods led to his later acquisition of statistical reasoning; and the application of sociological knowledge to social policy was a continuing interest.

There is no danger that the years ahead will see a neglect of the ideas of Burgess about the local community and the urban neighborhood. Within sociology "the future" of "the new community" appears bright. The danger rests rather in a distortion and exaggeration of the properties and the character of the emerging forms of constructed communities, and it would be good for at least some to pursue the eclectic yet vigorous theoretical and empirical approach of Burgess.

1

SOCIETY, THE COMMUNITY, AND THE GROUP

HUMAN NATURE and the person are products of society. This is the sum and substance of the readings in the preceding chapter. But what, then, is society—this web in which the lives of individuals are so inextricably interwoven, and which seems at the same time so external and in a sense alien to them? From the point of view of common sense, "society" is sometimes conceived as the sum total of social institutions. The family, the church, industry, the state, all taken together, constitute society. In this use of the word, society is identified with social structure, something more or less external to individuals.

In accordance with another customary use of the term, "society" denotes a collection of persons. This is a vaguer notion but it at least identifies society with individuals instead of setting it apart from them. But this definition is manifestly superficial. Society is not a collection of persons in the sense that a brick pile is a collection of bricks. However we may conceive the relation of the parts of society to the whole, society is not a mere physical aggregation and not a mere mathematical or statistical unit.

Various explanations that strike deeper than surface observation have been proposed as solutions for this cardinal problem of the social one and the social many; of the relation of society to the individual. Society has been described as a tool, an instrument, as it were, an extension of the individual organism. The argument

Reprinted from Ernest W. Burgess and Robert E. Park, *Introduction to the Science of Sociology* (Chicago: University of Chicago Press, 1921), pp. 161–67.

runs something like this: The human hand, though indeed a part of the physical organism, may be regarded as an instrument of the body as a whole. If as by accident it be lost, it is conceivable that a mechanical hand might be substituted for it, which, though not a part of the body, would function for all practical purposes as a hand of flesh and blood. A hoe may be regarded as a highly specialized hand, so also logically, if less figuratively, a plow. So the hand of another person if it does your bidding may be regarded as your instrument, your hand. Language is witness to the fact that employers speak of "the hands" which they "work." Social institutions may likewise be thought of as tools of individuals for accomplishing their purposes. Logically, therefore, society, either as a sum of institutions or as a collection of persons, may be conceived of as a sum total of instrumentalities, extensions of the functions of the human organism which enable individuals to carry on life-activities. From this standpoint society is an immense co-operative concern of mutual services.

This latter is an aspect of society which economists have sought to isolate and study. From this point of view the relations of individuals are conceived as purely external to one another, like that of the plants in a plant community. Co-operation, so far as it exists, is competitive and "free."

In contrast with the view of society which regards social institutions and the community itself as the mere instruments and tools of the individuals who compose it, is that which conceives society as resting upon biological adaptations, that is to say upon instincts, gregariousness, for example, imitation, or like-mindedness. The classic examples of societies based on instinct are the social insects, the well-known bee and the celebrated ant. In human society the family, with its characteristic differences and interdependences of the sexes and the age groups, husband and wife, children and parents, most nearly realizes this description of society. In so far as the organization of society is predetermined by inherited or constitutional differences, as is the case pre-eminently in the so-called animal societies, competition ceases and the relations of its component individuals become, so to speak, internal, and a permanent part of the structure of the group.

The social organization of human beings, on the other hand, the various types of social groups, and the changes which take place in them at different times under varying circumstances, are determined not merely by instincts and by competition but by custom, tradition, public opinion, and contract. In animal societies as herds, flocks, and packs, collective behavior seems obviously to be explained in terms of instinct and emotion. In the case of man, however, instincts are changed into habits; emotions, into sentiments. Furthermore, all these forms of behavior tend to become conventionalized and thus become relatively independent of individuals and of instincts. The behavior of the person is thus eventually controlled by the formal standards which, implicit in the mores, are explicit in the laws. Society now may be defined as the social heritage of *habit and sentiment, folkways and mores, technique and culture,* all of which are incident or necessary to collective human behavior.

Human society, then, unlike animal society, is mainly a social heritage, created in and transmitted by communication. The continuity and life of a society depend upon its success in transmitting from one generation to the next its folkways, mores, technique, and ideals. From the standpoint of collective behavior these cultural traits may all be reduced to the one term "consensus." Society viewed abstractly is an organization of individuals; considered concretely it is a complex of organized habits, sentiments, and social attitudes—in short, consensus.

The terms society, community, and social group are now used by students with a certain difference of emphasis but with very little difference in meaning. Society is the more abstract and inclusive term, and society is made up of social groups, each possessing its own specific type of organization but having at the same time all the general characteristics of society in the abstract. Community is the term which is applied to societies and social groups where they are considered from the point of view of the geographical distribution of the individuals and institutions of which they are composed. It follows that every community is a society, but not every society is a community. An individual may belong to many social groups but he will not ordinarily belong to more than one community, except in so far as a smaller community of which he is a member is included in a larger of which he is also a member. However, an individual is not, at least from a sociological point of view, a member of a community because he lives in it but rather because, and to the extent that, he participates in the common life of the community.

The term social group has come into use with the attempts of students to classify societies. Societies may be classified with reference to the rôle which they play in the organization and life of larger social groups or societies. The internal organization of any given social group will be determined by its external relation to other groups in the society of which it is a part as well as by the relations of individuals within the group to one another. A boys' gang, a girls' clique, a college class, or a neighborhood conforms to this definition quite as much as a labor union, a business enterprise, a political party, or a nation. One advantage of the term "group" lies in the fact that it may be applied to the smallest as well as to the largest forms of human association.

Classification of the Materials

Society, in the most inclusive sense of that term, the Great Society, as Graham Wallas described it, turns out upon analysis to be a constellation of other smaller societies, that is to say races, peoples, parties, factions, cliques, clubs, etc. The community, the world-community, on the other hand, which is merely the Great Society viewed from the standpoint of the territorial distribution of its members, presents a different series of social groupings and the Great Society in this aspect exhibits a totally different pattern. From the point of view of the territorial distribution of the individuals that constitute it, the world-community is composed of nations, colonies, spheres of influence, cities, towns, local communities, neighborhoods, and families.

These represent in a rough way the subject-matter of sociological science. Their organization, interrelation, constituent elements, and the characteristic changes (social processes) which take place in them are the phenomena of sociological science.

Human beings as we meet them are mobile entities, variously distributed through geographical space. What is the nature of the connection between individuals which permits them at the same time to preserve their distances and act corporately and consentiently—with a common purpose, in short? These distances which separate individuals are not merely spatial, they are psychical. Society exists where these distances have been *relatively* overcome. Society exists, in short, not merely where there are people but where there is communication.

The materials in this chapter are intended to show (1) the fundamental character of the relations which have been established between individuals through communication; (2) the gradual evolution of these relations in animal and human societies. On the basis of the principle thus established it is possible to work out a rational classification of social groups.

Espinas defines society in terms of corporate action. Wherever separate individuals act together as a unit, where they co-operate as though they were parts of the same organism, there he finds society. Society from this standpoint is not confined to members of one species, but may be composed of different members of species where there is permanent joint activity. In the study of symbiosis among animals, it is significant to note the presence of structural adaptations in one or both species. In the taming and domestication of animals by man the effects of symbiosis are manifest. Domestication, by the selection in breeding of traits desired by man, changes the original nature of the animal. Taming is achieved by control of habits in transferring to man the filial and gregarious responses of the young naturally given to its parents and members of its kind. Man may be thought of as domesticated through natural social selection. Eugenics is a conscious program of further domestication by the elimination of defective physical and mental racial traits and by the improvement of the racial stock through the social selection of superior traits. Taming has always been a function of human society, but it is dignified by such denominations as "education," "social control," "punishment," and "reformation."

The plant community offers the simplest and least qualified

example of the community. Plant life, in fact, offers an illustration of a *community* which is *not a society*. It is not a society because it is an organization of individuals whose relations, if not wholly external, are, at any rate, "unsocial" in so far as there is no consensus. The plant community is interesting, moreover, because it exhibits in the barest abstraction, the character of *competitive co-operation*, the aspect of social life which constitutes part of the special subject-matter of economic science.

This struggle for existence, in some form or other, is in fact essential to the existence of society. Competition, segregation, and accommodation serve to maintain the social distances, to fix the status, and preserve the independence of the individual in the social relation. A society in which all distances, physical as well as psychical, had been abolished, in which there was neither taboo, prejudice, nor reserve of any sort; a society in which the intimacies were absolute, would be a society in which there were neither persons nor freedom. The processes of competition and accommodation brought out in the description of the plant community are quite comparable with the same processes in animal and human communities. A village, town, city, or nation may be studied from the standpoint of the adaptation, struggle for existence, and survival of its individual members in the environment created by the community as a whole.

Society, as Dewey points out, if based on instinct is an effect of communication. *Consensus* even more than *co-operation* or *corporate* action is the distinctive mark of human society. Dewey, however, seems to restrict the use of consensus to group decisions in which all the members consciously and rationally participate. Tradition and sentiment are, however, forms of consensus quite as much as constitutions, rules, and elections.

Le Bon's classification of social groups into heterogeneous and homogeneous crowds, while interesting and suggestive, is clearly inadequate. Many groups familiar to all of us, as the family, the play-group, the neighborhood, the public, find no place in his system.

Concrete descriptions of group behavior indicate three aspects in the consensus of the members of the group. The first is the characteristic state of group feeling called *esprit de corps*. The enthusiasm of the two sides in a football contest, the ecstasy of religious ceremonial, the fellowship of members of a fraternity, the brotherhood of a monastic band are all different manifestations of group spirit.

The second aspect of consensus has become familiar through the term "morale." Morale may be defined as the collective will. Like the will of the individual it represents an organization of behavior tendencies. The discipline of the individual, his subordination to the group, lies in his participation and reglementation in social activities.

The third aspect of consensus which makes for unified behavior of the members of the group has been analyzed by Durkheim under the term "collective representations." Collective representations are the concepts which embody the objectives of group activity.

The totem of primitive man, the flag of a nation, a religious creed, the number system, and Darwin's theory of the descent of man—all these are collective representations. Every society and every social group has, or tends to have, its own symbols and its own language. The language and other symbolic devices by which a society carries on its collective existence are collective representations. Animals do not possess them.

2

THE GROWTH OF THE CITY

THE OUTSTANDING fact of modern society is the growth of great cities. Nowhere else have the enormous changes which the machine industry has made in our social life registered themselves with such obviousness as in the cities. In the United States the transition from a rural to an urban civilization, though beginning later than in Europe, has taken place, if not more rapidly and completely, at any rate more logically in its most characteristic forms.

All the manifestations of modern life which are peculiarly urban—the skyscraper, the subway, the department store, the daily newspaper, and social work—are characteristically American. The more subtle changes in our social life, which in their cruder manifestations are termed "social problems," problems that alarm and bewilder us, as divorce, delinquency, and social unrest, are to be found in their most acute forms in our largest American cities. The profound and "subversive" forces which have wrought these changes are measured in the physical growth and expansion of cities. That is the significance of the comparative statistics of Weber, Bücher, and other students.

These statistical studies, although dealing mainly with the effects of urban growth, brought out into clear relief certain distinctive characteristics of urban as compared with rural populations. The larger proportion of women to men in the cities than in the open country, the greater percentage of youth and middle-aged,

Reprinted from Robert E. Park, Ernest W. Burgess, and Roderick D. McKenzie, *The City* (Chicago: University of Chicago Press, 1925, reprinted 1967), pp. 47–62.

the higher ratio of the foreign-born, the increased heterogeneity of occupation increase with the growth of the city and profoundly alter its social structure. These variations in the composition of population are indicative of all the changes going on in the social organization of the community. In fact, these changes are a part of the growth of the city and suggest the nature of the processes of growth.

The only aspect of growth adequately described by Bücher and Weber was the rather obvious process of the *aggregation* of urban population. Almost as overt a process, that of *expansion*, has been investigated from a different and very practical point of view by groups interested in city planning, zoning, and regional surveys. Even more significant than the increasing density of urban population is its correlative tendency to overflow, and so to extend over wider areas, and to incorporate these areas into a larger communal life. This paper, therefore, will treat first of the expansion of the city, and then of the less-known processes of urban metabolism and mobility which are closely related to expansion.

Expansion as Physical Growth

The expansion of the city from the standpoint of the city plan, zoning, and regional surveys is thought of almost wholly in terms of its physical growth. Traction studies have dealt with the development of transportation in its relation to the distribution of population throughout the city. The surveys made by the Bell Telephone Company and other public utilities have attempted to forecast the direction and the rate of growth of the city in order to anticipate the future demands for the extension of their services. In the city plan the location of parks and boulevards, the widening of traffic streets, the provision for a civic center, are all in the interest of the future control of the physical development of the city.

This expansion in area of our largest cities is now being brought forcibly to our attention by the Plan for the Study of New York and Its Environs, and by the formation of the Chicago Regional Planning Association, which extends the metropolitan district of the city to a radius of 50 miles, embracing 4,000 square miles of territory. Both are attempting to measure expansion in order to deal with the changes that accompany city growth. In England, where more than one-half of the inhabitants live in cities having a population of 100,000 and over, the lively appreciation of the bearing of urban expansion on social organization is thus expressed by C. B. Fawcett:

One of the most important and striking developments in the growth of the urban populations of the more advanced peoples of the world during the last few decades has been the appearance of a number of vast urban aggregates, or conurbations, far larger and more numerous than the great cities of any preceding age. These have usually been formed by the simultaneous expansion of a number of neighboring towns, which have grown out toward each other until they have reached a practical coalescence in one continuous urban area. Each such conurbation still has within it many nuclei of denser town growth, most of which represent the central areas of the various towns from which it has grown, and these nuclear patches are connected by the less densely urbanized areas which began as suburbs of these towns. The latter are still usually rather less continuously occupied by buildings, and often have many open spaces.

These great aggregates of town dwellers are a new feature in the distribution of man over the earth. At the present day there are from thirty to forty of them, each containing more than a million people, whereas only a hundred years ago there were, outside the great centers of population on the waterways of China, not more than two or three. Such aggregations of people are phenomena of great geographical and social importance; they give rise to new problems in the organization of the life and well-being of their inhabitants and in their varied activities. Few of them have yet developed a social consciousness at all proportionate to their magnitude, or fully realized themselves as definite groupings of people with many common interests, emotions and thoughts.[1]

In Europe and America the tendency of the great city to expand has been recognized in the term "the metropolitan area of the city," which far overruns its political limits, and in the case of New York and Chicago, even state lines. The metropolitan area may be taken to include urban territory that is physically contiguous, but it is coming to be defined by that facility of transportation that enables a business man to live in a suburb of Chicago and to work in the Loop, and his wife to shop at Marshall Field's and attend grand opera in the Auditorium.

Expansion as a Process

No study of expansion as a process has yet been made, although the materials for such a study and intimations of different aspects of the process are contained in city planning, zoning, and regional surveys. The typical processes of the expansion of the city can best be illustrated, perhaps, by a series of concentric circles, which may be numbered to designate both the successive zones of urban extension and the types of areas differentiated in the process of expansion.

This chart represents an ideal construction of the tendencies of any town or city to expand radially from its central business district—on the map "The Loop" (I). Encircling the downtown area there is normally an area in transition, which is being invaded by business and light manufacture (II). A third area (III) is inhabited by the workers in industries who have escaped from the area of deterioration (II) but who desire to live within easy access of their work. Beyond this zone is the "residential area" (IV) of high-class apartment buildings or of exclusive "restricted" districts of single family dwellings. Still farther, out beyond the city limits, is the commuters' zone—suburban areas, or satellite cities—within a thirty- to sixty-minute ride of the central business district.

This chart brings out clearly the main fact of expansion, namely, the tendency of each inner zone to extend its area by the invasion of the next outer zone. This aspect of expansion may be called *succession*, a process which has been studied in detail in plant ecology. If this chart is applied to Chicago, all four of these zones were in its early history included in the circumference of the inner zone, the present business district. The present boundaries of the area of deterioration were not many years ago those of the zone now inhabited by independent wage-earners, and within the memories of thousands of Chicagoans contained the residences of the "best families." It hardly needs to be added that neither Chi-

CHART 1

THE GROWTH OF THE CITY

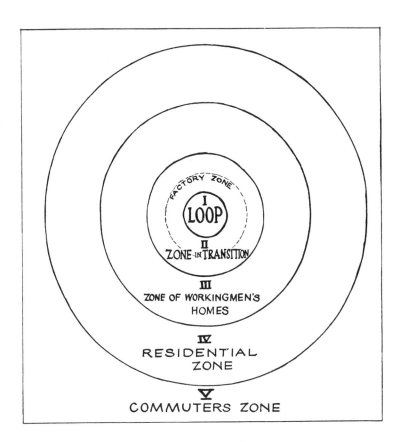

cago nor any other city fits perfectly into this ideal scheme. Complications are introduced by the lake front, the Chicago River, railroad lines, historical factors in the location of industry, the relative degree of the resistance of communities to invasion, etc.

Besides extension and succession, the general process of expansion in urban growth involves the antagonistic and yet complementary processes of concentration and decentralization. In all cities there is the natural tendency for local and outside transportation to converge in the central business district. In the downtown section of every large city we expect to find the department stores, the skyscraper office buildings, the railroad stations, the great hotels, the theaters, the art museum, and the city hall. Quite naturally, almost inevitably, the economic, cultural, and political life centers here. The relation of centralization to the other processes of city life may be roughly gauged by the fact that over half a million people daily enter and leave Chicago's "Loop." More recently sub-business centers have grown up in outlying zones. These "satellite loops" do not, it seems, represent the "hoped for" revival of the neighborhood, but rather a telescoping of several local communities into a larger economic unity. The Chicago of yesterday, an agglomeration of country towns and immigrant colonies, is undergoing a process of reorganization into a centralized decentralized system of local communities coalescing into sub-business areas visibly or invisibly dominated by the central business district. The actual processes of what may be called centralized decentralization are now being studied in the development of the chain store, which is only one illustration of the change in the basis of the urban organization.[2]

Expansion, as we have seen, deals with the physical growth of the city, and with the extension of the technical services that have made city life not only livable, but comfortable, even luxurious. Certain of these basic necessities of urban life are possible only through a tremendous development of communal existence. Three millions of people in Chicago are dependent upon one unified water system, one giant gas company, and one huge electric light plant. Yet, like most of the other aspects of our communal urban life, this economic co-operation is an example of co-operation without a shred of what the "spirit of co-operation" is commonly thought to signify. The great public utilities are a part of the mechanization of life in great cities, and have little or no other meaning for social organization.

Yet the processes of expansion, and especially the rate of expansion, may be studied not only in the physical growth and business development, but also in the consequent changes in the social organization and in personality types. How far is the growth of the city, in its physical and technical aspects, matched by a natural but adequate readjustment in the social organization? What, for a city, is a normal rate of expansion, a rate of expansion with which controlled changes in the social organization might successfully keep pace?

Social Organization and Disorganization as Processes of Metabolism

These questions may best be answered, perhaps, by thinking of urban growth as a resultant of organization and disorganization analogous to the anabolic and katabolic processes of metabolism in the body. In what way are individuals incorporated into the life of a city? By what process does a person become an organic part of his society? The natural process of acquiring culture is by birth. A person is born into a family already adjusted to a social environment—in this case the modern city. The natural rate of increase of population most favorable for assimilation may then be taken as the excess of the birth-rate over the death-rate, but is this the normal rate of city growth? Certainly, modern cities have increased and are increasing in population at a far higher rate. However, the natural rate of growth may be used to measure the disturbances of metabolism caused by any excessive increase, as those which followed the great influx of southern Negroes into northern cities since the war. In a similar way all cities show deviations in composition by age and sex from a standard population such as that of Sweden, unaffected in recent years by any great emigration or immigration. Here again, marked variations, as any great excess of males over females, or of females over males, or in the proportion of children, or of grown men or women, are symptomatic of abnormalities in social metabolism.

Normally the processes of disorganization and organization may be thought of as in reciprocal relationship to each other, and as co-operating in a moving equilibrium of social order toward an end vaguely or definitely regarded as progressive. So far as disorganization points to reorganization and makes for more efficient adjustment, disorganization must be conceived not as pathological, but as normal. Disorganization as preliminary to reorganization of attitudes and conduct is almost invariably the lot of the newcomer to the city, and the discarding of the habitual, and often of what has been to him the moral, is not infrequently accompanied by sharp mental conflict and sense of personal loss. Oftener, perhaps, the change gives sooner or later a feeling of emancipation and an urge toward new goals.

In the expansion of the city a process of distribution takes place which sifts and sorts and relocates individuals and groups by residence and occupation. The resulting differentiation of the cosmopolitan American city into areas is typically all from one pattern, with only interesting minor modifications. Within the central business district or on an adjoining street is the "main stem" of "hobohemia," the teeming Rialto of the homeless migratory man of the Middle West.[3] In the zone of deterioration encircling the central business section are always to be found the so-called "slums" and "bad lands," with their submerged regions of poverty, degradation, and disease, and their underworlds of crime and vice. Within a deteriorating area are rooming-house districts, the purgatory of "lost souls." Nearby is the Latin Quarter, where creative and rebellious spirits resort. The slums are also crowded to overflowing with immigrant colonies—the Ghetto, Little Sicily, Greektown, Chinatown—fascinatingly combining old world heritages and American adaptations. Wedging out from here is the Black Belt, with its free and disorderly life. The area of deterioration, while essentially one of decay, of stationary or declining population, is also one of regeneration, as witness the mission, the settlement, the artists' colony, radical centers—all obsessed with the vision of a new and better world.

The next zone is also inhabited predominatingly by factory and shop workers, but skilled and thrifty. This is an area of second immigrant settlement, generally of the second generation. It is the region of escape from the slum, the *Deutschland* of the aspiring Ghetto family. For *Deutschland* (literally "Germany") is the name given, half in envy, half in derision, to that region beyond the Ghetto where successful neighbors appear to be imitating

CHART 2

URBAN AREAS

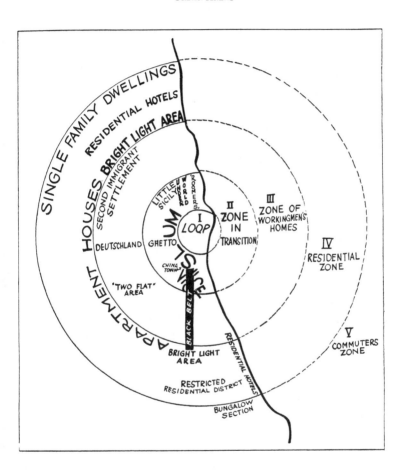

German Jewish standards of living. But the inhabitant of this area in turn looks to the "Promised Land" beyond, to its residential hotels, its apartment-house region, its "satellite loops," and its "bright light" areas.

This differentiation into natural economic and cultural groupings gives form and character to the city. For segregation offers the group, and thereby the individuals who compose the group, a place and a rôle in the total organization of city life. Segregation limits development in certain directions, but releases it in others. These areas tend to accentuate certain traits, to attract and develop their kind of individuals, and so to become further differentiated.

The division of labor in the city likewise illustrates disorganization, reorganization, and increasing differentiation. The immigrant from rural communities in Europe and America seldom brings with him economic skill of any great value in our industrial, commercial, or professional life. Yet interesting occupational selection has taken place by nationality, explainable more by racial temperament or circumstance than by old-world economic background, as Irish policemen, Greek ice-cream parlors, Chinese laundries, Negro porters, Belgian janitors, etc.

The facts that in Chicago one million (996,589) individuals gainfully employed reported 509 occupations, and that over 1,000 men and women in *Who's Who* gave 116 different vocations, give some notion of how in the city the minute differentiation of occupation "analyzes and sifts the population, separating and classifying the diverse elements."[4] These figures also afford some intimation of the complexity and complication of the modern industrial mechanism and the intricate segregation and isolation of divergent economic groups. Interrelated with this economic division of labor is a corresponding division into social classes and into cultural and recreational groups. From this multiplicity of groups, with their different patterns of life, the person finds his congenial social world and—what is not feasible in the narrow confines of a village —may move and live in widely separated, and perchance conflicting, worlds. Personal disorganization may be but the failure to harmonize the canons of conduct of two divergent groups.

If the phenomena of expansion and metabolism indicate that a moderate degree of disorganization may and does facilitate social organization, they indicate as well that rapid urban expansion is accompanied by excessive increases in disease, crime, disorder, vice, insanity, and suicide, rough indexes of social disorganization. But what are the indexes of the causes, rather than of the effects, of the disordered social metabolism of the city? The excess of the actual over the natural increase of population has already been suggested as a criterion. The significance of this increase consists in the immigration into a metropolitan city like New York and Chicago of tens of thousands of persons annually. Their invasion of the city has the effect of a tidal wave inundating first the immigrant colonies, the ports of first entry, dislodging thousands of inhabitants who overflow into the next zone, and so on and on until the momentum of the wave has spent its force on the last urban zone. The whole effect is to speed up expansion, to speed up industry, to speed up the "junking" process in the area of deterioration (II). These internal movements of the population become the more significant for study. What movement is going on in the city, and how may this movement be measured? It is easier, of course, to classify movement within the city than to measure it. There is the movement fom residence to residence, change of occupation, labor turnover, movement to and from work, movement for recreation and adventure. This leads to the question: What is the significant aspect of movement for the study of the changes in city life? The answer to this question leads directly to the important disinction between movement and mobility.

Mobility as the Pulse of the Community

Movement, per se, is not an evidence of change or of growth. In fact, movement may be a fixed and unchanging order of motion, designed to control a constant situation, as in routine movement. Movement that is significant for growth implies a change of movement in response to a new stimulus or situation. Change of movement of this type is called *mobility*. Movement of the nature of routine finds its typical expression in work. Change of movement, or mobility, is characteristically expressed in adventure. The great city, with its "bright lights," its emporiums of novelties and bargains, its palaces of amusement, its underworld of vice and crime, its risks of life and property from accident, robbery, and homicide, has become the region of the most intense degree of adventure and danger, excitement and thrill.

Mobility, it is evident, involves change, new experience, stimulation. Stimulation induces a response of the person to those objects in his environment which afford expression for his wishes. For the person, as for the physical organism, stimulation is essential to growth. Response to stimulation is wholesome so long as it is a correlated *integral* reaction of the entire personality. When the reaction is *segmental*, that is, detached from, and uncontrolled by, the organization of personality, it tends to become disorganizing or pathological. That is why stimulation for the sake of stimulation, as in the restless pursuit of pleasure, partakes of the nature of vice.

The mobility of city life, with its increase in the number and intensity of stimulations, tends inevitably to confuse and to demoralize the person. For an essential element in the mores and in personal morality is consistency, consistency of the type that is natural in the social control of the primary group. Where mobility is the greatest, and where in consequence primary controls break down completely, as in the zone of deterioration in the modern city, there develop areas of demoralization, of promiscuity, and of vice.

In our studies of the city it is found that areas of mobility are also the regions in which are found juvenile delinquency, boys' gangs, crime, poverty, wife desertion, divorce, abandoned infants, vice.

These concrete situations show why mobility is perhaps the best index of the state of metabolism of the city. Mobility may be thought of in more than a fanciful sense, as the "pulse of the community." Like the pulse of the human body, it is a process which reflects and is indicative of all the changes that are taking place in the community, and which is susceptible of analysis into elements which may be stated numerically.

The elements entering into mobility may be classified under two main heads: (1) the state of mutability of the person, and (2) the number and kind of contacts or stimulations in his environment. The mutability of city populations varies with sex and age composition, the degree of detachment of the person from the family and from other groups. All these factors may be expressed numerically. The new stimulations to which a population responds can be measured in terms of change of movement or of increasing contacts. Statistics on the movement of urban population may only measure routine, but an increase at a higher ratio than the increase of population measures mobility. In 1860 the horse-car lines of New York City carried about 50,000,000 passengers; in 1890 the trolley-cars (and a few surviving horse-cars) transported about 500,000,000; in 1921, the elevated, subway, surface, and electric and steam suburban lines carried a total of more than 2,500,000,-000 passengers.[5] In Chicago the total annual rides per capita on the surface and elevated lines were 164 in 1890; 215 in 1900; 320 in 1910; and 338 in 1921. In addition, the rides per capita on steam and electric suburban lines almost doubled between 1916 (23) and 1921 (41), and the increasing use of the autobomile must not be overlooked.[6] For example, the number of automobiles in Illinois increased from 131,140 in 1915 to 833,920 in 1923.[7]

Mobility may be measured not only by these changes of movement, but also by increase of contacts. While the increase of population of Chicago in 1912–22 was less than 25 per cent (23.6 per cent), the increase of letters delivered to Chicagoans was double that (49.6 per cent)—(from 693,084,196 to 1,038,007,854).[8] In 1912 New York had 8.8 telephones; in 1922, 16.9 per 100 inhabitants. Boston had, in 1912, 10.1 telephones; ten years later, 19.5 telephones per 100 inhabitants. In the same decade the figures for Chicago increased from 12.3 to 21.6 per 100 population.[9] But increase of the use of the telephone is probably more significant than increase in the number of telephones. The number of telephone calls in Chicago increased from 606,131,928 in 1914 to 944,010,586 in 1922,[10] an increase of 55.7 per cent, while the population increased only 13.4 per cent.

Land values, since they reflect movement, afford one of the most sensitive indexes of mobility. The highest land values in Chicago are at the point of greatest mobility in the city, at the corner of State and Madison streets, in the Loop. A traffic count showed that at the rush period 31,000 people an hour, or 210,000 men and women in sixteen and one-half hours, passed the southwest corner. For over ten years land values in the Loop have been stationary, but in the same time they have doubled, quadrupled, and even sextupled in the strategic corners of the "satellite loops,"[11] an accurate index of the changes which have occurred. Our investigations so far seem to indicate that variations in land values, especially where correlated with differences in rents, offer perhaps the best single measure of mobility, and so of all the changes taking place in the expansion and growth of the city.

In general outline, I have attempted to present the point of view and methods of investigation which the department of sociology is employing in its studies in the growth of the city, namely, to describe urban expansion in terms of extension, succession, and concentration; to determine how expansion disturbs metabolism when disorganization is in excess of organization; and, finally, to define mobility and to propose it as a measure both of expansion and metabolism, susceptible to precise quantitative formulation, so that it may be regarded almost literally as the pulse of the community. In a way, this statement might serve as an introduction to any one of five or six research projects under way in the department.[12] The project, however, in which I am directly engaged is an attempt to apply these methods of investigation to a cross-section of the city—to put this area, as it were, under the microscope, and so to study in more detail and with greater control and precision the processes which have been described here in the large. For this purpose the West Side Jewish community has been selected. This community includes the so-called "Ghetto," or area of first settlement, and Lawndale, the so-called "Deutschland," or area of second settlement. This area has certain obvious advantages for this study, from the standpoint of expansion, metabolism, and mobility. It exemplifies the tendency to expansion radially from the business center of the city. It is now relatively a homogeneous cultural group. Lawndale is itself an area in flux, with the tide of migrants still flowing in from the Ghetto and a constant egress to more desirable regions of the residential zone. In this area, too, it is also possible to study how the expected outcome of this high rate of mobility in social and personal disorganization is counteracted in large measure by the efficient communal organization of the Jewish community.

3

CAN NEIGHBORHOOD WORK HAVE
A SCIENTIFIC BASIS?

NEIGHBORHOOD WORK at present and as now practiced cannot, for two reasons, be said to be based upon science. First, the social sciences—and I refer to sociology in particular—have at present little to offer as a scientific basis for social work; secondly, what knowledge the social sciences have accumulated has been used little, or not at all, by neighborhood workers.

The Trend of Neighborhood Work to a
Scientific Basis

But if neighborhood work has not had a scientific basis, it has had, from its inception, as one of its conscious or unconscious motives, the search after knowledge as the basis of human relations. Settlement work, especially, represents not only the most devoted and the most idealistic, but also the most intelligent, phase of social work of the past generation. The settlement in its origin was an extension of the university. It carried over into a new environment the love of truth and, it may be added, the spirit of science. The residents of the settlement were brought at once into touch with social reality; that is, with the concrete facts of human life.

This early venture into intimate contact with social reality may accordingly be called the first stage in the trend of neighborhood

Reprinted from Robert E. Park, Ernest W. Burgess, and Roderick D. Mc-Kenzie, *The City* (Chicago: University of Chicago Press, 1925, reprinted 1967), pp. 142–55.

work toward a scientific basis. But settlement workers soon found that sympathetic understanding and intimate contacts failed to solve many of the actual problems of neighborhood work. The re-calcitrancy of the boys' gang, the opposition and manipulations of the ward boss, the competition of commercialized recreation, the unsolvable cultural conflict between immigrant parents and Ameri-canized children are only a few of the many perplexing conditions of neighborhood life in immigrant areas which resisted the spirit of good will of settlement workers. They therefore began to study their communities in the attempt to state the factors at work by an analysis of the elements in the situation. *Hull House Maps and Papers, The City Wilderness,* and *Americans in Process* are illustra-tions of the careful study and keen observation of these very early efforts to determine and to take account of the many and different conditions affecting neighborhood work. This interest in the dis-covery of factors in the social situation may therefore be called the second stage in the trend of neighborhood work toward a scien-tific basis.

Science, however, is concerned not with factors, but with forces. The distinction is not always clearly drawn between a factor and a force. "Factors are the elements that co-operate to make a given situation. Forces are type-factors operative in typical situations."[1] A factor is thought of as a concrete cause for an individual event; a force is conceived to be an abstract cause for events in general so far as they are similar. A particular gang of boys, the Torpedo gang, of which Tony is the leader—and which is made up of eight street Arabs—is a factor in the situation which a certain settlement in an Italian colony in Chicago faces. But as soon as the attention shifts from this one gang and this particular settlement to settle-ments in general and to gangs in general the transition is made from a factor to a force. A gang is a factor to a given settlement; the gang is a force from the standpoint of all settlements.

The Study of Social Forces in the Community

If neighborhood work can have a scientific basis, it is be-cause there are social forces in community life—forces like geographical conditions, human wishes, community consciousness —that can be studied, described, analyzed, and ultimately measured. In a series of research projects now in progress in the Department of Sociology in the University of Chicago, studies are being made of the social forces of community life. While the city of Chicago is used as the laboratory for this investigation, it is assumed that the processes of urban life in one community are in certain ways typical of city life throughout the United States.

The term "community" is widely used by sociologists, neighborhood workers, and others, but often with widely divergent meanings. In research in any field it is necessary to define our concepts and to make relevant distinctions. In the literature of the subject there is a growing disposition to emphasize as one of the fundamental aspects of the community its geographical setting. Whatever else the community may be, it signifies individuals, families, groups, or institutions located upon an area and some or all of the relationships which grow out of this common location. " 'Community' is the term which is applied to societies and social groups where they are considered from the point of view of the geographical distribution of the individuals and institutions of which they are composed."[2]

Upon reflection it is evident that markedly different social relationships may have their roots in the conditions of a common territorial location. Indeed, it is just these outstanding differences in communal activities, viewed in relation to their geographic background, which have caused much of the confusion in the use of the term "community." For community life, as conditioned by the distribution of individuals and institutions over an area, has at least three quite different aspects.

First of all, there is the community viewed almost exclusively in terms of location and movement. How far has the area itself, by its very topography and by all its other external and physical characteristics, as railroads, parks, types of housing, conditioned community formation and exerted a determining influence upon the distribution of its inhabitants and upon their movements and life? To what extent has it had a selective effect in sifting and sorting families over the area by occupation, nationality, and economic or social class? To what extent is the work of neighborhood or community institutions promoted or impeded by favorable or unfavorable location? How far do geographical distances within or without the community symbolize social distances? This apparently "natural" organization of the human community, so similar in the formation of plant and animal communities, may be called the "ecological community."

No comprehensive study of the human community from this standpoint has yet been made. A prospectus for such a study is outlined by Professor R. D. McKenzie, under the title, "The Ecological Approach to the Study of the Human Community."[3] Yet there are several systematic treatises and a rapidly growing literature of scientific research in the two analogous fields of plant ecology and animal ecology. The processes of competition, invasion, succession, and segregation described in elaborate detail for plant and animal communities seem to be strikingly similar to the operation of these same processes in the human community. The assertion might even be defended that the student of community life or the community organization worker might secure at present a more adequate understanding of the basic factors in the natural organization of the community from Warming's *Oecology of Plants* or from Adams's *Guide to the Study of Animal Ecology* than from any other source.

In the second place, the community may be conceived in terms of the effects of communal life in a given area upon the formation or the maintenance of a local culture. Local culture includes those sentiments, forms of conduct, attachments, and ceremonies which are characteristic of a locality, which have either originated in the area or have become identified with it. This aspect of local life may be called "the cultural community." This relationship of cultural patterns to territorial areas has not yet been adequately studied unless in the phenomena of language. What, for example, are studies in dialect but one illustration of how local areas with their entailed isolation differentially affect customs of speech? Concrete materials for a wider study of culture in relation to location are increasing, notably upon preliterate peoples and upon retarded groups geographically isolated, as the southern mountaineers or the remote inhabitants of Pitcairn Island.

The immigrant colony in an American city possesses a culture unmistakably not indigenous but transplanted from the Old World. The telling fact, however, is not that the immigrant colony maintains its old-world cultural organization, but that in its new environment it mediates a cultural adjustment to its new situation. How basically culture is dependent upon place is suggested by the following expressions, "New England conscience," "southern hospitality," "Scottish thrift," "Kansas is not a geographical location so much as a state of mind." Neighborhood institutions like the church, the school, and the settlement are essentially cultural institutions, and recognition of this fact has far-reaching implications for the policies and programs of these local centers.

There remains a third standpoint from which the relation of a local area to group life may be stated. In what ways and to what extent does the fact of common residence in a locality compel or invite its inhabitants to act together? Is there, or may there be developed upon a geographical basis, a community consciousness? Does contiguity by residence insure or predispose to co-operation in at least those conditions of life inherent in geographic location, as transportation, water supply, playgrounds, etc.? Finally, what degree of social and political action can be secured on the basis of local areas? This is the community of the community organization worker and of the politician, and may be described as "the political community." It is upon this concept of the community as a local area that American political organization has been founded.

These three definitions of the community are not perhaps altogether mutually exclusive. They do, however, represent three distinctly different aspects of community life that will have to be recognized in any basic study of the community and of community organization. A given local area, like Hyde Park in Chicago, may at the same time constitute an ecological, cultural, and political community, while another area like the lower North Side in the same city, which forms a distinct ecological unit, falls apart into several cultural communities and cannot, at any rate from the standpoint of a common and effective public opinion, be said to constitute a going political community. The Black Belt in Chicago comprises one cultural community but overflows several ecological areas and has no means of common political action except through ward lines arbitrarily drawn.

It follows that the boundaries of local areas determined ecologically, culturally, and politically seldom, if ever, exactly coincide. In fact, for American cities it is generally true that political boundaries are drawn most arbitrarily, without regard either to ecological or cultural lines, as is notoriously the case in the familiar instance of the gerrymander. Therefore it is fair to raise the question: How far are the deficiencies in political action through our governmental bodies and welfare action through our social agencies the result of the failure to base administrative districts upon ecological or cultural communities?[4]

This analysis of the community into its threefold aspects suggests that the study of social forces in a local area should assume that the neighborhood or the community is the resultant of three main types of determining influences: first, ecological forces; second, cultural forces; and third, political forces.

Ecological Forces

The ecological forces are those which have to do with the process of competition and the consequent distribution and segregation by residence and occupation. Through competition and the factors which affect it, as trade centers, etc., every neighborhood in the city becomes a component and integral part of the larger community, with a destiny bound up by its relation to it. In the study of the growth of the city it is found that the life of any neighborhood is determined, in the long run, not altogether by the forces within itself, but even more by the total course of city life. To think of the neighborhood or the community in isolation from the city is to disregard the biggest fact about the neighborhood.

Studies of urban growth reveal that the city grows outward from its central business district (1) in a series of expanding zones.[5] There is a "zone of transition" (2) encircling the downtown area. This is the area of deterioration, the so-called "slum," created in large part by the invasion of business and light manufacture. A third area (3) is inhabited by workers in industry who have escaped from the area of deterioration (2) and who desire to live within easy access of their work. Beyond this zone is the "residential area" (4) of high-class apartment buildings or of exclusive "restricted" districts of single family dwellings. Still farther, out beyond the city limits, is the "commuters' zone" (5) of suburban areas or satellite cities within a sixty-minute ride of the central business district.

Within these zones of urban growth are to be found local districts or communities, and these in turn subdivide into smaller areas called neighborhoods. In the long run, geographical factors and the process of competition fix the boundaries and the centers of these areas. It is important that neighborhood work be in accordance with, rather than in opposition to, these silent but continuous influences. A map of local communities was prepared to show the way in which rivers, railroads, large industrial establishments, parks, and boulevards divide the city into its constituent local communities—residential and industrial.

The centers of local communities are to be found at the point of highest land value in the intersection of two business streets. These local community centers are also characterized by the concentration of retail business, of banks, of restaurants, and of the large and magnificent palaces of amusement, like motion picture houses and public dance halls. If high land values indicate the center of the community, the lowest land values generally define its periphery.

But if the intersection of two business streets determines the trade center, these same streets divide it into neighborhoods. In Chart I on page 44 is offered a schematic representation of a Chicago local community, Woodlawn, with its economic center at the intersection of the two main business streets of Sixty-Third Street and Cottage Grove Avenue. At this intersection land values are five thousand dollars a front foot. Woodlawn falls into four neighborhoods, A, B, C, and D, divided from each other by these same intersecting business streets. It is interesting that each of these neighbor-

CHART 1

SCHEMATIC REPRESENTATION OF THE DIVISION OF A COMMUNITY INTO
NEIGHBORHOODS BY THE INTERSECTION OF TWO BUSINESS STREETS.

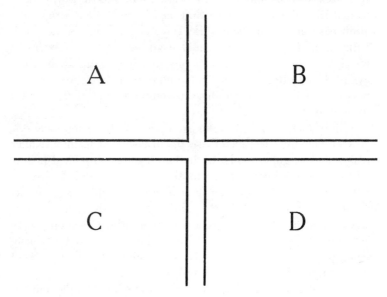

hoods has its own public school. Even more significant is the fact
that an attempt to unite two struggling churches of the same
denomination in two of these neighborhoods into one strong church
failed because neither would surrender its location.

It sems almost axiomatic to state that community and neighborhood work must take into account the operation of these silent but
continuous ecological forces and work with them rather than
against them. Yet how often are social centers located on the edge,
rather than at the center, of a neighborhood. In the location of a
neighborhood center the consequences which flow from the play of
ecological forces must be heeded, because they condition the development of its work and the radius of its influence.

Cultural Forces

Ecological or economic forces are naturally basic to the
play of cultural forces. Culture, as the social heritage of the group,

implies both a locality to which it is indigenous and a constant, rather than a changing, social situation. Chicago, like other large cities, has its cultural communities, each of which has, if not a local area, at least a local center. Hobohemia, Bohemia, Philistia, the Ghetto, and the Gold Coast are cultural communities.

Movement in the person, as from one social location to another, or any sudden change as caused by an invention, carries with it the possibility or the probability of cultural decadence. The cultural controls over conduct disintegrate; impulses and wishes take random and wild expression. The result is immorality and delinquency; in short, personal and social disorganization. An illustration of cultural decadence as a result of movement is the excessively high rate of juvenile delinquency among the children of immigrant parents. To what extent have neighborhood workers gauged the effect of the daily newspaper, the motion picture, the automobile, and the radio, in releasing the child, the youth, and the adult from the confines of the neighborhood and of bringing them into contact with the city-wide, nation-wide, and world-wide life of our time?

These changes taking place in community life may be observed in a dramatic form in commercialized recreation. The day of the neighborhood public dance hall and the neighborhood motion picture show has passed, or at least is passing. Young people are deserting the neighborhood recreation centers and are thronging to centers outside the local community, to the high-class, magnificent dance gardens and palaces, and to the so-called "wonder" theaters of the "bright light" areas.

A realignment of the leisure-time movements of urban young people is taking place, which every agency engaged in neighborhood work must take into account. Is the neighborhood as a factor in the lives of youth soon to become a situation of the past? Can settlements and social centers expect to hold back the tide of the forces of city life?

A map of the residences of dance hall patrons which shows both the disappearance of the small public dance hall from the neighborhood and the concentration of large dance halls in "bright light" areas is all the more significant because it portrays the phenomenon of promiscuity. By promiscuity is meant primary and intimate behavior upon the basis of secondary contacts. In the village type of neighborhood, where everyone knows everyone else, the social relationships of the young people were safeguarded by the primary controls of group opinion. But in the public dance hall, where young people are drawn from all parts of the city, this old primary control breaks down. Is not this the basic reason why social workers find the dance hall so recurring a factor in personal disorganization and delinquency? As yet, however, we have no satisfactory study of the dance hall as a social world of youth. Two new social types— the "sheik" and the "flapper"—have been created by the dance hall and the motion picture, but they are regarded as subjects for jest rather than for serious study.

A study by Miss Evelyn Buchan of girl delinquency shows the effect of the increasing mobility and promiscuity of city life upon the behavior of youth, and suggests an interesting method of study. To bring into clearer relief the rôle of mobility and promiscuity as factors in behavior, a device called "the delinquency triangle" was employed. The three points of the triangle were located by spotting the home of the girl, the home of her male companion, and the place of delinquency. Three typical forms of the triangle soon appeared.

Form 1 represents the traditional form of sex delinquency, where all three points of the triangle are within the community. This may be called the "neighborhood triangle." In this case the intimacy of the boy and girl might be little more than the continuance in this country of old-world folkways, but without the protection for the girl in subsequent marriage which the European peasant mores afford.

Form 2, which is "the mobility triangle," stands for delinquency of the type related to increased freedom of movement, where two points of the triangle or its base, formed by the homes of the girl and the boy, lie within the same community, but where its apex, or the place of delinquency, is situated outside. In this case the bright-light area becomes a place of freedom from the narrower, distant controls of the home and the neighborhood.

In form 3, delinquency is of the type of promiscuity, because here all the points of the triangle lie in different communities. The

FORM 1. THE NEIGHBORHOOD TRIANGLE.
FORM 2. THE MOBILITY TRIANGLE.
FORM 3. THE PROMISCUITY TRIANGLE.

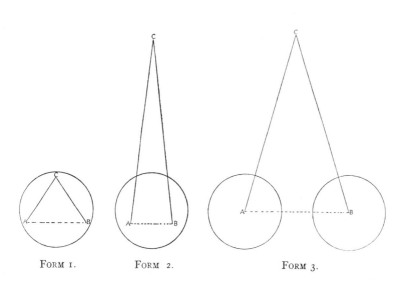

FORM 1.   FORM 2.   FORM 3.

intimacy developing from the casual acquaintance of the metal
worker from the steel mills with the girl from the West Side whom
he "picked up" at an amusement park may be so transient that
neither knows the family name or the address of the other.

The total effect of city life, like mobility and promiscuity, upon
the neighborhood and upon our traditional culture seems to be
subversive and disorganizing. Particularly is this true of deteriorating areas, where neighborhood work originated, and where it is
still, in any completely developed state, for the most part confined.
A series of maps has been prepared which shows graphically what,
of course, is known to social students—that the zone of deterioration and the areas of the greatest mobility in the city have the
greatest concentration of poverty, vice, crime, juvenile delinquency, divorce, desertion, abandoned infants, murder, and suicide.

Political Forces

The political forces have to do with the more formal control of public opinion and law. Neighborhood work is concerned with political forces whenever social action is desired. Our whole scheme of social work may be regarded, from this standpoint at least, as social politics. But has the social worker, who is the social politician, the same intimate knowledge of his neighborhood that the professional politician possesses? A minimum of information which he needs is a card catalogue of, plus some direct contact with, all the local dynamic personalities, including gang leaders, pool hall proprietors, leaders of all the neighborhood organizations, and of all professional persons, like representatives of social agencies, physicians, lawyers, clergymen, at work in his locality. More than that, he needs to know the basic interests, the driving wishes, and the vital problems of the men and women, the youth and the children, living in the community.

The knowledge of these forces in neighborhood life will suggest feasible projects and programs. Too often, however, attempts at social control rise from ignorant good will rather than from the facts of the situation. This is particularly true of the many futile efforts to impose neighborly relationships upon areas which are no longer neighborhoods.

What, then, is our answer to the question, Can neighborhood work have a scientific basis? It can have a scientific foundation if it will base its activities upon a study of social forces. But the social forces of city life seem, from our studies, to be destroying the city neighborhood. Is the neighborhood center to engage in a losing fight against the underlying tendencies of modern urban society? This question should be squarely faced: Is neighborhood work prepared to base its justification for existence upon facts rather than upon sentiment?

There are those who are convinced that the function of the neighborhood center is passing with the decay of the neighborhood in the city. For myself, I am not so certain. Surely the work of the neighborhood center must now be conceived and planned in terms of its relationship to the entire life of the city. The work of neighborhood centers, like that of all other social agencies, must increasingly be placed upon the basis of the scientific study of the social forces with which they have to deal. Especially are studies desired of the actual effect and rôle of intimate contacts in personal development and social control.

A feasible way for neighborhood centers to place their work upon a scientific basis would be to stress the impulse to research that has always been associated with the settlement movement. Thirty years ago Mr. Robert A. Woods read a paper on "University Settlements as Laboratories in Social Science." The argument for research in its relations to neighborhood work is contained in that article. He conceived the advantage of research both to social science and to the settlement. The growing fluidity and complexity of urban life has but increased the force of his argument.

Neighborhood work, by the logic of the situation, if it is to evolve a successful technique, will be compelled more and more to depend upon research into the social forces of modern life.

4

RESIDENTIAL SEGREGATION IN AMERICAN CITIES

SEPARATION by residence of the Negro from the white exists in some form in all American cities. In none of them is there complete segregation. No large American city is entirely white or entirely Negro, as is the case with certain smaller communities. There is no Negro quarter in any city in this country with the absolute line of demarkation which separated Jew from Gentile in the ghettoes of the Middle Ages in European cities.[1]

T. J. Woofter, Jr., in his survey of racial separation in urban communities found wide differences within the same city and between different cities.

Each city visited has examples of all degrees of separation. Some servants live under the same roof as their employers, and occasionally white and Negro families occupy the same apartment-houses or duplex dwellings. There are many cases, both in the South and in the North, where white and colored people are mixed in the same block, and in other instances the dividing line can be more or less definitely traced along streets.

Each city has a pattern of its own determined by the percentage of Negroes in the total, the distribution of Negro employment, the distribution of the areas where property is within the means of colored families, the attitude of the people toward segregation, and the rate of expansion of business and manufacturing sections. Where there is wide variation from city to city, several general patterns may be described.[2]

Reprinted from *The Annals of the American Academy of Political and Social Science* 140 (1928) : 105–15.

The residential separation of white and Negro has almost invariably been treated by itself as if it were a unique phenomenon of urban life. In fact, however, as recent studies clearly prove, this is only one case among many of the workings of the process of segregation in the sorting and shifting of the different elements of population in the growth of the city. There are immigrant colonies, the so-called Ghettoes, Little Sicilies, Chinatowns, as well as Black Belts. There are also economic and cultural areas which often cut across or transcend racial and nationality classifications like the Hobohemias, Bohemias, Suburbias and Gold Coasts of our metropolitan cities. The city upon analysis is divided and subdivided into residential areas and neighborhoods, each of which is or tends to be predominantly inhabited by some one racial and immigrant group, or economic and social class.

This paper accordingly proposes to inquire into the residential separation of the Negro from the rest of the community in its setting in the larger process of urban segregation. From this perspective may perhaps be gained a clearer understanding of the interplay of the factors and forces which determine the location and the movement of Negro neighborhoods within the larger community.

City Growth and Urban Zones

Every community as it grows expands outward from its center. This radial extension from the downtown business district toward the outskirts of the city is due partly to business and industrial pressure and partly to residential pull. Business and light manufacturing, as they develop, push out from the center of the city and encroach upon residence. At the same time, families are always responding to the appeal of more attractive residential districts, further and ever further removed from the center of the city.

As the result, then, of business and industrial encroachment, on the one hand, and of the corresponding residential motive of escape, on the other, the city tends to take form and to become organized on a pattern approximating that of concentric zones as shown in Chart I. These zones are: I. The Central Business District Zone. II. The Zone in Transition. III. The Zone of Workingmen's

Homes. IV. The Residential Zone. V. The Commuters' Zone. (See page 27 above.)

Any discussion of the movement and location of immigrant and racial groups in American cities requires, as a first condition of clarity, explicit reference to this basic classification of urban zones.[3] Accordingly, a brief description of each of these zones follows:

I. The central business district tends in American cities to be at once the center of retail, financial, recreational, civic and political activities. By day its skyscrapers and canyon-like streets are thronged with shoppers, clerks, and office workers. During the evening, crowds of pleasure seekers swarm into theaters, restaurants and cafés and out again into the blaze of the white way of the streets with their towering edifices brilliantly adorned with displays of multicolored signs of salutation and invitation. Aside from transients in hotels, homeless men as hoboes and "home guards" (casual resident workers), and dwellers in Chinatown, the central business district has few inhabitants.

II. The zone in transition has been described as an interstitial area in the throes of change from residence to business and industry. This region is "the port of first entry" for incoming racial and immigrant groups. The areas of first settlement are located here, as Little Italy, the Ghetto, and the Black Belt, from which their most enterprising members are seeking to escape. In this zone of transition, but close to the central business district and branching out along the main thoroughfares running out from it, are situated the rooming house districts with their mobile and mixed population of youth and old age, aspiring and defeated individuals, pleasure-seeking Bohemians and hard-working students, rural Fundamentalists and radical freethinkers, and of law-abiding citizens and professional criminals.

III. The zone of workingmen's homes finds its location at that distance beyond the factory belt surrounding the central business district, which is still accessible, often within walking distance, to the worker. In American cities the zone of workingmen's homes is generally an area of second immigrant settlement. Its inhabitants are constantly being recruited from those making their escape from the zone of transition, but at the same time are being depleted by those who are seeking more desirable residences in the zone beyond.

IV. The better residential zone is inhabited chiefly by the families of persons engaged in professional and clerical pursuits who have had high school if not college education. Their intellectual status is manifested by the type of books and magazines in the home, by the prevalence of women's clubs and by independence in voting. This is the home of the great middle class with ideals still akin to those of rural American society. In this zone are also located apartment and residential hotel areas with their urbanized and sophisticated tenants.

V. The commuters' zone comprises the suburban districts of the city which combine the atmosphere of village residence with access by rapid transit or by automobile to the downtown metropolitan center for work, shopping, and entertainment. Residence in restricted suburban communities implies an economic rating sufficient to acquire a bungalow costing more than a stipulated minimum figure and an automobile of commensurate rank.

If radial extension were the only factor affecting the growth of American cities, every city in this country would exhibit a perfect exemplification of these five urban zones. But since other factors affect urban development as situation, site, natural and artificial barriers, survival of an earlier use of a district, prevailing city plan and its system of local transportation, many distortions and modifications of this pattern are actually found. Nevertheless, so universal and powerful is the force of expansion outward from the center that in every city these zones can be more or less clearly delimited.

Applying the Pattern

In applying this pattern of urban zones to the problem of residential segregation of racial and immigrant groups, certain interesting facts at once emerge which suggest clues for further study. In the main, the material from which the following conclusions have been derived has been drawn from the Chicago situation but, wherever feasible, checked with the facts in other cities.

In the first place, in cities in the North, Negro and immigrants alike seem to be concentrated in settlements, the largest of which are in the zone of transition (II). In Chicago, the majority of Negroes, Poles, Lithuanians, Italians, Greeks, and Chinese are to be found in this interstitial region between residence and industry. Until recently the larger number of Bohemian and Russian Jews were also inhabitants of this zone. Woofter's series of maps in his book *Negro Problems in Cities* indicate that the bulk of the Negroes in Buffalo, Dayton, Gary, Indianapolis, and Philadelphia, are in this area lying immediately beyond the central business district. This is also the case both for the Negro and for recent immigrant groups of other northern cities not included in his survey, as Cleveland, Kansas City, Minneapolis and St. Louis. Although Harlem is the last of a series of Negro settlements on Manhattan, as a port of first entry for newcomers from the South and the West Indies, it exhibits many of the characteristics of an area in transition (II). Even before the Negro invasion, Harlem, as the northern extension of the East Side Ghetto, had already become an area of first settlement for the newly arriving immigrant Jew.

The concentration and scatter of Negroes and recent immigrants like the Poles, Lithuanians, and Italians, seem in general the same. Chart II indicates the degree to which concentration of population is similar for Negroes, Italians, and Poles, as shown by an examination of their distribution by wards in Chicago, Cleveland, Detroit, Manhattan borough of New York, Philadelphia and Pittsburgh. The fact that for each city the number of wards having ten per cent or more of Negroes, Italians and Poles is practically the same for each group points to common factors at work which influence the distribution of all three population groups.

When, however, the highest percentage of each population group is ascertained for any ward the Negroes show the greatest concentration of population for every city selected except Philadelphia, where the Italians have the highest percentage.

For Chicago, Cleveland and New York statistics are available by census tracts for the distribution of racial and foreign-born groups. The following data on Chicago has been furnished by Mr. E. Franklin Frazer.[4] He found that out of a total of 499 tracts into

CHART II

CONCENTRATION OF THREE POPULATION GROUPS, NEGROES, ITALIANS AND POLES IN SIX CITIES IN THE UNITED STATES

| Cities | Population, 1920 | | | Total Number of Wards | Concentration by Wards* | | | | | |
| | Negro | Italian | Polish | | Number of Wards with 10 Per Cent or More of Each Population Group | | | Highest Per Cent of Population of Each Group in Any Ward | | |
					Negro	Italian	Polish	Negro	Italian	Polish
Chicago	109,458	59,215	137,611	35	2	2	2	43.5	25.6	12.2
Cleveland	34,451	18,288	35,024	26	3	2	2	34.1	27.5	23.0
Detroit	40,838	16,205	56,624	21	2	3	4	25.5	21.0	17.6
New York (Manhattan borough)	109,133	184,546	64,514	23	2	3	3	34.3	22.6	21.5
Philadelphia	134,299	63,723	31,112	35	1	3	1	11.5	21.6	10.0
Pittsburgh	37,725	15,371	15,537	27	2	2	3	27.5	18.0	20.7

*In case of Manhattan by assembly districts.

which Chicago was divided for purposes of the 1920 federal census, 364 had one or more Negro residents, 95 had one per cent or more Negroes in its population, 51 had 5 per cent or more, and 16 had 50 per cent or more. The distribution of Negroes by wards for Cleveland and New York suggests that an analysis of census tracts would give similar findings for these cities.

Point of Entry

Each new group as it enters the city finds a place of most favorable entry. For all new groups with one or more of the following characteristics—an alien culture, a low economic status and a different race—this point of arrival naturally tends to be in or near the central business district. A commercial district, a business street or a rooming house area puts up notoriously slight resistance to the intrusion of a new group. At the present time in Chicago, representatives of the most recent immigrant groups, Mexicans, Philippinos, Syrians and Assyrians are found at certain definite points within Zones I and II. In 1884, when Chicago had only 155 Negroes out of its total population of 10,864, all but 66 of these resided in the two wards containing the business district. The five pieces of property then held by Negroes were all in the downtown neighborhood.[5] The first homes of the German and Russian Jews in Chicago were also in and near the business district. The evidence available all seems to point to a similar situation in the origins and growth of racial and immigrant neighborhoods in other cities.

Chinatowns are first established and long remain within or in close proximity to the central business district, as is the case in San Francisco, New York, and Chicago. Indeed, it would seem that Chinatowns have the characteristics of the Medieval Ghetto, namely, isolation, an alien culture, obedience to a government administered within its group. The Negro communities in American cities, on the contrary, while they possess their own institutions and unique modes of behavior are, in general, much more of an integral part of American life than are Polish and Italian communities. What James Weldon Johnson says of Harlem applies with almost equal force to Negro communities in other American cities.

Harlem grows more metropolitan and more a part of New York all the while. I shall give the three reasons that seem to me to be important in their order: First, the language of Harlem is not alien, it is not Italian nor Yiddish; it is English. Harlem talks American, reads American, thinks American. Second, Harlem is not physically a "quarter." It is not a section cut off. It is merely a zone through which four main arteries of the city run. Third, the fact that there is little or no gang labor gives Harlem Negroes the opportunity for individual expansion and individual contacts with the life and spirit of New York.[6]

Population Movements

The movement of Negro population into new residential areas is often considered as different in kind from that of other racial, immigrant, or economic groups. When studied, however, from the standpoint of human ecology, it appears to vary little, if at all, from those of other groups.

In Chicago these main population movements have been charted and the chief factors governing their direction and rate defined, if not as yet numerically determined. The great arterial business streets of the city have been and remain the highways of invasion. In Chart III these movements of immigrant groups outward from the central business district have been charted.

On the North Side the main line of (1) northward invasion has been along Clark Sreet, a highway traversed first by Germans and Scandinavians with Hungarians and Italians at a respectable distance behind. On the West Side are six great highways: (2) the northwest march of the Poles along Milwaukee Avenue, crowding fast behind an earlier German and Scandinavian movement; (3) the outward Italian expansion following the winding of Grand Avenue even outside the city limits into Maywood; (4) the westward penetration of the Negroes following Lake Street; (5) the extension of the cosmopolitan rooming house district westward on West Madison Street, the "main stem" of Hobohemia; (6) the migration of the Russian Jews along Roosevelt Road; and (7) the Czech journey from Pilsen through South Lawndale to Cicero and Berwyn along 22nd Street. On the South Side the three main radial lines are: (8) the Polish settlements southwest following Archer Road; (9) the Irish southern movement down Halsted Street and (10) the Negro invasion of the South Side along State Street.

The direction of these lines of migration, although fixed by the physical features of the city plan, also conform to the principle of radial extension. The rate of movement of a population group is

CHART III

RADIAL EXPANSION OF RACIAL AND IMMIGRANT GROUPS

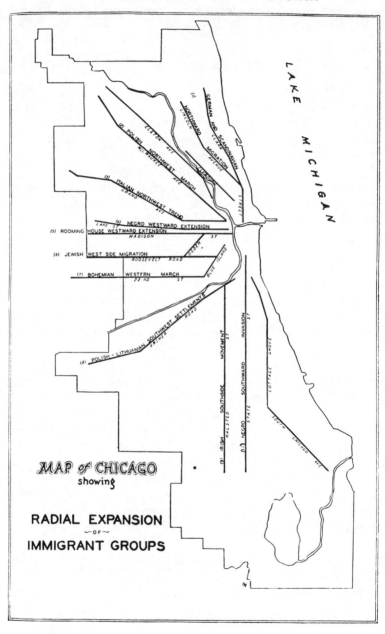

LAKE MICHIGAN

(1) GERMAN AND SCANDINAVIAN MIGRATION

NORTHWARD

(1) POLISH NORTHWEST MARCH

(1) ITALIAN NORTHWEST TREND

(4) NEGRO WESTWARD EXTENSION

(5) ROOMING HOUSE WESTWARD EXTENSION

(6) JEWISH WEST SIDE MIGRATION

(7) BOHEMIAN WESTERN MARCH

(8) POLISH - LITHUANIAN SOUTHWEST SETTLEMENTS

(9) IRISH SOUTHSIDE MOVEMENT

(0) NEGRO SOUTHWARD INVASION

MAP of CHICAGO
showing

RADIAL EXPANSION
~OF~
IMMIGRANT GROUPS

the product also of the radial character of urban growth and the peculiarities of the physical formation of the city, but complicated by the relative mobility of different immigrant groups. Jews seem, for example, to have a higher rate of movement than Bohemians; Italians, Poles, Lithuanians and Mexicans rank much lower than either. The mobility of the Negro is relatively low due to the strong resistance encountered by him in his invasion of white neighborhoods.

These population movements, from the center toward the periphery of the city as the resultant of outward pressure and local community, take the form, therefore, of successive waves of invasion. Succession as a process has been studied and its main course charted as (1) *invasion,* beginning often as an unnoticed or gradual penetration, followed by (2) *reaction,* or the resistance mild or violent of the inhabitants of the community, ultimately resulting in (3) the *influx* of newcomers and the rapid abandonment of the area by its old-time residents, and (4) *climax* or the achievement of a new equilibrium of communal stability.

Every residential community offers resistance to the intrusion of a new group of imputed inferior status whether on the basis of race, economic standing, or cultural difference. This resistance may manifest varying degrees of intensity. In the face of Negro invasion it may go to the extremes of violent opposition.

This antagonism in northern cities appears to have been particularly intense with the Irish and at an earlier period with the Germans. Carter G. Woodson in his volume *A Century of Negro Migration* notes the rise early in the nineteenth century of race prejudice in northern cities against the free Negro.

The first exhibition of this prejudice was seen among the lower classes of white people, largely Irish and German, who, devoted to menial labor, competed directly with the Negroes. It did not require a long time, however, for this feeling to react on the higher classes of whites where Negroes had settled in large groups.[7]

At any rate, no instance has been noted in the literature where a Negro invasion succeeded in displacing the Irish in possession of a community. Yet, frequently, as notably in New York and

Chicago, Negroes have pushed forward in the wake of retreating Jews. At the present time the Negroes in Chicago are invading two new areas, the Ghetto on the West Side and Little Sicily on the Lower North Side. It is rather significant to point out in passing the frequent propinquity of Negroes and Italian settlements in our larger cities. The proximity of Negro and Italian communities in New York and Chicago is well known. Three of the other four cities, namely, Cleveland, Detroit, and Pittsburgh, analyzed above for concentration of population groups, contained a ward with over 10 percent of the total Italian and Negro population of the city. In no one of the six cities, however, were wards found containing 10 per cent of both the Negro and the Polish population.

This contrast suggests the importance of further study of the relative resistance of different immigrant groups in determining the direction of the movement of Negro population in northern cities.

Further Projects for Study

It would seem, in general, that the residential distribution of Negroes in northern cities in the United States conforms to the location and movement of other population groups. Nevertheless, important differences have been observed which deserve further study from the standpoint of the ecological organization of the city into its five chief urban zones. The following projects are, therefore, suggested as promising lines of inquiry:

1. *A comparative study of the movement of Negro population in Northern and Southern cities.* The material and findings presented in this paper have been drawn from northern cities where in recent years the Negroes, rapidly increasing in number, have taken the rôle of an immigrant group. Obviously, the factors determining the location and shifting of population groups are quite different in the South. For example, Jesse F. Steiner in an unpublished study of the distribution of Negroes in New Orleans finds significant correlations of Negro population movement with the varying number of feet of depression of various areas below the level of the Mississippi River.

2. *A comparative study of different types of Negro communities within a city.*[8] In a term paper on the distribution of Negro communities in St. Louis, Berenice O'Fallon makes an interesting comparison of different rôles taken by the various neighborhoods in the larger Negro community corresponding with their position in the five urban zones. Extending from the central business district (I) into the zone of transition (II) are (a) the Negro slums along the river frontage frequented by hoboes, dope fiends, drunkards; (b) a low grade rooming house district with certain streets given over to prostitution, inhabited by low paid workers in nearby railroad yards and factories; and (c) better furnished rooms where dwell men employed as porters, waiters, policy vendors, professional card sharks and women working out in service as cooks, maids, chambermaids in hotels and laundresses, and where is located such institutions of night life as the dance hall, the cabaret and the club house. In the workingmen's zone (III) is located (d) a workingman's district with low rents and little repair on dwellings where the men do various kinds of laborious work for a weekly pay check of twenty to twenty-five dollars, and the women work in laundries and factories, scrub office buildings and do housework by the day. In the residential zone (IV) are found (e) a good residential section of fine, large homes lately acquired by the Negroes from wealthy owners who have moved into palatial apartment buildings or into exclusive suburban sections, and (f) a bungalow district in which reside men who are postal clerks, mail carriers, small business men and highly paid skilled workingmen with weekly incomes of forty-five to fifty-five dollars, and women who are housewives, stenographers, and elevator and stock girls in department stores. In the suburban zone (V) there are located (g) near the wealthy suburban districts several small Negro settlements whose inhabitants are mainly mulattoes.

The statement has been made by Robert E. Park that Negro society is not at all homogeneous as erroneously thought by most outsiders, but has actually as many, if not more, economic and social gradations as white society. In his study of the Negro family in Chicago, E. Franklin Frazier is engaged in developing a technique to measure with some degree of precision these differences in economic and social status implied in this impressionistic analysis, from the standpoint of location, of the social structure of Negro society in St. Louis.

3. *A study of changes in land values incident to Negro invasion of an area.* The entrance of the Negro into a white community results in an immediate apparent depreciation in land values.[9] This also results, but not always so rapidly, from any other racial or immigrant intrusion or from commercial and industrial encroachment. No study has, however, been made of the long time effect upon land values of Negro settlement. A cursory examination of the trend in land values from 1912 to 1928 as entered in "Olcott's Land Values Blue Book" of Chicago seems to indicate that in time residential values tend slowly to recover from their losses, but that commercial values with little or no check, forge rapidly ahead.

The fact is that Negroes frequently acquire sites in the direction of business and industrial growth. A Negro once owned property on Wall Street in New York. Two Negro churches with locations in and near the loop in Chicago were able to realize on the sale of their property enough to clear their mortgages and to purchase suitable sites further south in districts to which their parishioners had migrated. In the case of the Bethel American Methodist Episcopal Church this was only possible through the generous assistance of a wealthy white friend who advanced the sums necessary to prevent foreclosure of the mortgage.[10]

More frequently, however, Negro property owners are not in position to take advantage of the future rise in land value. They have not been able in New York, for example, to profit as have certain institutions which have moved several times because they were able to hold the property until they could capitalize on each occasion upon the increase in land values.

In certain cases where clashes have occurred upon the invasion by the Negro of a white residential area, a period of quiet follows in which it would seem that the Negroes have been kept out. But actual study shows that in many cases the reverse is true. The Negro really had acquired property and his progress of penetration continued peacefully until he had obtained possession of the neighborhood. These situations merit further investigation.

4. Density of population in Negro settlements—height of buildings. Woofter in his volume *Negro Problems in Cities*[11] shows that the density per acre is much greater for Negroes than for whites in the same city. He also indicates that the density in Negro settlements varies widely. An examination of the census tracts for Chicago showed, however, that the density of population in certain immigrant settlements, particularly the Polish, was much higher than in any Negro neighborhood. In general the density of population in Negro neighborhoods was practically the same as that of other neighborhoods in the same urban zone. Further study should be made in order to determine whether or not in other cities the density of population is greater or less in Negro and in white neighborhoods in the same urban zone. In any study of rates of density of population, it is always desirable to distinguish between neighborhoods by prevailing type of dwellings and height of buildings as between single homes, two flat and tenement or apartment houses, and one story, two story, or many story structures.

5. A study of rents in Negro neighborhoods. All investigations of rents in Negro areas show that on the average rents are higher for Negroes than for whites. These studies, however, are generally made in times of a housing crisis for the Negroes and in periods of Negro immigration into the city. It would be desirable to study rents for the different types of Negro neighborhoods in the city to determine more accurately the factors making for higher rent and, if possible, the conditions under which rents are stabilized at the level prevailing in white neighborhoods.

6. A study of the proximity of vice resorts and Negro districts. In many cities, as Chicago, Kansas City, Buffalo, Springfield (Illinois), Fort Wayne (Indiana), Topeka (Kansas), vice has been located in openly recognized segregated districts or in concealed resorts within or adjacent to Negro districts. Presumably the Negro has been forced to seek these areas for residence because of his difficulty in gaining entrance into better residential districts.[12] With the abolition of segregated districts new institutions have made their appearance in the city like the cabaret and the closed dance hall. So-called "black and tan" cabarets and night clubs run openly in New York, Chicago, Los Angeles. No adequate study of the rôle and function of these institutions has as yet been made. They demand further study as one phase of the interesting drama of race relations in our largest American cities.

This list of projects does not in any sense exhaust the number that might be suggested. They are probably sufficient to indicate the way in which certain aspects of residential segregation may be approached from the standpoints and methods of human ecology. The trend of the discussion in this paper may also tend to the conclusion that the residential segregation of the Negro in northern cities in this country is, in the main, not the product of race prejudice alone but the result of the interplay of factors in urban growth which determine the location and movement of all groups, institutions, and individuals.

II. The Family

Introduction

BY LEONARD S. COTTRELL, JR.

OVER A HALF century ago in 1915, a brash young bachelor from Kingfisher College, Oklahoma, offered a course on the family at Ohio State. No one else in the Department of Sociology there would teach the course, and Dr. Burgess, being the junior member, had to take it. He was "under thirty" and had been awarded his Ph.D. degree at the University of Chicago just two years previous. As would be expected, therefore, his course was "revolutionary" in conception and content. He tells a little about it in a paper of pivotal significance, "The Family as a Unity of Interacting Personalities," reprinted below as chapter 5.

From that spirited start and throughout the next generation, Professor Burgess, bachelor, was America's Mr. Family. Rare indeed were the courses, research articles, doctoral dissertations, textbooks, family agency programs that did not draw heavily on his work. In fact, almost as strong a claim can be made for the present time. After he retired from active duty as a member of the faculty at the University of Chicago in 1951, he continued a substantial publication program up into the early sixties.

One who studies the Burgess contribution and then takes a look at the current handbooks, textbooks, and course outlines gains a strong impression that were Professor Burgess alive today and should he drop in on a college course on the family, he would feel quite at home. Were he asked to lecture on any topic on the outline, he could do so with complete relevance and little or no disruption of the continuity of the course. This he could do, not because the field has become dormant and static. During the past two decades, there has been a continuously mounting volume of published materials. His at-homeness would derive from the fact that the basic categories and issues he had identified in the early twenties are still the chief current concerns.

In the syllabus of a contemporary course of study in the family, there would undoubtedly be a section on comparative institutional studies. This, of course, would be familiar territory, for he not only had cut his eye teeth on the great classics in the historical and anthropological studies, but had his students do likewise. Moreover, he had them adapt the approach to the study of family forms in different subcultures in our own contemporary society. In the halcyon days of what came to be known as the "Chicago School" of sociology, Professors Park and Burgess conducted a research seminar in what was known as "The Temple"—an old residence of the gay nineties vintage across the Midway from the campus which was used as the headquarters of the many studies of the City of Chicago being conducted by the various members of the social science departments in the university. Many members of the seminar were doing research on what were identified as "natural" areas of the city as opposed to administratively defined areas. These natural areas were seen as emerging from the ecological and sociopolitical processes that characterized the modern city. They were defined by distinctive subcultural features. Of special interest to Professor Burgess was the hypothesis that each type of natural area had a distinctive pattern of family life. This idea was given explicit formulation and tested by one of Burgess's well known students, Ernest R. Mowrer, in *Family Disorganization* (University of Chicago Press, 1927).

Another study emerging from Burgess's comparative interest and Park's interest in the Negro was the definitive study *The Negro Family in Chicago* by E. Franklin Frazier (University of Chicago Press, 1932).

As these and other similar studies show, Burgess went well beyond the comparative descriptive interest that characterized the older classical studies. He pointed to the method as a means of testing a wide variety of hypotheses as to the relationship among cultural variables and forms and functions of the family. This interest, of course, led him in the direction of what today has been elaborated into the structural-functional conceptual framework. In his article "The Family as a Unity of Interacting Personalities," he had clearly indicated his opinion that systematic functional interrelationships would be found to exist between the various familial forms and functions and the cultural systems in which they were embedded.

This correlation between cultural areas of the city and types of family life is no fortuitous coincidence. It suggests the ways in which family life is related to the ecology of the city. The pattern of family life develops under certain life conditions and thrives only in conformity with the folkways and mores of the local community. [Below, chap. 6.]

In later years, he elaborated his ideas more explicitly in "The Changing American Family" (*Religious Education* 23 [1928]: 408–15), "The Family in a Changing Society" (*American Journal of Sociology* 53 [1948]: 417–22), and a collaborative work with Harvey J. Locke, *The Family: From Institution to Companionship* (American Book Company, 1945). Thus, the issues in the ongoing debate on structural-functional theory of research studies were ones to which Burgess had given considerable thought. His ideas would not show the elaboration or the level of abstraction of the current theorists, but they would have the vitality and penetration that comes from long and intimate contact with the concrete phenomena.

The present-day emphasis on interaction within the family for Professor Burgess would have been especially gratifying, for it was this area that he early perceived as the most promising for progress in the development of research on the family. I have referred to Burgess's article "The Family as a Unity of Interacting Personalities" as pivotal. It helped determine both his own professional career and the direction of sociological research on the family during the ensuing several decades.

In this article two things are clear: One, that Professor Burgess clearly grasped the nature and importance of historical, comparative institutional, and structural-functional, as well as interactional modes of study; and two, that he believed the neglect of the study of the internal dynamics of the family seriously restricted our understanding of its nature and functioning. It was to supplying this lack that Professor Burgess devoted a major portion of his research career. The productivity of his diagnosis and the influence of his leadership is amply documented in the bibliography of the research literature on the family during the forty years that followed his "declaration."

The basic conceptualizations and working assumptions with which Professor Burgess studied the processes and products of intrafamilial interaction can be stated in skeletal form as follows. Men and women emerge from the interactive experience in their own families of origin with specific patterning of organic drives, conceptions of themselves and expectations of others in familial situations, and socially relevant skills and capabilities. These patternings play a major part in selection of and interaction with potential marriage partners. The nature of the new dyad is the resultant of the interplay between past patterns of the mates and the particular interactive experiences in the developing relation. With the coming of children, the aging of the parents, the changes in the developmental stages of family life, and the changes in conditions in which the family exists, the patterns of interactions change, latent roles appear, or new roles emerge. Thus, even in highly stable cultures the family is never a static "structure" but a dynamic and changing process. While in the latter part of his career Professor Burgess was interested in research on the cyclic developmental changes and role progressions in the family, especially with respect to the later years of life (see this volume, chap. 9), he was chiefly interested in the dynamics of the modern family as it confronted changing socioeconomic and cultural conditions (chap. 10).

Burgess found himself increasingly preoccupied with the dynamics of the marital relationship. It was he more than anyone else of his time who saw that the cultural supports and sanctions and the role conceptions and expectations of a more stable period of family history would lose their power and would be replaced by internal bonds that would give whatever stability modern marriage might retain. Among these bonds, be it noted, Burgess did not number "romantic love." When he looked at marriage and the family in the 1920s, he did not find it to be in shambles nor see it as a vanishing form of human association. His comment on the "free unions of our Greenwich Villages" is characteristic.

Hardly a day passes but the public is shocked and outraged by some new form of wild and reckless behavior, particularly of youth in revolt no longer regulated by customary controls.

But these random and aimless variations away from the basic pattern of family life are not, as some believe, an indication of the future of family life and sexual relationships. They are only the symptoms in the present, as in similar times in the past, that society is undergoing change. When an equilibrium is re-established a new pattern of family life will emerge, better adapted to the new situation, but only a different variety of the old familiar pattern of personal relationships in the family." ["The Romantic Impulse and Family Disorganization," *Survey* 57 (1926): 290–94.]

It was this insistence on seeing the family in the realities of behavioral processes and products rather than through the lenses of cultural and legal institutional forms that made Burgess so "relevant" during his own time and continues to make him relevant today.

The foregoing citation was the initial statement of a theme that became progressively more clearly articulated and central in Burgess's work on marriage and the family. He early became convinced that the vigor and stability of the family in Western society could not depend on the authority of traditional cultural forms and sanctions. He further held that, while the sexual bond was indeed important, it alone could not be relied upon to supply the foundation of a stable relationship in marriage.

During the 1920s and '30s there was no lack of prophets, including some sociologists, who were predicting the early demise of the family. And indeed the crumbling of its authoritative traditional patterns, the progressive loss of many of its functions, and the changing sexual mores appeared amply to justify the predictions. Professor Burgess, however, thought otherwise. To him the processes of urban industrialization with its accompanying fragmentation and depersonalization of lives would intensify the felt need for a stable, intimate, congenial personal relationship. Thus, the conditions that would make for a lasting and satisfying marriage would be those that supported companionship. The family, therefore, would not disappear but would change its form and foundations. Burgess expressed this in his phrase "from institution to companionship." This theme was made more explicit in his statement of his conceptual orientation to the problem of predicting adjustment in marriage (see this volume, chap. 8). The theme of marital adjustment is found in the two texts which Professor Burgess published with two of his students—*The Family: From Institution to Companionship*, with Harvey Locke (American Book Company, 1945), and *Engagement and Marriage*, with Paul Wallin (J. B. Lippincott Company, 1953).

Another thing that made and still makes Burgess's work so fresh and vital was his unwillingness to commit himself to any single theoretical system. He was an eclectic par excellence, not in the manner of a dilettante, but as a versatile workman who used theories pragmatically as tools. Typical is the way Professor Burgess utilized various behavioral theories in his analysis of the family. The conceptualizations with which he viewed the processes and outcomes of interaction of the family members are perhaps best described in chapters 2, 3, and 6 of *Introduction to the Science of Sociology*, which Burgess coauthored with Robert E. Park. Biological determinants are explicitly recognized not only in the form of limited reflexes, biochemical processes and very general motivational states. Upon this substrate is erected a superstructure of behavior patterns and capabilities acquired through the learnings precipitated from interaction with the environment, the most important part of which is the behavior of other persons and groups. This view is best epitomized by Robert Park: "Man is not born human. It is only slowly and laboriously, in fruitful contact, co-operation and conflict with his fellows, that he attains the distinctive qualities of human nature" (*Introduction to the Science of Sociology*, p. 79).

No specific motivational theory is adopted or developed, though Burgess uses W. I. Thomas's theory of the four fundamental wishes when that formulation appears useful (cf. Thomas, *The*

Unadjusted Girl: With Cases and Standpoint for Behavior Analysis
[Little, Brown and Company, 1933]). No specific theory of learning is utilized, though E. L. Thorndike's principles of learning are occasionally referred to (cf. Thorndike, *Educational Psychology*, vols. 1–3 [Teachers' College of Columbus University, 1913–14]).

The same eclectic freedom marked Burgess's use of Freudian theory. Both Park and Burgess referred to the work of Freud more or less in passing in their *Introduction to the Science of Sociology*. But while Park was inclined to reject psychoanalytic theory, Burgess was intrigued by it. He early introduced readings in Freudian literature in his course on the family and made John Carl Flugel's book *The Psychoanalytic Study of the Family* (London, 1921) a major reference in his syllabus for the course as soon as the work appeared. He encouraged his students to tap earliest childhood memories in preparing their autobiographical studies, and to record recurring dreams. He did not put much stock in the concept of the Unconscious, but was aware of the significance of unconscious attitudes, motives, and fears. He appreciated the significance of Freud's discovery of the Oedipal dynamics, but was not inclined to make of it the nucleus of personality. He was especially interested in the processes of importation of parental roles into the self-other patterns of the person, but was not inclined to give much credence to the notion of "the primordial patricide" and the alleged "racial unconscious" roots of the superego.

So far as I know, Professor Burgess never tried "the couch." A good many of his students and colleagues had a go at it with varying results. He was always quite curious as to how much difference the psychoanalytic experience or "training" made in the way the person interpreted behavioral data. He once remarked that for some the experience seemed to make them more sensitive and alert to subtle cues and changes in interpersonal interaction; others appeared to become so bound by orthodox psychoanalytic interpretations that they actually became less competent observers of what went on in interaction. His article on "The Influences of Sigmund Freud upon Sociology in the United States" (*American Journal of Sociology* 45 [1940]: 356–74) makes clear his interest in Freud.

Both Park and Burgess regarded their central theoretical orientation to be interactional and found the conceptualizations of George Herbert Mead of great relevance (cf. Mead, "The Social Self," *Journal of Philosophy* 10 [1913]:374–80; *Mind, Self, and Society* [University of Chicago Press, 1934]). Burgess exercised the same prerogatives of the eclectic in his use of Mead's social behaviorism. Those who find it necessary to classify sociologists place Burgess in the interactional category, and he would agree to this placement. But he was not a "follower of George Herbert Mead" (as Harold T. Christensen describes him in *Handbook of Marriage and the Family* [Rand NcNally, 1964], p. 62). He certainly made use of some of Mead's ideas and concepts such as the social self, and he saw human behavior as both process and product of social interaction rather than as manifestation of attributes of the individual. But his model of the interaction process remained at pretty much the level of "mutual influence" theory characteristic of most non-Meadian sociologists today. Mead, of course, pushed the concept of interaction further to include the processes of "mutual interpenetration," whereby the behavior of the self and other became a single integrated process and the property of each participant in the interact. Burgess's analysis of cases frequently implied this latter conception of interaction, but he did not make consistent use of it. Furthermore, when the practical demands of a research problem dictated it, Burgess could operate with an attribute or trait model of behavior with little apparent strain on his interactionist "conscience" (see, for example, *The Adolescent in the Family: A Study of Personality Development in the Home Environment* [Appleton, 1934]). In fact, methodological and technical limitations made research with attribute models almost inevitable. Even today it is almost impossible to do research of any considerable size and complexity with a strict interactionist model.

Strictly speaking, Professor Burgess was more artist than scientist in his analysis and interpretation of the human personality. This does not mean he lacked objectivity and analytic skill. In fact, he usually appeared more objective than many who were adherents of one or another theory of behavior. As noted above, he had a substantial grasp of Freudian theory, Meadian social behaviorism, and

Thorndikian and Hullian learning theories. But when he undertook to explain behavior of the person, he relied heavily on his own keen perceptiveness and penetrating empathic grasp. His skill in this area is seen in his brilliant use of case study, life history, and interview materials (see this volume, chaps. 6, 11, 15). To be sure, his illuminating interpretations were informed by conceptualizations of various theoretical systems, but he was thrall to none. Burgess's empirical work on personality development and functioning in the family has not provided systematic formal testing of clear-cut hypotheses derived from a specific theoretical system. But it has dramatically expanded our perceptions and understandings of the realities of the processes and products of interaction in the family. In doing this, it has stimulated a widespread development of research on all aspects of familial behavior.

Among students of the family as well as among the general public, Professor Burgess is best known for the pioneer work he and his collaborators did in their efforts to identify critical factors affecting relationships in marriage and to use these factors in predicting marital adjustment. When in 1930 he proposed a research project aimed at predicting "success or failure in marriage" (a project in which I cooperated with Burgess; see this volume, chap. 7), he did so with a substantial amount of confidence based on successful efforts to predict parole violation rates of various categories of prisoners (chap. 12). Moreover, the practical value of the parole prediction procedure induced a similar practical slant in the approach to the marriage study. The emphasis, therefore, was not on testing theoretically derived hypotheses so much as on identifying efficient predictors.

This did not mean that we were without benefit of any theoretical framework—rather that theory had to be elastic, and theory testing tended to give way to practical "hunch" as to what looked promising as a predictor. However, most of the data collected from our sample did in fact bear on a general working hypothesis which may be stated as follows. The level of adjustment in marriage depends on the assimilability of the partners in an intimate, mutually supportive relation—a companionship in Professor Burgess's terms. The degree of attainment of such a relation is determined in substantial part by the interaction of the cultural patterns, normative expectations, and role patterns acquired by the partners in the cultural, class, and family matrices to which these partners have been socialized. Identification and appropriate weighting and combination of indicia of these patterns should yield an approximate quantitative index of the probability of specified levels of adjustment.

Resource, technical, and "state of the art" limitations permitted only approximate testing of the hypothesis. But results (see this volume, chaps. 7, 8) were of sufficient significance and promised to encourage further, somewhat more refined efforts along the same lines. These include Lewis Madison Terman's *Psychological Factors in Marital Happiness* (McGraw Hill, 1938); three articles by Burgess and Wallin, "Homogamy in Social Characteristics" (*American Journal of Sociology* 49 [1943]: 109–24), "Predicting Adjustment in Marriage from Adjustment in Engagement" (ibid. 49 [1944]: 324–30), and "Homogamy in Personality Characteristics" (*Journal of Abnormal and Social Psychology* 39 [1944]: 475–81); and two books, mentioned earlier, coauthored by Burgess—*Engagement and Marriage* (with Wallin) and *The Family: From Institution to Companionship* (with Locke).

Notwithstanding its limitations, the 1936 study did demonstrate the feasibility of quantification and prediction in a very complex human relationship. There have been numerous replications of the original research, none of which have reversed the essential findings of that study. Beginning with Terman, many investigators have made use of substantial parts of the original test items. The results and the research questionnaire have been used extensively by marriage counselors and instructors in courses on marriage. Columnists who offer advice on personal problems still cite some of the findings; and the study may properly claim what some might regard as a dubious credit for the basic ideas and a good deal of the specific content of computer dating and matchmaking.

In many respects, this pioneering study of marriage provided an ideal vehicle for the expression of the essential Burgess. One marked characteristic of Professor Burgess was his unfailing curiosity about people and their frailties and foibles. When one of his students, assigned to write a description of her family, complained that her family was completely lacking in any interesting experiences or problems, Professor Burgess remarked that in the course of reviewing several hundred life histories and family descriptions he had yet to encounter one that was not interesting. He had a keen relish for what some might regard as gossip—not the malicious kind, but the kind that gave the "low down" on what was going on "off stage." It would be easy to point out plausible psychoanalytic interpretations as to the roots of this intense curiosity. But it is clear to anyone who knew Professor Burgess that these components had been thoroughly sublimated into highly fruitful and constructive motives to understand human beings and to discover ways that might assist them in coping with their problems. Son of a protestant minister, reared in a conventional middle-class, somewhat puritanic, small-town setting, this rather timid and withdrawn and very discrete bachelor possessed a perceptiveness and understanding of people from every position on the human spectrum that was a byword among his students and colleagues.

Another "fit" between the marriage prediction research and the essential Burgess was due to the freedom this research gave to his heterodox orientation to theory. Professor Burgess respected serious theories and those who sought to test them. He had little time or patience for "theological" debate, exegesis, and similar word games. He was interested only when he encountered empirical testing of theories. He never found a single theoretical system that ordered all the phenomena that interested him. He was therefore inclined to use any conceptualization that promised to give him a window on what was going on. The study of marital behavior allowed, nay required, the eclecticism so congenial to him.

The same freedom characterized Professor Burgess in his utilization of methods. He was, of course, highly expert in the use of case studies—a skill that unfortunately has languished, to the great detriment of our discipline (see this volume, chap. 17). When he found he needed statistical methods, he took courses, tutored, and practiced until he had a reasonable command of those procedures required by his problems. He was delighted when in the midst of the prediction study, Professor L. L. Thurstone came up with his multiple factor method for reducing large numbers of variables to a few "basic factors." Richard O. Lang, who was at that time my assistant, and I took Professor Thurstone's course and gained enough proficiency in the method to apply it to the marriage data. We gave Burgess a short course in the method, and he was not only highly gratified with the results, but was pleased that our study represented the first sociological application of the method. In this connection it should be remembered that, whereas today a multiple factor analysis can be done in minutes with the computer, in the early 1930s one problem of the size of ours took two or three months. It is important at this point to observe that while Professor Burgess was convinced of the necessity for sociologists to move strongly toward greater competence in the development and use of quantitative techniques, he would regard as something of a disaster the current policy of many departments of sociology to make virtuosity in statistics the principal if not the sole criterion of competence required of a sociologist. He would almost certainly attribute the anemic and inconsequential character of much that passes for sociological research to the widespread lack of capacity to make penetrating and meaningful qualitative observations and interpretations of human behavior and the almost complete absence of systematic training in these skills.

Underlying all of Professor Burgess's devotion to sociology as a science was a concern for improving the capability of human beings to cope with problems and build a more satisfying life. Marriage, with its potential for great human happiness and unrelieved agony, was a compelling field of interest. And the utilitarian value of knowledge that would throw light on and provide some guidance to conduct in marital life played a major role in Burgess's long commitment to research, teaching, and practical social action in that field. It is well known that he was a prime mover in numerous national efforts to provide a wider understanding of the problems of the family and the resources available for improvement of family life. Of special note was his role in the establishment of the National Council on Family Relations, on which he served as president in 1942. Another agency closely connected with the family was the American Gerontological Society. He was active in the development of the program of this society and served as its president in 1952. The Family Study Center at Chicago is another type of activity that resulted from his efforts. This organization, connected with the University of Chicago, is devoted to research and the application of research findings to the solution of problems of the family. The emphasis on research and applications of research findings that will be found in organizations like the Social Science Research Council, the American Sociological Association, the Society for the Study of Social Problems, and other professional organizations bear the mark of his interest and activity.

Following completion of the Burgess-Cottrell study, Professor Burgess, as we have previously indicated, continued his investigations, pushing into the field of courtship interaction and in further study of the transition of marriage from traditional institutional forms to freer, more varied patterns of what he termed companionship. The matured results of investigations covering two decades following the initiation of the original prediction study were published in 1945 (*The Family: From Institution to Companionship*) and 1953 (*Engagement and Marriage*). Though greatly expanded and elaborated with empirical material, the basic themes of these books had already been articulated in Burgess's 1926 paper.

This perennial quality in Burgess may be attributed in large part to certain personal qualities and to the kind of training environment provided him when he was a young graduate student at the University of Chicago. As a person, Burgess was marked by unusual empathic ability. Though this skill was masked by a somewhat timid, withdrawn, formal, and stiff manner, it was there and covered an extraordinary range in the spectrum of human experience. This great perceptiveness and comprehension was matched by an essential good will and friendliness for people. He was no "bleeder" who made saints of all the unfortunate and downtrodden, but he had a strong sense of fairness and justice and good will. To these must be added an intense curiosity about people, what they thought and felt and did behind their facades.

With these highly potent resources, Burgess had the additional good fortune to land at the University of Chicago Sociology Department in the early phases of its most creative period. The chairman of the department, Albion Small, was insisting that the chief responsibility of the graduate students was to render what their professors were teaching them "out of date as soon as possible." There was a revolt against large, abstract, theoretical systems. The main thrust was getting out and finding out how people actually behaved. The watchword was "know your data intimately and don't stray too far from it when you theorize about it." No situation could have been more congenial to young Burgess's basic disposition and skills. It was a case of love at first sight and lifelong commitment. This particular combination of personal capability and professional training was not likely to produce a towering theoretical system, but it should produce the highly durable insights and understandings that always characterize the classical in art and science. It should and it did in Ernest Burgess.

5

THE FAMILY AS A UNITY OF
INTERACTING PERSONALITIES

NINE YEARS ago I gave for the first time a course on the family. There was even then an enormous literature in this field. But among all the volumes upon the family, ethnological, historical, psychological, ethical, social, economic, statistical, radically realist, or radically idealist, there was to be found not a single work that even pretended to study the modern family as behavior or as a social phenomenon. It has been studied as a legal institution but it had not been studied as a subject of natural science, *i.e.* (as Professor Park once said of the newspaper), in the way in which the biologist studies the potato bug.[1] So far as I know, the description by Professor Thomas of the large family group among the Polish peasants was the first study of the family as a living being rather than as a dead form.[2]

Because of this lack of social psychological studies of the family, the work of the course was planned upon two principles. The first was to select from the literature of psychiatry, psychology, social psychology, and sociology, statements of concepts that seemed to have a bearing upon research in family life, as sexual instinct, maternal sentiment, wish for response, monogamy as in the mores, birth control as a folkway, family conflict, accommodation, and assimilation. The second was to assemble, from all possible sources, case studies of family life. These were taken from the

---

Reprinted from *The Family* 7 (1926) : 3–9. Paper read at meeting of the section on the Family of the American Sociological Society, New York, 29 December 1926.

works of ethnologists, from histories of manners and customs, from biography and autobiography, from fiction, from drama, from records of social agencies, from any source where realistic pictures of family life might be secured. In addition, my students have contributed several hundred case studies, which often, with more or less intimate detail, describe their own families.

In reading these cases, reflecting upon them, and seeking to analyze them, certain facts began to emerge and finally to crystallize in rather clear form. The first was that in spite of the undoubtedly great differences between individual families or between family life in various cultural groups, there was a family type in general. In the last analysis, the essential characteristics of the family were found to be everywhere the same. And what are these characteristics? The whole body of familial sentiments which naturally and inevitably grow out of and maintain the relationships of husband and wife and parents and children. The rôle of the mother, for instance, we immediately recognize as basically the same, despite the apparent superficial differences in the care of children among Eskimos, Turks, or Englishmen.

My next discovery was a sudden perception of the tremendous difference between the modern family and the family of the past. How many of us realize how modern a phenomenon is the small family of father, mother, and children emancipated from the control of the wider kinship group of grandparents, uncles, aunts, and cousins? Do we perceive that it is to be found as a typical specimen perhaps only in cities, and particularly in the urbanized areas of our very largest American cities? The small family group in apartment houses or residential hotels is, no doubt, the most notorious illustration of effectual detachment from the claims of kinship. The absence in the city home of "the spare bedroom," that famous institution of the country-side, serves as a convenient defense against invading relatives.

At the same time, the family in modern life is undergoing changes and modifications which can hardly be appreciated or understood except in the perspective of the past or by an opportunity for comparison with a contemporary organization of the large family in process of disintegration, such as China affords.

But, as the large family was organized in the interests of the older generation to resist change, and so to perpetuate the family pattern, the modern family is exposed to change since it begins in a certain sense anew with every marriage and is thus at the mercy of the new romantic notions of the younger generation.

In contrasting the small family of these city areas with the kinship or large family group—whether in ancient Israel, Greece, or Rome, or in contemporary India, Japan, or China, or even with the large peasant family of Poland or Russia, or with the kinship clans of American rural communities—differences are at once apparent. The large family group tends in every culture to be impressed in one standardized form; while within the same culture the small family tends to exhibit a variety of patterns. Already in American society are to be found the following patterns classified by size of family: the childless family or the so-called "companionate"; the one-child family; the two-child family; the family with three or more children. And these are not merely biological or economic classes, they are in large part determined by custom, or by new fashions in the folkways. Dr. Mowrer[3] has even classified areas of the city by types of family life, the non-family areas with their Hobohemian and Bohemian centers; areas of the so-called emancipated family in the rooming-house regions; the patriarchal family areas of the immigrant colonies; the equalitarian family areas of apartment house districts; and finally, in the so-called dormitory suburbs that new type of family where the husband leaves for down-town before the children are awake and returns after they are asleep, the modern matriarchal family, or perhaps more accurately, the matricentric family. This correlation between cultural areas of the city and types of family life is no fortuitous coincidence. It suggests the ways in which family life is related to the ecology of the city. The pattern of family life develops under certain life conditions and thrives only in conformity with the folkways and mores of the local community.

Next I found peculiarly revealing a classification of families by the pattern of personal relationships between husband and wife and parents and children. Two contrasted patterns soon presented themselves: the highly integrated family and the unintegrated or loosely integrated family. These in turn might be subdivided into several varieties. Upon analysis it was found that the highly integrated family possessed one or more of the following traits: elaborate ritual, rigorous discipline, sentimental interdependence; stimulating co-operative activities or objectives; while the unintegrated or loosely integrated family had little or no ritual, exerted slight control either through discipline or sentimental attachment and its members were only in small degree unified by common family aims to which individual purposes were subordinated. The typical orthodox Jewish family has in marked degree all the traits that are positive for the highly integrated family. The Puritan family, stigmatized by the younger generation as the Puritanical family, is a conspicuous illustration of integration through the characteristics of rigorous discipline and dominant family objectives.

This study of the patterns of personal relationships in family life led directly to the conception of the family as a unity of interacting persons. By a unity of interacting personalities is meant a living, changing, growing thing. I was about to call it a superpersonality. At any rate the actual unity of family life has its existence not in any legal conception, nor in any formal contract, but in the interaction of its members. For the family does not depend for its survival on the harmonious relations of its members, nor does it necessarily disintegrate as a result of conflicts between its members. The family lives as long as interaction is taking place and only dies when it ceases.

In a recent work (soon to be published) on *Family Disorganization*, Dr. Ernest R. Mowrer points out that interaction as a principle of family life applies not only to inter-communication within the family but to the relations which the family sustains to the environing society. He says:

The sociological concept of the family as a unity existing in interaction has two chief aspects. It signifies, first of all, that the family is an interplay of personalities rather than purely a common fixation of sexual, parental, and filial instincts. The sociological description of family interaction will then naturally be in terms of impulses socially defined, as wishes, attitudes and sentiments.

The family also exists in interaction with the larger society of which the family and its members are component parts. The status of the family in the neighborhood, its rôle as defined in the mores, in public opinion and by law, the changes in the family which result from the play of social forces in the community, are all illustrations of the significance for the family and its members of interaction with society.[4]

The family is even more than an interaction of personalities. In this interaction, the family develops a conception of itself. When this conception of familial relations is recognized by the community, the family acquires an institutional character. This is what is meant by the family as a social institution. A family that had no conception of its rôle in the community, or of the responsibilities of its individual members would not be an institution, perhaps not even a family. It is just these natural relationships of family life, the obligations and responsibilities spontaneously assumed in family interaction, which the community seeks first through custom and then through law to define, to make contractual, and to enforce. But everywhere, and always, by those who are dealing with problems of family life it is paramount to recognize that the family as a reality exists in the interaction of its members and not in the formalities of the law with its stipulations of rights and duties.

Often too the family is thought of as a mere collection of interacting individuals rather than a unity of interacting persons. Herein lies the value for research of the technical distinction, made by Professor Park, between the individual and the person.

The person is an individual who has status. We come into the world as individuals. We acquire status, and become persons. Status means position in society. The individual inevitably has some status in every social group of which he is a member. In a given group the status of every member is determined by his relation to every other member of that group. The individual's self-consciousness—his conception of his rôle in society, his "self," is based on his status in the social group or groups of which he is a member.[5]

This definition of the person as an individual with status has thrown a flood of light upon family interaction. The members of the family do react to each other as individuals and that is important. But they react to each other as persons and that is also important. For every person has, with more or less awareness, a conception of his rôle, not only in society, but in all groups of which he is a member. Not only does the person have a lively conception of his own rôle in the family, but he has a sense of the rôles of all the other members of the family and notions of what family life is or ought to be. The rôles of the good father, the good mother, and the good child enter powerfully in determining the conception which each member holds of his place in the world of family life.

In a stable, homogeneous society, ideas of family life and the rôles of its different members are relatively fixed and constant. In a changing society composed of heterogeneous elements, familial attitudes are almost inevitably in a state of flux. Instead of a common pattern of family life intrenched in tradition and crushing out all impulse to variation by the sheer weight of universal conformity, our American society presents what at first sight seems to be a chaotic conglomeration of every conceivable pattern of family organization and disorganization, from the patriarchal kinship groups of our Southern Mountain highlands to the free unions of our Greenwich Villages. Hardly a day passes but the public is shocked and outraged by some new form of wild and reckless behavior, particularly of youth in revolt no longer regulated by customary controls.

But those random and aimless variations away from the basic pattern of family life are not, as some believe, an indication of the future of family life and sexual relationships. They are only the symptoms in the present, as in similar times in the past, that society is undergoing change. When an equilibrium is re-established a new pattern of family life will emerge, better adapted to the new situation, but only a different variety of the old familiar pattern of personal relationships in the family.

The general currents of the social influences affecting the family can, however, be outlined. They were ably presented in a paper by Professor Ernest R. Groves[6] read before this group last year in Chicago. The passing of man's dominance, the emancipation of woman, and her entrance into all fields of economic, social, and civic life, parenthood by choice, the transition from the homestead family to the home in the small apartment or the hotel—these are only a few of the influences affecting family interaction in new and disturbing ways. More intangible but even more dynamic are the subtle changes taking place in our conception of the family and of the rôle of its members. It is only by contrast that we realize the revolutionary nature of the changes in our attitudes, as for example the difference between the attitudes of the Sicilian immigrant and the native American toward divorce.

In Little Sicily in Chicago, Dr. Mowrer found not a single case of desertion or divorce recorded in the Court of Domestic Relations or in the Superior or Circuit Courts. An Italian social worker in this district reported that she had never known a bona fide case where a Sicilian husband deserted his family, although this is one of the areas where poverty abounds. Divorce or desertion does not enter into the thought of the Sicilian as a conceivable solution for family difficulties. His prevailing code of conduct, his mores, and his religious sentiments effectually exclude any evasion of family responsibility afforded by desertion or the divorce courts. But separation and divorce, once under the ban of American mores, have now, at least for certain causes, tacitly received the sanction of the community. At any rate, the possibility of family disruption enters as a factor into the complex of familial attitudes, where it was almost absent in the American society of fifty years ago.

In his penetrating paper, Professor Groves gave a particularly illuminating explanation of the influence of conflicting conceptions of family life. The modern husband conceives the rôle which his wife should play in the family in the likeness of his mother (a sociological adaptation of the theory of the mother image) while the wife thinks of her rôle as a realization of some embodiment of the new woman. What family can be found in which this very natural divergence in family ideals has not been the crux of a conflict, perhaps slight or perhaps severe, and how interesting it would be to know the different solutions that have been worked out?

The following excerpts from a case studied by one of our graduate students depict the influence upon family life of conflicting patterns of family ideals. It will be called the Marx family, not because that is its name but because it suggests the German ancestry of the father. The father, like so many parents, acquired his notions of the rôle of parents and children from the family pattern in which he was reared.

In the early eighties the Marx family, consisting of the paternal grandparents and a son, a child of two, emigrated from Germany to Cincinnati, Ohio. There the grandfather worked as a teamster and in a few years as a teaming contractor. The oldest son, the Mr. Marx of our small family group, at twelve worked with his father as a teamster during the heavy season. Another son and daughter were soon added to the family and the economic struggle became severe. At the age of fourteen he was taken out of school and set to work ten or twelve hours a day. His wages were given over to his father, and he was "glad to have a dime to spend on the Fourth of July." At the age of eighteen he joined the cavalry in the Spanish American War and saw active service later in the Philippines. Returning overland after his discharge, he stopped in a small town to visit a friend. There he met Mrs. Marx and married her.

This picture of the paternal family pattern, while not detailed, suggests the characteristic features of the German-American immigrant family: the exercise of the paternal authority, rigorous discipline, the subordination of the individual members to the aim of the economic security and success of the family. A brief sketch of family history will bring us down to date for a description of family interaction at the present time.

Since his father died soon after his marriage, Mr. Marx and his bride moved to Cincinnati taking over the dwindling contracting business. His mother had grown rather harsh and melancholic during his absence and in every way he tried to defer to her wishes and render her the respect and obedience due to one who had done so much for him. In accordance with her wishes the first child was named Wilhelm (William). Four years yater Henry came and only a year later, Joseph. At the outbreak of the World War Mr. Marx enlisted and was in camp near Columbus where the family took up its abode. Late in 1919 he was honorably discharged. He immediately took a commission in the National Guard commanding a cavalry troop stationed in a small city where the widowed maternal grandmother lived.

Mr. Marx noticed that William had begun to grow rapidly during his absence and this continued until now he is six feet tall and only sixteen. At the same time Mr. Marx noticed that he was "acting up," was becoming lazy, was failing in school, and avoided strangers. He played with smaller boys and disobeyed his mother who gave up in despair and began to rely on the whippings administered by his father. These had little effect and William left school and went to work. Since then he has lost every job he has held after a few weeks or a month. He continues to dress slovenly, to loaf, and to disobey. William is the family problem; they have all come to take a hand in discussing him and in saying what he should do.

Mr. Marx conceived his rôle as the head of the family according to his mental picture of himself as taking his father's place. His military experience but confirmed his belief in the efficacy of what Professor Thomas has called the ordering and forbidding technique.

Mr. Marx is quite open and objective, saying what he thinks, occupied with the concrete happenings of family life and its immediate plans. He tries to dominate the family and especially to control William. The father believes in doing what you are told, in respecting your elders and superiors, and in venerating the common virtues of honesty, thrift, and industry as the sum and substance of the way of life. He is frequently heard quoting something that he did as a boy or that his parents did or expected of him. Mr. Marx attempts to "put over" his father's family idea but fails. He apparently does not find himself capable of adjusting himself to any other plan of family control; the army and his military training saw to that. Denied contacts with middle class men that would give him some conception of other family patterns, he is helpless and vainly struggles toward an impossible goal.

The maternal pattern of family life and the rôles appropriate to it are derived from the girlhood life of Mrs. Marx.

Mrs. Marx told the writer about her own home life as a young woman and as a girl but she does not speak of it much in the family circle. Nevertheless it is very potent in the formation of her attitudes, and these attitudes remain in conflict with attitudes of her husband to the present day. Democratic family life, independence, initiative, and mutual respect on equal terms of all the members of the family, are the American notions she carries over from her girlhood family life.

Mrs. Marx is more introspective than any other member of the family. She worries about being a failure, thinks about death and imagines all sorts of calamities that might happen to the family. She looks for spiritual values, liberty, artistic expression (she finds that her violin helps more than anything else to make life worth living). To raise her boys to be good and noble men is her idea of success in life and because they do not seem to be turning out right she feels that she is a failure. Moreover, she feels helpless to change the family situation.

The oldest son, William, has already been termed the "family problem." He has all the problems of the boy of the awkward age and others in addition. Existing in the family as an outcast, he attempts to find a social world outside the home in which his wishes may be expressed.

William is sensitive about his stature, secretive, avoiding the society of others. He has a very decided feeling of inferiority and seeks the company of boys young enough to look up to him or at least not old enough to torment him. He is virtually an outcast from the family at present and goes his own way as much as he can. He says little but so far as his actions indicate he sees life as getting food and shelter with the least effort possible. His "bumming around" and disobedience bring on a conflict usually ending in violence on the part of Mr. Marx. His parents marvel that he has not taken to the road and become a bum. Bill takes it all without resisting but continues to disobey. Mrs. Marx expressed her opinion to the writer that it galls her to see this and that if she were a boy his size she would fight back even though defeat was inevitable. Bill has evidently been beaten so often that all the "fight" has been taken out of him, and lacking a satisfactory status in the family he has nothing to protect by fighting back. He has accepted the rôle of the "dog"—without a bit of spirit—whipped and defeated already in life, accepting a mean, hand-to-mouth existence.

The two younger brothers, Henry and Joseph, exhibit marked temperamental differences, but time does not permit a description of their personal traits nor an account of their attitude of superiority to their older brother.

The status of the different members of the family is disclosed quite unmistakably by the seating at meals.

Each has his position at table, Henry at the right and Joseph at the left of their father, William at his mother's left. There is indication of status in the seating arrangement: (1) Mr. Marx; (2) Mrs. Marx; (3) Henry; (4) Joseph; (5) William. Their attitude toward their places is one of "rights" and they feel disturbed if they are made to sit anywhere else, except for a guest.

The interpretation made in this case study of the Marx family life follows:

One is struck in studying the family that it is not one family but three. Mr. Marx's family lives on through him and the patterns that it conformed to persist. While the family lived with the paternal grandmother this was probably the dominant pattern in the family life. During the taste of independence offered by Mr. Marx's absence, the maternal family's pattern, that of freedom and mutual respect developed. With the father's return a conflict arose between the paternal and maternal pattern, conflict made more intense by the training the father had received in the army. The children began to assert their own "rights" and to resent the paternal discipline. The family pattern which the children drew from their associates was formulated in the processes of interaction which took place between them and the parents. This may be called the third family pattern. At any rate three distinct patterns are to be found existing in the attitudes of father, mother and children, and more important is the fact that they have not been integrated into a single, more or less consistent and harmonious, resultant pattern upon which successful family life could be built. Hence family control is labelled "anarchy"—the family as a group is disorganized. Three family patterns are in conflict, that of the father's family, that of the mother's family, and that of the children's group of associates. All of the patterns have failed to realize adequate expression.

This case is only one among many that might have been selected to illustrate the effect on family life of conflicting rôles. Like any case study it raises more questions than it answers. Among all the many questions that might be asked, one interests me the most. What is going on in the inner life of William? What changes are taking place in his conception of himself and of his attitude toward his father that may lead him to rebel, or to escape, or to go insane?

But the case at any rate does indicate the possibilities for research of an analysis of family life in terms of family patterns and rôles.

In a recent brilliant article on "Social Images Versus Reality,"[7] Dr. Trigant Burrow defines social images in terms of what Professor Cooley has called "the looking-glass self,"[8] but he challenges the reality of these social images or rôles as natural phenomena:

Each of us occupies a position professionally, politically, economically, personally. There is one's relationship to one's wife, to his child, to his mother, his friends, his servants, and to every class and condition of people. In all these relationships the individual is constantly measuring his behavior according to the estimate of those in front of him. All of them give back his personal image in the social mirror they present to him. To the servant we play the master: to royalty we play the slave. The more we consider this self-reflective tendency the more we may realize how readily we fall into this, that, or the other characterological rôle in response to the image or rôle that is unconsciously being played opposite us.

Dr. Burrow regards these images or rôles as illusions:

What is called the mother-image is but the sum of the impressions reflected by the mother from the social environment about her. The mother-image bears no relation whatever to the mother-organism and our impression of this early impression of our childhood is totally unconnected with the personality from whom we receive it. . . . The image we unconsciously cherish is not the image of the mother's personality. It is the image of the social suggestion that has surrounded the mother. For I think we must ultimately come to see that the child automatically replaces the biological reality of the parent-organism with the *social image* that is artificially reflected to him by the patient.

Our "mother-image," according to Dr. Burrow, is an illusion, the reality is the biological organism. But, speaking of illusions, is not the biological organism as a mother even more of an illusion? How is it possible for a human being to be a mother without some notion of the rôle of a mother, which is just what a social image is? All her natural feelings, her affection for her children compel her to function as a mother. She becomes highly conscious of herself as a mother the moment she encounters different modes of bringing up children, or when her own methods of child rearing are criticized.

These social images, these conceptions of ourselves and of others which Dr. Burrow regards as nefarious illusions, seem to many of us the very substance of human nature and personality. Surely our reflexes, our instincts, and our endocrine secretions are not the distinctive characteristics of human nature, no matter how greatly they influence it. What is human nature but the capacity to have social images, to put oneself in the other person's place and look at oneself, so far as one is able, in the mirror of the attitudes of other persons? Cooley has defined human nature as "sympathy and the innumerable sentiments into which sympathy enters, such as love, resentment, ambition, vanity, hero-worship, and the feeling of social right and wrong."[9]

For the study of human nature, personality, and groups like the family, the basic reality is just this social image, this conception of one's rôle in the family, in the congenial group and in the community. Intimate studies of family life reveal that the actual problems of human beings center, in general, around the struggle to realize our conceptions of our rôles—as was vividly illustrated by the case of the Marx family. Any program of treating this case, to be even intelligent, not to say successful, would lie not in assessing the proportionate share of the blame upon Mr. Marx, or upon Mrs. Marx, or upon William, but in an understanding of their attitudes in the light of each one's conception of his rôle in family life.

For it is in his social images, his memories, his wishes, his dreams, his illusions, his faiths that a human being really lives. Take from him his social images of motherhood and brotherhood, of truth and justice, of immortality and God, and life would not be worth living. Yet, for these social images, the so-called illusions of home and country, friendship and honor, humanity and right, man has always been willing to put forth the utmost effort, to make the most heroic sacrifices, even to life itself.

However, in dealing with human rôles as the social reality of personality, it is necessary to regard them not as absolutes, but as relative to the social situation. Changes in life conditions render time-honored rôles obsolete. Where is the grandmother with her black bonnet of the last generation? Where is the ideal that a woman's place is confined to the home? Why is it that the rôle which made the mother as a girl the belle of the village leaves her old-fashioned daughter a wall-flower at a dance? Why is it that the father who in the country was the center of all the activities of the family, economic and cultural, seems in many city homes to be reduced to the negative rôle of saying "no" to the plans of the other members of the family?

Then too, even the personal rôles of family life may become so formal and mechanical that they lose the spontaneity and the human quality that originally and essentially belonged to them. "Are Parents People?" is the impertinent phrasing of this question in the title of a recent motion picture. Or a similar reaction against the formalism that may ossify familial rôles and sentiments was some time ago expressed in the flippant lines of a ragtime song, "They say the family is an institution, but who wants to live in an institution?" It is well to realize that even the least institutional of institutions may become so impersonal and mechanical as to take on the characteristics of a secondary instead of a primary group.

The scientific study of the family is still in its infancy. I have attempted briefly and I know inadequately to touch on certain of the aspects of family life that, in the studies which we have made, have seemed to be important for future research. These are: first, to push further the effort to describe, analyze, and classify the patterns of family life; second, to recognize that the family as a going concern depends more on the natural unity that arises and develops through the personal interaction of its members than upon any attempt to enforce the family obligations which the law imposes; and third, to test the assumption that the family as a reality inheres in the conception which society and its members have of it and of their rôles as husbands and wives, parents and children.

6

THE FAMILY AND THE PERSON

THE HISTORICAL FAMILY has been recognized by all students in the social sciences as an institution; indeed, as the original institution. In comparison, other institutions, as the schcol, the church, industry, and even the state, may be regarded as subsequent and derivative.

Historically, as these and other institutions have evolved, the family has lost one by one its original collective activities, until the question may be raised whether the modern family is any longer an institution. Is it now anything more than a mere unity of interacting personalities?

Certainly the modern family of husband and wife and three, two, one, or no children, living in a rear apartment on the tenth floor of a skyscraper apartment in New York City, is a family in a somewhat different sense from the large Chinese kinship group of grandparents, married sons and their wives and children, sixty-odd in number, living for twenty generations in one large household worshiping the same ancestral gods and obedient to the one recognized family head. The Chinese family seems, at first glance, to be an institution in a degree and in a sense which the modern family is not.

Psychiatrists and psychoanalysts who by reason of their treatment of behavior problems of individuals have been led into the study of family relationships are preconditioned to treat, as they

Reprinted from *Publication of the American Sociological Society* 22 (1928) : 121–33.

do, of family life as a state of emotional harmony or of emotional conflict of its component individuals. Count Hermann Keyserling, of the school of wisdom (who is not a psychiatrist, but a philosopher), in his article "The Correct Statement of the Marriage Problem," defines marriage as "essentially a tragic state of tension."

These two cursory references are sufficient to indicate the large group of biologists, psychiatrists, psychologists, and others who look upon the modern family as a collection of individuals temperamentally compatible or incompatible, emotionally in harmony or in conflict.

It is evident that an institution means more than mere temperamental or emotional solidarity. The family as an institution is the form of relationships between husband and wife, parents and children, sanctioned, if not prescribed, by society. These rôles that constitute the family are, in fact, cultural patterns, and, like all cultural patterns, have a history and are subject to social change. At the same time these familial rôles are idealized by the members of the family. The stern but just father, the loving and prudent mother, the dependable and honest son, the dutiful and virtuous daughter are ideals toward which conduct is directed and by which shortcomings are measured.

Thus it comes about that the family as an institution performs what seems to be a double function, but what actually is a unitary function. The family still remains the chief social agency both for transmitting the cultural heritages from the older to the younger generation and for the development of the personality of its members. It is, indeed, in the circumstances of this cultural transmission and in the interaction of the family and its members with the environing community that modifications and conditionings of the personality of all the members of the family take place. Herein for the family lies the significance of the definition by Thomas of personality as "the subjective aspect of culture."

It is not only that in the family its members assume rôles consistent with the cultural tradition, and in which they feel a vested personal interest, but the family itself sets up claims and obligations which tend to become sacred and to transcend the rights and even the individuality of its members.

This brief introductory statement is preliminary to the presentation of a life-history in which the influence of the family in its interrelations with the community upon the development of the personality may be more concretely stated and perhaps more simply and clearly defined. One document was selected in preference to reading extracts from several documents in order to give a longer perspective of personal growth. Cues to interpretation, however, are derived in part from similar and different cases. The following life-history is that of Marie, the daughter of a German-American family who lived in several culturally different communities, some German-American, and others native American. The interaction of the family and its members to these variable cultural environments provides the setting for the personal development of the child.

The first childhood memories often focus upon conflict situations. Not infrequently the young child takes an attitude of objectivity or even levity toward objects and ideas that to the adult are sentimental or sacred.

This seems to me to be my first clear memory of my mother: My father had driven to town, nine miles away, and Mother and I were having lunch together. I said or did some naughty thing and my mother told me that God would see me. I said that I'd pull down the blind and then He couldn't see.

"Oh, but He sees everything. He can see through the blind."

I looked up into the sky. In my imagination I saw an old gray-bearded man with human attributes. I took a superior attitude toward my mother, and thought "How could anyone be so stupid as to believe that He could see through a blind?" I wondered if she *really* believed it; I didn't think so.

I felt detached from this young and rather pretty creature sitting across the table from me. There was none of the feeling toward her that poets sing of.

This detached, almost perverse, attitude of the child toward its mother and the culture of its group is an expression, perhaps, of what the Calvinistic theory defined as "the innate depravity of man."

The way in which the discipline imposed by the family is mediated by affection is revealed in the first recollection of her father:

The first memory of my father was when, one time, I took a hatchet and started to chop at one of the porch posts. I knew that I shouldn't, but I thought they wouldn't know that I knew that I shouldn't. I was playing that I was in a forest cutting down trees. My father nearly spanked me. I remember his black hair and those brown eyes. I was somewhat afraid of my father, and yet I felt like a pal with him also.

The nervousness and German mannerisms that annoyed me so much a little later did not bother me at this period. I thought my father was a pretty fine daddy.

How the person's conception of his rôle is created not so much by his own behavior but by the reaction of the members of the family toward it is revealed by certain oft-repeated family anecdotes.

This story my father told with pride:

"We never let anyone frighten her of the dark or anything else if we can help it. You see, she goes any place now in the dark. One night after dark we missed her, and there she was out in the granary piling handfuls of wheat out of the bin onto the floor." After hearing this told, of course I was never afraid; at least I would not let myself be.

I think I was quite an egotistical little thing. I felt superior to my mother; I felt real pals with my dad. I played quite an important rôle and I knew it.

The appearance of the second child may, unless the situation is skillfully and sympathetically handled by the parents, create a crisis for the older child.

The following impression of my mother and father I remember vividly: I was over four. It was dusk. They were sitting side by side on a lounge, holding hands, I think, when I came into the room. They asked me if I didn't want a little brother. I was embarrassed. I said I thought I did, but I felt uneasy and left the room.

When I was five, my brother came. Now the tables turned. It developed later that he was a paralytic. He was always ill. He cried a very great deal. My mother was not well. We had a "hired girl" all the time. At first I *demanded* attention. Once I asked my mother to comb my hair. She did not have time right then. "But you simply have to!" I shrieked at her, and she proceeded to tame me down.

Mother is naturally undemonstrative. I remember sometimes standing by her chair and wanting to put my arms around her, but being afraid that she would not pay any attention, or worse still, that she would not understand and ask me to run away. One day when I was seven I made some remark that drew from her, "Why, don't you think I love you?" I wanted to cry. I didn't know what to say. At last I said, timidly, without resentment, "No!" I think she sensed some of the situation, for she said, with real warmth, "Why, of course I love you!" What a relief! I was happy for days! Did my intense love for children and the lavish affection I bestowed upon them in my adolescence grow partly out of the memories of this situation? I have always said that no child should go hungry-hearted around me. I have thought it was because I understood.

Even the preadolescent child makes comparisons between its family and the others in the community. The feelings of inferiority or superiority of the child are bound up with the status of its family.

I saw that my home was different from others, but everything was always spotlessly clean. We did not have all the nice little things that give the home touch. I had a little playroom upstairs, and here my chum and I fixed up things to my heart's content. This should be charming like other homes.

In comparing my family with other families I felt at once proud and humble also. My father took his place among the leading farmers. I was always proud of that, but his emotional mannerisms and his broken English annoyed me before my friends.

This conflict, which I am sure every child of an immigrant feels, had begun.

The new adjustments in adolescence have caused it to be designated as a period of stress and strain. In this case a new change of residence of the family into another and an American community intensified the personal and social maladjustments. Conflicts between standards and ideals of the family and the values of the community lead to emotional disturbances, confusion, and restless, anomalous behavior.

When I was twelve we bought a little ranch near Y, a little town of about five thousand inhabitants. There was a mortgage on it; we guarded this secret very carefully.

My parents seemed to be disturbed because I had no girl friends my own age. They showed this in the form of teasing. I wished that I had a girl friend, too, but I didn't know how to make friends with any of the girls. They all had their chums. They were nice to me, and sometimes went to see one another on Sunday afternoons, tame formal calls, no spontaneity.

This period became one of tears, storm, and stress. I wept over the least little thing; my mother did not understand what made me act so strangely. My father began to get disgusted with me at times and to let me know it, and then I wept more than ever.

The village was one of the "toughest" places in which we had ever lived. Whenever any of us girls had to go by a place where young fellows were grouped together, the boys would make remarks. I was terribly sensitive over this, and it was not the least of my worries.

Sometimes when I wept I felt that I should like to die. What was the use of living? What was I heading for? At last a dream began to formulate. I should like to be a teacher; I loved children. Everyone remarked about my hold on them. I remember the day the idea became very real to me. I was given to day dreaming, anyway, but this day was different. I walked as in a haze all day. I saw the profession with all the ardor of a romantic and idealistic adolescent. In my eyes it was not ordinary now—it was glorified.

I guarded my secret carefully. It was almost too sacred a thing to discuss. Finally I told my mother that I should like to go to work to earn some money. I wanted to go to high school. Falteringly I said I'd like to be a teacher. To my joy she was pleased. I believe she had been worrying more over me than she let me see, for she had always said, "I shall see that my daughter has an *education*. She shall not *have* to get married."

My parents did not want to let me go; they said they could still afford to send me to school; but I finally prevailed and I went to a nearby state institution to work. My father was displeased with the type of men and women with whom I worked and soon saw that I came home. I had earned about seventy-five dollars. In the summer I picked grapes.

My father wanted to have me help with the corn, which was much easier work, but I felt that I must earn money. It was not customary in that locality for children to go to high school, and I felt that if I wanted to go I must help myself.

Finally the grand day came and I started to high school. I was nervous about it. I was slight and undeveloped physically, and although I was sixteen, I passed for one of the little thirteen- or fourteen-year-olds. This made it possible for me to enter into the school life quite freely.

Since many of the other freshmen were from out of town also and were strangers, I soon made friends. I soon became enthusiastic about high-school life and wanted to enter into it. When the class was organized, I found myself on a committee. Since there were over a hundred in the class I felt happy over even this small distinction. But the committee always met after school and I had to take the car home even before three. Now that I was going to high school, I had to hustle up my work at home to get it all finished.

I helped my mother with the washing and ironing on Saturday and with all the mopping and cleaning. I felt very keenly my responsibility for helping my mother. Soon I was placed on another committee, and here I was also unable to serve. I was always too busy. I realized that I must be content with only a formal education.

I owed my help to my parents. In my scholastic standing I always excelled. I did not tell any of my friends that I wanted to become a teacher. Perhaps they might think that I would not have the ability.

I did tell my class teacher. I knew that she was fond of me; but she said, "No, I don't think you should go into teaching. I think that you are too nervous." It was as if someone had given me a mortal wound—*me*, with all my dreams; didn't my attitude count for something? She herself had some definite nerve trouble and could not hold a class's attention. Soon my money was nearly all gone. I would never be successful as a teacher probably, so why waste my parents' money? I decided to stay at home.

I said nothing, but just simply didn't get ready to go to school one morning. My mother came out into the kitchen about 8:30 and found me there finishing up the work. "But why are you here?" I told her that I was going to quit. I had no more money. "Why, of course you haven't. I knew it wouldn't last very long; but now that you have started to school you go on and finish." And she proceeded to give me one of those talks that played such a vital part in my life during this period when I was so unadjusted. To this day my mother holds my admiration for this ability. I would feel that the whole world was against me, and before she would get through with me I could face anything. So calmly and wisely she saw my problems. Sometimes I needed disciplining, and her talks usually toned me down. I felt at the time that she did not understand all the high-school problems. Very often at this period I did feel horribly misunderstood. At times I resolved that when I grew up I should be the friend of every adolescent girl. This I still hold as a hobby. I was working rather hard; I was commuting nine miles to school; I was ambitious in my studies.

Marie goes to school, but has no time for social activities. She must assist with the household work.

I helped my mother a great deal. I worried over the financial situation. I probably suffered from malnutrition. Very often I was so tired that I did not feel life worth living. One day someone said something about how joyous were the days of youth, and I flared back, "Huh, if the rest of life is worse than this, I'm sure I don't want to live!" This sort of thing perplexed and worried my mother.

Finally, one day, I discovered an article in the *Ladies' Home Journal* on adolescent girlhood. There I was, all described, and it said that this was only a period of adjustment. This was a great relief. I had thought that I should always be as I was now.

In high school my art and English teacher was my idol. She had a keen mind, a charming personality, and was the most popular instructor of the school. I decided to ask her if she thought I could ever become a teacher. I put it off as long as I could, and, finally, on the last day of school, at noon, I went up timidly and asked her. She was busy, but she took time for me. "Why, I think you would make an excellent teacher." She asked me to come back again in the afternoon; then she gave me a long talk on personality development. I was in the clouds again and determined now that I would go through with anything that was reasonably within my ability.

In this account of adolescent unadjustment four points should perhaps be made: First, there is the crystallization of a vocational life-goal out of the main trends of her attitudes and interests. This solved her problem by giving direction and meaning to her life. Then, as in many other cases, it is the mother who understands, not completely, but in the light of her own girlhood experience. So, also, she gained from reading the article on adolescence the realization that her personal problems were not unique but universal, and not insolvable. Finally a sympathetic teacher who personified her ideal gave her the encouragement and inspiration necessary to put forth every effort to achieve her goal.

The persecution of German-Americans in the World War solidified the family and brought to the daughter a sense of cultural unity with her parents.

This life-history is, it must be admitted, an incomplete, and in all probability an imperfect, record of the unfolding of the person in the family and community environment. It is only the person's own story of the memorable events in his career, to the exclusion, no doubt, of many other incidents and circumstances. What, then, is the value, if any, of such a document, or of documents like these, when they must be discounted at once as fragmentary and subjective?

I must confess that I cannot answer all these objections in a fashion that would be convincing to you, nor even to myself.

Yet, admitting all these and other criticisms that might be raised, there is a certain type of knowledge or understanding that comes from the examination of personal documents which one does not obtain in dissertations on the origin and nature of personality, nor from psychological, psychiatric, or psychoanalytic classifications of personality types.

This life-history, taken as a whole, does throw much light on the actual process by which a child comes to self-consciousness and obtains a conception of his rôle, first as a member of the family and then as a participant in the wider life of the community.

The dialectic of personal growth, however, as pictured in this life-history, is widely different from the celebrated abstract definition of it made by J. Mark Baldwin. The achievement by the person of self-consciousness in the family situation is no logical consistent process, as described here. What is suggested by this case is quite the opposite. Before the person arrives at some stable conception of his rôle—before, as we say, "his character gets set"—he is subject to the play of many diverse and conflicting impulses. The great variety of attitudes and the wide range of random, mischievous, and even devilish, behavior in children is suggestive both of the possibilities of personality development in children and of the order which the conventional discipline of the family imposes upon the chaotic tendencies to behavior in the young child. Out of the child's own struggle with his conflicting impulses and wishes within first the code of family life, and then with the conflicting patterns of the freer community life, does he assume a rôle and achieve some coherent consistency in his behavior.

It becomes obvious, then, why the ordering of a child's behavior is a comparatively simple matter where the mores of the community are of one pattern with the standards of conduct of the family, and the reason why the problem of personal organization always becomes more acute with the degree of divergence between familial and communal ideals.

This and similar life-histories give a picture of the family and the interrelations of parents and children which departs widely from the legal definitions of the rights and duties of parents and children, and is scandalously at variance with our cherished ideals of family life. For in the law and in the mores the obligations of the members of the family are defined in their external and formal aspects with reference to what are regarded as norms of familial behavior.

This conventional schematization of familial interrelationships is not to be dismissed as unimportant. To the contrary, it is an expression of our deepest sentiments and of our most profound convictions of what family life ought to be. But as a matter of fact, these moral and legal conceptions of the family are totally different from what family life actually is. This life-history does give us a sense of family interrelationships that are living and changing, of family bonds that loosen and tighten, and of shifts and mutations of attitudes rather than the static and permanent ordering of relationships of affection and duty subsumed under the conventional theory of the family.

It is interesting to speculate upon the way in which psychologists, psychiatrists, and psychoanalysts would label this case. Interpretation by instinct has indeed gone out of fashion. Freud doubtless would point out evidence for the Electra complex; Jung might well enter it as an introvert type; Adler would start his analysis from feelings of inferiority. Kretschmer would perceive the schizoid type. Others would place emphasis upon this or that glandular type.

These classifications are all helpful, no doubt; but they seem arbitrary, mechanical, and even somewhat irrelevant when compared with the process concretely set forth in this document by which the person, out of the cultural conflict of the family with the other groups in the community, out of the warring impulses in his own bosom, out of shameful experiences and praiseworthy endeavor, out of lonely reverie and social contacts, organizes his life and directs it to some goal of achievement.

This life-history, as well as other life-histories, seems to show how little we have reckoned with the flood of feelings and emotions, impulses, and ideas that color and give individuality to our lives, especially in childhood.

Then, even more important, is the fact, which all of us realize when once our attention is called to it, that, particularly as children, many or most of our multitudinous impulses never eventuate in our acts. They find expression but in play, in day-dreaming, or in a great variety of attitudes that to adults may seem inexplicable, amusing, perverse, or diabolical. Certainly in the mind of the child a world of events is transpiring which are beyond the perception of even the most sympathetic and discerning outside observer.

Most important for the understanding of the process of personal development is a recognition of the rôle of these uncompleted acts. In the uncompleted act the person is thrown back upon himself. These conflicts and maladjustments, distressing and painful as they are, provide the situations necessary for the development of the subjective life of the person. As one reflects over his past life is it not significant that the attention is fixed upon conflict situations? It is in these that the child and the youth works out slowly and painfully a conception of his rôle in society and a philosophy of life about which his impulses become organized and his character becomes formed.

This inner life of the individual, of unexpressed impulses, of concealed memories, and of secret ambitions, seems to him private and personal, the essential nucleus of his personality and of his individuality. And so, at least to the sociologist, it actually is.

What constitutes the intensity of the problem of the child is its isolation, its loneliness, its feeling that its own subjective life is unique. No matter how objective the child is in many realms of his activities, there always are those regions of life which are mysterious, where he gropes as in the dark, where he feels confused and bewildered.

A first clue to the understanding of one's self and to the solution of the enigma of one's relation to others seems to be the perception, as in the case of Marie, that one's problems are not unique, but are common to others. Through this human finding the person not only tends to obtain mastery over his own experience and problems, but he begins the discovery of the world about him. He is able to sympathize, to enter into the feelings and attitudes of other persons. Through making his own adjustments and in solving his own problems he acquires a skill in detecting and in assisting others in their problems.

Finally, in life-history materials we may expect to discover the conditions under which mutations in personality occur, as in religious conversion, or, as in the case of Marie, of secular conversion to teaching as a vocational career. These critical experiences, to use the phrase of W. I. Thomas, are not, so this case indicates, bolts out of the blue, but rather the crystallization of trends of impulses, aptitudes, and interests which are then projected in some organized form into the future. The significance of further knowledge of personality mutations is only too evident to need elaboration.

The life-history method is in its infancy. Attempts doubtless will be made to standardize the technique of securing and interpreting them. It is to be hoped, however, that this method will not become so formalized and the interpretations of cases so abstract that the unique value of the personal document will be lost. For in the life-history is revealed, as in no other way, the inner life of the person, his moral struggles, his successes and failures in securing control of his destiny in a world too often at variance with his hopes and ideals.

THE PREDICTION OF ADJUSTMENT
IN MARRIAGE

The Problem

WE DO NOT FEEL it necessary to justify an effort to increase skill in guessing right about the future. Particularly is this true of fields of experience wherein correct guesses are relevant to immediate acts of personal adjustment. Hence without apology we submit a brief outline of an exploratory effort at predicting adjustment in marriage.

Briefly stated, the problem in this study was to discover what prediction as to adjustments in marriage could be made from a knowledge of certain items in the background of prospective husbands and wives. The background items selected were those which would not require the subtle powers of the psychologist or psychiatrist to detect, but were chosen purposely on the basis of the case with which the information could be elicited from persons willing to co-operate in the study.

Such a choice of items should in no sense be taken to imply that we discount the importance of more elusive psychological and physiological factors in marital adjustment. Indeed, in the work of collecting schedule data we accumulated information on personality factors in marital adjustment that appeared more basic than any of the items on our schedules.

We wish to reiterate, however, that we were after background material which would be easily obtainable and which could be used

Reprinted from *American Sociological Review* 1 (1936) : 737–51.

for predicting the probabilities of successful adjustment in marriage. A precise description of the relationships obtaining between our various items and marital adjustment was not the central interest in this study.

The Population-Sample Studied

The materials upon which this study was based were taken from schedules returned by couples who were living in the state of Illinois, and who had been married not less than one and not more than six years. Certain characteristics of the group will enable the reader to place it approximately as to its position in the social-economic order.

Over 70 percent had been married from two to four years. The median age at the time of marriage was 27.2 years for husbands and 23.1 years for wives. Fifty-six percent of the husbands and 52 percent of the wives had completed one or more years of college or graduate work at the time of marriage. Only 10 percent of the husbands and 5 percent of the wives had less than a high school education at the time of marriage. Most of the sample was from an urban environment, only 10 percent coming from places of less than 10,000 population. Seventy percent were from cities of over 200,-000 population, which in this case means that most of them came from Chicago. Slightly over half of the husbands and 58 percent of the wives were brought up in the city, while less than 10 percent of the total were reared on the farm.

Our group for the most part were from the middle class. Forty-three percent lived in moderate rent apartment house areas and another 43 percent lived in the better class single family residential and suburban communities. Only 10 percent were from immigrant, rooming house and similar communities of low social-economic status.

Only about 25 percent of the husbands had experienced as much as one month or more of unemployment since marriage, and over half of the wives had held positions since marriage. The occupation of husbands and wives were for the most part white-collar and professional.

Only 10 percent of our sample had bought or were buying their homes, and 25 percent stated they were planning to buy. The majority were renting and not planning to buy homes.

Practically all of our sample were native white. Fifty percent of the husbands and 58 percent of the wives had fathers who were native white Americans. Fifty percent of the husbands and 58 percent of the wives were Protestant in religious affiliation, while 15 percent of the husbands and 9 percent of the wives claimed no religious affiliation. There was about an even distribution of the remainder among the Catholic, Jewish and other faiths.

These characteristics point to the conclusion that we had a roughly homogeneous, middle class, native-white, urban American group.

The data on this group were collected on eight-page printed schedules that were filled out anonymously. Many students, colleagues, friends and a few social organizations participated in getting nearly 7000 schedules into the hands of possible subjects. About 1300 couples responded. Of these, 526 conformed to the requirement that they be residents of Illinois and that their marriage date be not less than one year and not more than six years in the past at the time of filling out the schedules. Most of the schedules were collected during 1931–33.

With this description of our sample and method of collection of data we may now turn to a description of the way the materials were handled.

A Criterion of Adjustment in Marriage

Any attempt at predicting adjustment in marriage calls for some definition of what is meant by adjustment, and some method of indicating varying degrees of adjustment.

A highly generalized definition of a well adjusted marriage might be the following: A well adjusted marriage is a marriage in which the attitudes and actions of each of the partners produces an environment which is highly favorable to the proper functioning of the personality structures of each partner, particularly in the sphere of primary relationships.

Four corollaries follow from this definition: (1) The degree to which the indicated conditions are met would be the degree of adjustment realized. (2) Since personality structures differ from individual to individual it follows that a particular combination highly favorable to a given personality would be entirely unsuited for another. (3) Since personalities are not unitary but are composites of role patterns, a marriage which is favorable to the functioning of one part of the personality may not be favorable for another part of the structure. (4) Since personalities are not static but are in process of development, a combination favorable to the functioning of the personality at one time may not be so for a later period in the development; and hence recurring periods of poor adjustment are necessary conditions of "growth" until a relatively mature and stable level of personality organization is achieved.

Setting aside all questions of the relative adequacy of this definition and its corollary propositions, it is quite evident that it would be extremely difficult, if not impossible, to give it a direct quantitative expression. However, in this as in other instances where a numerical index is desirable, it is possible to give symptoms of adjustment a quantitative expression even though we may not be able to measure directly the variables operating in adjustment. This means, of course, that we do not measure adjustment directly but must be content with an inferential criterion. Moreover, we are measuring present adjustment only.

In constructing a numerical index of adjustment it was necessary to make certain assumptions. We assumed that those subjects whose marriages approximated our definition would make statements which would indicate: (1) That the individual regards his marriage as happy. (2) That there is essential agreement on critical issues in the relationship. (3) That there is a substantial amount of common interests and activities. (4) That there are frequent demonstrations of affection. (5) That there is a minimum of regret concerning the marital choice and a minimum of complaint about the marriage or the partner.

If our assumptions are correct, then we should expect replies to questions centering around the above points to have some value for indicating the degree of adjustment realized in a given marriage. Moreover, if the replies to such questions were appropriately weighted or scored, a composite of these individual weights should give at least a rough numerical index of the degree of adjustment in marriage.

Proceeding on such an assumption we assigned numerical values to the various types of replies on a list of twenty selected questions. At first we were disposed to assign values arbitrarily but finally decided on a more empirical method. We correlated replies to each of the selected questions with the way the subjects rated the degree of happiness of their marriages. The replies were then weighted according to their correlation with happiness ratings. How these weights were assigned and the score computed is described below.

Since the ratings of happiness in marriage were used as a guide in the assignment of weights to the various replies, we should first devote our attention to these ratings. We asked each subject to rate his marriage on a scale with five steps designated as "very happy," "happy," "average," "unhappy," "very unhappy."

Now happiness is a nebulous and elusive affair, especially when one attempts to define it. Offhand one would expect a great deal of variability in the way a subject would rate the happiness of his marriage from time to time. It might be expected also that husbands and wives would rate the marriage differently. Moreover, one would expect that an outsider's rating of a marriage would differ from that of the marriage partners.

Thus far these expectations have not been borne out by our experience. The following data show that there is a rather consistent agreement in: (1) Independent ratings given by the two partners in a given marriage. (2) The ratings given by outsiders more or less familiar with the marriage and one of the marriage partners. (3) The rating of a given marriage by two outsiders. (4) The rating given by the same person at different times.

Table I shows a comparison of the way husbands and wives independently rated their marriages.

Of the 252 pairs of ratings 180, or 71.4 percent, agree; 62, or 24.6 percent, disagree by only one scale step, and only 10, or

TABLE I

COMPARISION OF THE WAY HUSBANDS AND WIVES RATED THE HAPPINESS
OF THEIR MARRIAGE

| Ratings | Husband's Rating | | | | | | |
	Very Unhappy	Un-happy	Average	Happy	Very Happy	Total	Percentage Distribution
Wife's rating:							
Very happy	1		3	24	112	140	55.6
Happy			12	38	12	62	24.6
Average		3	14	7	6	30	11.9
Unhappy	1	11	2			14	5.5
Very unhappy	5	1				6	2.4
Total	7	15	31	69	130	252	100.0
Percentage distri-bution	2.8	5.9	12.3	27.4	51.6	100.0	

4.0 percent, disagree by two or more scale steps. The tetrachoric correlation between the two sets of ratings is $+.89$.

Table II shows the comparison of ratings of a marriage, one rating being by one of the marriage partners and one being by an outsider who is well acquainted with the couple. The ratings were of course given independently, and the persons who were being rated were not aware of the fact.

In this comparison we find that 132, or 48.5 percent, are iden-

TABLE II

COMPARISON OF THE RATING OF MARRIAGES BY A MARRIAGE PARTNER
AND AN OUTSIDER

| Ratings | Marriage Partner's Rating | | | | | | |
	Very Unhappy	Un-happy	Average	Happy	Very Happy	Total	Percentage Distribution
Outsider's rating:							
Very happy			4	16	57	77	28.3
Happy		2	4	31	35	72	25.5
Average	1	4	6	16	8	35	12.9
Unhappy	10	27	20	3		60	22.0
Very unhappy	11	11	5	1		28	10.3
Total	22	44	39	67	100	272	100.0
Percentage distri-bution	8.1	16.2	14.3	24.6	36.8	100	

tical ratings; 116, or 42.7 percent, vary by only one scale step; and 24, or 8.8 percent, disagree by two or more scale steps. The tetrachoric correlation coefficient for the table is +.91.

Husbands and wives were asked to give independent ratings of the happiness of their parents' marriages. Table III shows the way husband and wife rated the marriage of the wife's parents.

TABLE III

COMPARISON OF RATINGS BY HUSBAND AND WIFE OF WIFE'S PARENTS' MARRIAGE

Ratings	Husband's Rating						
	Very Unhappy	Un-happy	Average	Happy	Very Happy	Total	Percentage Distribution
Wife's rating:							
Very happy			4	15	41	60	31.7
Happy			16	38	7	61	32.3
Average		2	37	5	2	46	24.3
Unhappy	2	8	5	1		16	8.5
Very unhappy	6					6	3.2
Total	8	10	62	59	50	189	100.0
Percentage distri-bution	4.2	5.3	32.8	31.2	26.5	100	

One hundred and thirty, or 68.8 percent, of the ratings are the same; 52, or 27.5 percent, of the ratings differ by one scale step, and only 7, or 3.7 percent, differ by two or more scale steps. The tetrachoric coefficient of correlation is +.90.

The same comparison was made of the way husbands and wives rated the marriages of the husbands' parents. Here again we found very close agreement. Only 3 percent of the ratings differed by two or more scale steps. The tetrachoric correlation coefficient was +.91.

On a small number of cases (34) we made careful reports of case interviews. These interviews, properly disguised, were read by two competent judges. The judges gave what they regarded as a correct rating of the happiness of the marriages. In all the comparisons made: between rating of judge number one and the rating by the subject; between judge number two and the subject; and between the ratings of the two judges, there was very close agreement. None of the coefficients of correlation fell below +.95.

A small number of subjects (38) were available for a second rating after a lapse of time varying from eight months to two years.[1] A comparison of the first and second ratings of this group showed that only four of the ratings differed by as much as two scale steps. The correlation coefficient was +.86.

This study of happiness ratings suggests that the rating scale has sufficient reliability and validity to allow its use as a guide in selecting questions which discriminate between good and poor adjustment and in assigning proper weights to the various answers to such questions.

By correlating the replies to each of our questions with the happiness ratings, we were able to select twenty questions. These questions elicited replies that were indicative of the degree of adjustment.

The twenty questions include such things as the following: (a) Extent to which couple engages in common activities. (b) Extent of agreement on a number of points such as handling finances, recreation, friends, dealing with in-laws, manners, intimate relations, etc. (c) Extent to which affection is demonstrated. (d) Extent to which partners confide in one another. (e) The number of complaints listed regarding the marriage or the partner.

Replies to each question were given numerical values which varied with the proportion of "very happy" subjects giving the reply. Thus, if in our sample, 40 percent of those who rated their marriage as very happy gave answer "a" to question "x" and only 5 percent gave answer "b," the numerical value assigned to answer "a" would be roughly 8 times as great as that assigned to answer "b." This procedure can be best illustrated by showing a few tables in which replies to certain of the questions are correlated with the ratings of happiness.

In Table IV the replies to the question on extent of agreement in ways of dealing with in-laws are correlated with the rating of happiness.

As one might expect, replies indicating essential agreement on the in-law question are much more frequent among those who rate their marriage as very happy or happy than are replies indicating serious disagreement.

TABLE IV

COMPARISON OF RATINGS OF HAPPINESS IN MARRIAGE WITH EXTENT OF AGREEMENT
ON WAYS OF DEALING WITH IN-LAWS. PERCENTAGE DISTRIBUTION

Extent of Agreement	Rating of Happiness					
	Very Unhappy	Un-happy	Average	Happy	Very Happy	Number of Cases
Always agree	3.8	2.7	11.5	19.2	62.7	182
Almost always agree	4.5	6.3	17.1	29.7	42.3	111
Occasionally disagree	7.7	20.0	23.1	20.0	29.2	65
Frequently disagree	18.6	25.6	23.2	16.3	16.3	43
Almost always disagree	20.0	50.0	20.0	5.0	5.0	20
Always disagree	38.2	38.2	11.8	8.8	2.9	34
All cases	9.1	12.9	16.0	20.5	41.5	455

In the "very happy" column the percentage of those who checked "always agree" is about twenty times as great as the percentage who checked "always disagree." Hence we may assign a value of twenty to the answer "always agree" and zero to the answer "always disagree." We followed this procedure in principle. When the distribution on all of the "agreement" questions were averaged and the two scale steps "almost always disagree" and "always disagree" were combined to get enough cases to make the proportion stable, we found it desirable to give a maximum value of ten to the answer "always agree" and zero to the answer "always disagree" for all questions of that type.[2] The intermediate answers were given values graded down evenly from ten to zero.

Table V shows the comparison of happiness ratings with the extent to which couples engage in outside activities together.

Here again the expected distribution results. The proportion of the "very happy" group who say they engage in all outside activities together is about fifteen times as great as those engaged in few or none of their outside activities together. Hence we may assign a value of 15 to the answer "all of them" and zero to the answers "few of them" and "none of them."

This procedure was followed for each of the twenty selected questions, and resulted in a numerical value for each possible reply to each of the questions. This done, it was possible to take a sched-

TABLE V

COMPARISON OF RATINGS OF HAPPINESS IN MARRIAGE WITH EXTENT TO WHICH
HUSBAND AND WIFE ENGAGE IN OUTSIDE ACTIVITIES TOGETHER. PERCENTAGE
DISTRIBUTION

Number Joint Activities	Rating of Happiness					
	Very Unhappy	Unhappy	Average	Happy	Very Happy	Number of Cases
All of them	3.9	2.6	6.5	19.6	67.3	153
Some of them	5.3	12.8	20.2	24.4	37.2	226
Few of them	27.6	34.5	22.4	10.3	5.2	58
None of them	36.4	31.8	13.6	13.6	4.5	22
All cases	9.1	12.9	16.0	20.5	41.5	459

ule properly filled out and compute a marriage adjustment score
by summing up the numerical values on replies to the twenty
questions.

Table VI shows the frequency distribution of adjustment scores
for the whole group and for each happiness rating group.

TABLE VI

FREQUENCY DISTRIBUTION OF MARRIAGE ADJUSTMENT SCORES BY HAPPINESS
RATING CATEGORIES

Adjustment Score	Happiness Rating							
	Very Un- happy	Un- happy	Aver- age	Happy	Very Happy	No Rating	Total	Percentage Distribution
180–199				7	65		72	13.7
160–179			5	31	118	1	155	29.4
140–159			12	34	32	1	79	15.0
120–139	2	9	27	24	6	2	70	13.3
100–119	3	13	23	8			47	8.9
80– 99	13	19	5	3		1	41	7.8
60– 79	15	17	3		3		38	7.2
40– 59	7	8		1			16	3.2
20– 39	2	5	1				8	1.5
Total	42	71	76	108	224	5	526	
Percentage distribution	8.0	13.5	14.4	20.5	42.6	1.0		100.0

Mean score $= 140.8$; $\sigma = 38.8$

As would be expected the adjustment scores show a fairly close correlation with the ratings of happiness, since the ratings were used as guides in assigning the score values to the individual questions. The tetrachoric coefficient of correlation between scores and ratings is +.92.[3]

Table VII shows that the score does discriminate between groups who are divorced or separated on the one hand and those whose marriages have not been broken on the other. Furthermore, among those not divorced or separated the score discriminates between those who state they have considered breaking their marriage and those who claim not to have contemplated this step.

TABLE VII

DISTRIBUTION OF MARRIAGE ADJUSTMENT SCORES BY GROUPINGS INTO THOSE WHO ARE DIVORCED, SEPARATED, HAVE CONTEMPLATED DIVORCE OR SEPARATION AND HAVE NOT CONTEMPLATED DIVORCE OR SEPARATION

Adjustment Score	Marital Status					
	Divorced	Separated and Not Divorced	Have Contemplated Divorce or Separation	Have Not Contemplated Divorce or Separation	No Reply	Total
180–199				64	8	72
160–179	3		4	141	7	155
140–159	1	6	8	54	10	79
120–139	9	6	19	29	7	70
100–119	10	13	13	11		47
80– 99	15	12	9	4	1	41
60– 79	12	18	4	3	1	38
40– 59	6	8	2			16
20– 39	5	2	1			8
Total	61	65	60	306	34	526

This table would suggest that our score has considerable validity.

Some evidence of the reliability of the score is seen in the fact that scores computed from schedules filled out independently by husbands and wives have a fairly high correlation ($r=+.88\pm.03$).

Having constructed a score to measure indirectly the present marital adjustment, we then attempted to use certain background information to predict the adjustment score.

Construction of a Prediction Score

The schedules used in this study called for information on certain items in the premarital backgrounds of husband and of wife. This information covered such things as age; place in the family; health; education; occupation; employment history; earnings; amount saved at time of marriage; religious affiliation and activity; participation in other organized social groups; friendships with men and women; length of courtship and engagement; attachments to and conflicts with parents; happiness of parents' marriages; and certain items on the occupation, religion, education and social-economic status of the parents of each.

Our problem with respect to these data was to devise a method of combining the information on each of the schedules into single numerical expressions, whose variations would correlate as closely as possible with the variations in the marriage adjustment scores.

The procedure followed in constructing such a prediction score was similar in most respects to our procedure in constructing the adjustment score. Since we were trying to predict the adjustment score we used that score as a guide in assigning numerical values to replies on questions regarding premarital information.

Each item of information on the premarital backgrounds of husband and of wife was correlated with the adjustment score. Those items which showed a significant relationship were selected for use in constructing the prediction score. Twenty-one items in the husband's background material and twenty items in the wife's background were selected for this purpose. Each type of reply was then given a numerical value in accordance with its frequency in the "very high" adjustment score group.

Table VIII illustrates the procedure. In this table is presented the relationship between level of educational achievement at the time of marriage and marriage adjustment score.

The data in this table indicate that in our sample the higher the educational level at the time of marriage the greater the chances

TABLE VIII

PERCENTAGE DISTRIBUTION OF MARRIAGE ADJUSTMENT SCORES AT DIFFERENT
EDUCATIONAL LEVELS

	Marriage Adjustment Score*				
	Very Low	Low	High	Very High	Number of Cases
Husband's education					
Graduate work	3.8	8.6	36.2	51.4	105
College	9.8	15.1	26.8	48.3	205
High school	15.1	24.3	27.0	33.6	152
Grades only	21.6	19.6	21.6	37.2	51
No reply					13
Wife's education					
Graduate work	0.0	4.8	38.7	56.5	62
College	9.2	18.9	22.9	48.9	227
High school	14.4	16.3	32.2	37.1	202
Grades only	33.3	25.9	25.9	14.8	27
No reply					8
All cases	11.8	16.7	28.4	43.2	525

* For convenience in presentation, the adjustment scores were grouped as follows: very low, 20–79; low, 80–119; high, 120–159; very high, 160–199.

are that the marriage adjustment score will be high. It also seems that contrary to certain recent pronouncements on the college girl as a poor marriage risk, the wife's educational achievement makes more difference in the chances for a high adjustment score in marriage than does the husband's.[4]

The numerical values assigned to the different educational levels were determined (with certain variations that we do not have space here to discuss) by the procedure already described in the discussion of the adjustment score. In the case of husbands, we gave twenty points to replies stating that the husband was in a graduate level of educational achievement at the time of marriage; 15 if he was in, or had completed, college; zero if he was in, or had completed, high school; and five points if his education did not exceed the grades.

In the case of the wife's schedule we gave forty points for the graduate level at time of marriage, thirty for collegiate level, twenty for high school level, and zero for the grade school level.

Table IX shows the relation between the number of social organizations the persons belonged to at the time of marriage and the marriage adjustment scores.

This table seems to suggest that persons with proclivities for joining organized social groups are better risks for marriage adjustment than those who lack such tendencies. This item seems to be more discriminating for husbands than it does for wives.

Scores assigned husbands' answers were: 20 for membership in three or more organizations; 10 for membership in two; 5 for one; 0 for none. For the wives' answers the scores were: 15 for membership in three or more organizations; 5 each for two and none; and zero for membership in one.

This procedure was followed for each of the forty-one items used in constructing the premarital background or prediction score. It is an admittedly crude procedure and doubtless has a number of serious fallacies. It is encumbered with such apparent inconsisten-

TABLE IX

RELATION BETWEEN MEMBERSHIP IN SOCIAL ORGANIZATIONS AT TIME OF MARRIAGE AND MARRIAGE ADJUSTMENT SCORE. PERCENTAGE DISTRIBUTION

Number Organizations	Marriage Adjustment Score				
	Very Low	Low	High	Very High	Number Cases
Husband:					
Three or more	8.6	9.9	27.2	54.3	81
Two	8.7	16.3	27.9	47.1	104
One	11.9	18.1	27.1	42.9	210
None	13.3	17.3	37.3	32.0	75
No reply					56
Total					526
Wife:					
Three or more	4.2	18.9	22.1	54.7	95
Two	13.3	15.9	25.7	45.1	113
One	13.0	14.3	34.2	38.5	161
None	12.5	17.0	28.4	42.0	88
No reply					69
Total					526
All cases	11.8	16.7	28.4	43.2	

cies as giving more score points to wives who were members of no organizations than to those who were members of one; or to take another instance, of giving more value to a grade school level of education of the husband than to a high school level. The differences in score values cited were not great, but they violate one's feeling for consistency. However, we preferred to be consistent in our empirical procedure rather than violate that procedure for the sake of consistent weightings in some of our items.

It will be noted that the maximum score values vary from item to item and are not the same for the same item for husbands' and wives' answers. In each case the maximum score is approximately equal to the difference between the highest percentage and the lowest percentage in the column headed "very high" adjustment scores. Thus in Table IX, the percentages of replies from husbands in marriages with "very high" adjustment scores varied from 32.0 to 54.3, a range of approximately 20. The percentage of replies from wives in marriage with "very high" adjustment scores varied from 38.5 to 54.7 or approximately 15 points.

By following this method we were able to assign values which varied roughly in accordance with the discriminal value of the item.

With a numerical value determined for all types of answers to questions on the 41 selected items, we were in a position to take any given schedule on which a couple had answered the required questions, assign the numerical value to the replies, sum them and thus compute a background or prediction score. The background scores were computed for each of the 526 couples and these scores were correlated with the marriage adjustment scores. The Pearsonian coefficient of correlation was $+.51$.

Table X gives a better idea of the relation between the two scores.

It was of course to be expected that, since the adjustment score was used as a guide in assigning numerical values to the replies upon which the premarital score is based, the two scores would correlate fairly closely. However, our confidence in the prediction value of the score is increased somewhat by noting the relation between the background score and the status of the marriage.

TABLE X

RELATION BETWEEN THE PREDICTION SCORES AND MARRIAGE
ADJUSTMENT SCORES, PERCENTAGE DISTRIBUTION

Prediction Score	Marriage Adjustment Score				
	Very Low	Low	High	Very High	Number Cases
700–799	0.0	10.0	10.0	80.0	10
620–699	1.5	12.1	25.8	60.6	66
540–619	5.8	21.9	29.2	43.1	137
460–539	27.6	29.4	25.9	17.1	170
380–459	39.8	31.1	15.1	14.0	93
300–379	57.2	25.7	11.4	5.7	35
220–299	75.0	25.0	0.0	0.0	8
Total					519*

Mean prediction score = 516.0; σ = 98.8.

* Seven cases thrown out because subjects failed to answer a sufficient number of background questions for computation of their scores.

Table XI shows the percentage distribution of prediction scores for 73 divorced couples; 61 separated couples; 64 couples who state they have considered divorce or separation; and 342 couples who claim not to have contemplated breaking their marriage.

TABLE XI

PERCENTAGE DISTRIBUTION OF PREDICTION SCORES FOR THOSE WHO ARE
DIVORCED, SEPARATED, HAVE CONTEMPLATED DIVORCE OR SEPARATION
AND HAVE NOT CONTEMPLATED DIVORCE OR SEPARATION

Prediction Score	Marital Status				
	Divorced	Separated	Have Contemplated Divorce or Separation	Have Not Contemplated Divorce or Separation	Number of Cases
700–789	0.0	0.0	9.1	90.9	11
620–699	2.9	0.0	5.9	91.2	68
540–619	2.9	4.3	6.5	86.3	139
460–539	13.9	15.0	13.9	57.2	173
380–459	25.0	17.0	16.0	42.0	100
300–379	34.2	21.9	21.9	21.9	41
220–299	50.0	37.5	12.5	0.0	8
Number of cases	73	61	64	342	540*

* Fourteen cases were added to the original sample of 526.

With our scoring procedure established, the important question was whether or not the scores would behave the same way when applied to a new sample. Schedules were collected from a new sample of 155 couples in the same general social-economic level from which we drew our first group. Their replies were scored in the manner described above. Notwithstanding the fact that the ranges in the adjustment and prediction scores were narrower than those of the original sample, the correlation coefficient was +.48.

While our procedure will doubtless either amuse or irritate the sensitive statistician, there is no denying that the study does point to possibilities of a more thorough and adequate application of prediction techniques to the problem of marriage adjustment.

We are confident that by refining our schedule questions and our method of scoring, as well as adding certain items not now included in the score, we can increase considerably the precision of our predictions.

ADJUSTMENT IN MARRIAGE

As ANCIENT as human nature is the problem of the adjustment of man and woman in marriage. But in the past domestic discord was regarded almost entirely as a private question confined to the two interested persons. The recognition of marital incompatibility not only as a ground for the dissolution of a marriage, but as a social problem and therefore a subject of public concern, is only recent.

Marital Adjustment as a Social Problem

Historically, the emergence in Western society of marital adjustment as a social problem is to be traced to the individualistic movement ushered in by the Renaissance and the Reformation.[1] The transition from the conception of marriage as a sacrament to that of marriage as a contract was essentially a change from subordinating the person to the institution of marriage to making his interests paramount. If marriage be a contract rather than a sacrament, then divorce, as John Milton, the poet of Puritanism, argued, is the remedy for an unsatisfactory union.[2]

In the United States it was, in fact, the increasing divorce rate that called public attention to the problem of adjustment in marriage. The number of married people who sought the secular

Reprinted from Ernest W. Burgess and Leonard S. Cottrell, Jr., *Predicting Success or Failure in Marriage* (Englewood Cliffs, N. J.: Prentice-Hall, 1939), pp. 1–15.

release of divorce from the holy bonds of matrimony multiplied in something like a geometric ratio. While the population increased only 215.7 per cent from 1870 to 1930, the number of divorces increased 1,647.8 per cent. The divorce rate grew from 28 per 100,000 population in 1870 to an estimated 193 per 100,000 in 1937.[3] So rapidly has divorce gained upon marriage that in 1932 there was one divorce for every six marriages.

There is no conclusive evidence that the growing divorce rate actually indicates an increase in marital maladjustment. In fact, by terminating unhappy unions divorce may represent a decrease in marital discord. But divorce does constitute a social problem in that it has aroused public concern as to the cause of domestic discord and the possibility of its treatment and prevention.

If the increasing divorce rate does not represent increasing marital unhappiness, it does indicate a profound change in mores as to the inviolability of marriage. Fifty years ago the sanction of American mores was still enforced against divorce as inimical to social welfare. Today our mores condone, if they do not approve, divorce as one solution of the problem of marital unhappiness.

To be understood, marriage adjustment, like any other problem, must be examined in the context of culture and of social change. A perspective, then, of marital adjustment in American society is to be gained through comparison of its status in our culture with its status in other cultures, through an examination of trends in family life, and through a survey of the changes now in progress in sex and marriage mores.

Marriage in the Orient and the Occident

"Falling in love" is, in the United States, the right and proper basis for marriage. In China, and elsewhere in the Orient, love comes after rather than before marriage, if it comes at all. Even in marriage respect has priority over love.

In American mores, marriages are arranged by the young people themselves, and parental interference is not sanctioned. During courtship and engagement the youth and the maiden are expected to find out whether they are really in love and well suited to one another. Chinese marriages are arranged by the parents or through a matchmaker, and the young people have little or nothing to say in the matter. Before marriage the bride and groom meet each other only formally.

Our mores encourage the newly married couple to set up a separate domestic establishment, and disapprove of their living after marriage with the parents of either the bride or the groom. In their own home they therefore have freedom to institute desired innovations. In India and Japan, as well as in China, the traditional course is for the young married couple to live after marriage with the bridegroom's parents. The bride becomes the assistant of her mother-in-law in the performance of the household tasks. Ceremonial forms regulate and control the relations of the young couple to each other and to the larger family group. It is difficult if not impossible for them to make innovations, since the whole situation is organized to perpetuate the customary and sanctioned ways of family life.

In the Orient the roles of husband and wife, parent and child, and the relation of a member of the small family to the large family group are clearly defined and regulated by custom. In the United States recent social changes have caused an increasing ambiguity in the definition of these roles, which ambiguity leaves the person without social orientation and therefore makes more important the individual patterns of behavior in adjustment in marriage.

In short, the entire course of selection of mates, marriage, and marital adjustment is regulated by Oriental mores with a minimum of personal freedom and initiative and a maximum of familial and social control. In American society the mores ensure a maximum of personal freedom in courtship, engagement, and marriage, but in a time of rapid social change provide little or no guidance for adjustment in married life.

Social Trends and the Family

The rapidity of social change in American society has outrun attempts to make the necessary institutional adjustments. The problems of marital adjustment need to be considered in their relation to past and present trends in family life.

In *Recent Social Trends* William F. Ogburn has described in detail the changes now taking place in the family and its functions. He thus states the two outstanding conclusions indicated by his data:[4]

One is the decline of the institutional functions of the family, as for example its economic functions. Thus the family now produces less food and clothing than it did formerly. The teaching functions of the family also have been largely shifted to another institution, the school. Industry and the state have both grown at the family's expense. The significance of this diminution in the activities of the family as a group is far-reaching.

The other outstanding conclusion is the resulting predominant importance of the personality functions of the family—that is, those which provide for the mutual adjustments among husbands, wives, parents and children and for the adaptation of each member of the family to the outside world. The family has always been responsible to a large degree for the formation of character. It has furnished social contacts and group life. With the decline of its institutional functions these personality functions have come to be its most important contribution to society. The chief concern over the family nowadays is not how strong it may be as an economic organization but how well it performs services for the personalities of its members.

Certain specific instances of shifts in functions of the family and the behavior of its members may be briefly summarized from *Recent Social Trends* (pp. 664–700) to substantiate the above conclusions:

1. Many household economic activities, such as baking, canning, laundering, cleaning, dyeing, and sewing, have already been largely transferred from the home to outside industries.

2. Between 1920 and 1930 the number of married women working outside the home increased 60 per cent, while their total number in the population rose only 23 per cent.

3. An increasing number of labor-saving devices and conveniences have been introduced into the home.

4. Multi-family dwelling is on the increase. In recent years

about one-half of the newly constructed homes in cities were apartment buildings, and only about one-third were one-family dwellings.

5. Protective functions such as health conservation, security against old age, unemployment insurance, and control of child labor are now largely in the hands of the state.

6. Family attendance at church and family prayers, as reported by one study, are twice as frequent in rural as in urban areas. This fact is perhaps indicative of the decline of religious influence upon the city family.

7. Recreational activities outside the home have greatly increased in recent decades, although the radio may be cited as one instance of a reversal of this general trend.

8. The status of the family is apparently declining in importance as the individualization of its members takes place. Increasing although not complete recognition has been given by law to the individualization of the married woman.

9. Since 1890, contrary to widespread opinion, the percentage of population in the United States that is married has increased with each decade and is larger in the rural than in the urban areas.

10. The study of a sample of families from different communities indicates that the average size of the family household has declined from 4.30 persons in 1900 to 4.01 in 1930. The per cent decreases for different types of areas from 1900 to 1930 are: farms, 0.6 per cent; small towns, 3.5 per cent; cities, 4.5 per cent; and the metropolis, 21.2 per cent.

11. The average size of the unbroken family (husbands and wives and children living at home) has only slightly decreased, the decrease being from 3.67 in 1900 to 3.57 in 1930.

12. The number of unbroken families without children increased from 28 per cent in 1900 to 31 per cent in 1930.

13. Homes broken by death decreased from 7.6 per cent in 1900 to 4.9 per cent in 1930, but those broken by divorce, annulment, or separation increased from 6.7 per cent in 1900 to 9.8 per cent in 1930.

14. In 1930 there were 36 divorces for 10,000 married persons, as compared with 20 in 1900. In 1930, 37 per cent of the

divorces occurred within five years after marriage; in the period 1887–1906 only 28 per cent occurred within that time.

These changes in the functions and structure of the family have been accompanied by the emancipation of woman. The wife and mother has been freed from the slavery of the kitchen and relieved of the greater part of household drudgery. She is winning her right to an independent career outside the home either in an occupation or in some social, civic, or welfare activity.

The continuing loss of functions by the family may, in fact, make all the more important those remaining; namely, affection, companionship, and the rearing and informal education of children. This may mean that the family today, more than ever before in human history, is specializing in its intrinsic functions of providing persons with the satisfactions of intimate personal relationships.

A knowledge of the trends now taking place in family life is an aid in giving the background necessary for an analysis of the factors underlying marital maladjustment in our society. Many of the problems of the family are incidental to the transition from a rural to an urban civilization. The concepts of "cultural lag" and "cultural conflict" serve to identify and, in part, to explain the maladjustments which are concomitant with a period of social change.[5]

The family at present is in a process of adjustment to changes in our society in which the functioning of institutions and the attitudes and behavior of persons are being gradually accommodated to the technological conditions of modern existence, changes which may perhaps best be summed up by the use of the term "urbanization." Nowhere has the influence of urbanization been more profound than in the fields of child care, marital adjustment, and attitudes toward sex. In these fields vast changes have taken place in the folkways and the mores.

Changes in the Mores

In the field of child rearing the commandments of the mores have been definitely displaced by the authority of science. The young mother no longer asks her own mother how to bring up her child but appeals to the pediatrician and to the latest book on child psychology. Rapid has been the development of child study groups and associations, child research institutes, and journals for child welfare.[6]

In the area of husband-and-wife relations, the authority of tradition has been broken, but no substitute in science has yet been provided. Marriage consultation centers have been advocated and many have been instituted, but they are still in the experimental stage.[7]

The problem of the adjustment of modern youth in social relations, in courtship, in engagement, and in marriage needs to be placed in the perspective of the great changes in sex mores which have accompanied the lifting of the Puritan taboo upon sex.

A main objective of the movement to end the policy of silence surrounding sex was to give children information upon the "facts of life." The new freedom of sex discussion was quickly capitalized upon by newspapers, popular magazines, "bestseller" books, and the stage, and was exploited by the "yellow" press and by melodramatic, risqué, sensational, and semipornographic publications. The motion picture, the new means of mass entertainment, quickly discovered in themes of love, sex, and the eternal triangle a sure way of increasing attendance and box-office receipts. Competition soon forced producers to vie with each other in "giving the public what it wanted." The study *Movies and Conduct* by Herbert Blumer[8] portrayed and analyzed the impelling influence of the motion picture on the fantasies, lovemaking, and general patterns of behavior of adolescents and youths.

Illustrations *ad infinitum* might be marshaled to indicate the profound effects of this revolution in sex mores. The Methodist Episcopal Church lifted its ban on dancing. Liberal denominations sponsored dances. The Y. W. C. A. conducted "charm" classes. Agitation for the introduction of sex instruction in the public schools has been continuous. Cigarette smoking is now permissible for youths of both sexes. In the isolated Southern mountain community where William Jennings Bryan and Clarence Darrow debated the pros and cons of evolution, newspaper reporters noted that lipstick and the vanity case had already arrived. The public is markedly responsive to advertising with "sex appeal." The bathing-beach costumes of last summer if worn 20 or even 10 years ago would have been sufficient cause for arrest on the charge of indecent exposure or disorderly conduct. And, to cite an extreme case of social change, witness the growth of the cult of nudism.

Most dramatic of all the changes in sex mores was the hard-fought struggle regarding the limitation of the size of the family by means of contraception. Birth control, which had been a folkway of the educated classes for over a generation, has now entered the mores with the sanction both of the Federal Council of Churches and, in 1937, after many years of resistance, of the American Medical Association.

Syphilis, a long-neglected health problem of vital importance to the family, is now being attacked with unanimous public approval by the available scientific technique in the public health field.

No discussion of changes in the sex mores would be adequate or complete without recognition of the influence of psychiatry and particularly psychoanalysis. The popularization of the discoveries of Dr. Sigmund Freud had much to do in directing attention of the public to sexual maladjustment as the chief cause of marital unhappiness. This marked emphasis upon the sexual aspect of life by the followers of Freud may be regarded as a reaction to the earlier extreme of minimizing its influence upon human behavior. Through the growing number of psychiatrists, through the mental hygiene movement, through child guidance clinics, and through the psychiatric social worker, psychiatric study and treatment are now being given to many types of personality maladjustment, both within and outside of family relationships.

The impact of these changes upon the sex mores has naturally been strongest among youth. Undoubtedly sex is much more in the consciousness and in the conduct of young people of the present than it was in past generations.[9] Symptoms of this are the emergence of "necking" and "petting" and the interest in the "art of lovemaking." There is widespread evidence of increasing frequency of premarital sexual relations.[10] Little or no reliable information, however, is available about the repercussions of these changes in attitude and behavior upon adjustments in married life.

Marital Adjustment Defined

Modern marriage in America differs widely not only from marriage in the Orient but from marriage in the United States of yesteryear. Marriage is becoming more and more an intimate and informal personal affair with less and less traditional control. It is regarded by young people as the fitting culmination of a romance rather than as a socially sanctioned institution. Marriage tends now to be considered as a continuation of a companionship instituted and tested in the period of courtship and engagement.

Marital adjustment must, then, be defined in the context of the modern conception of marriage. Adjustment is not insured here, as it is in the Orient, by customs and ceremonies minutely regulating the conduct of the young married people. If marriage has become a personal rather than a social relation, adjustment is to be defined in terms of personalities, their conflicts and accommodations, and the degree of assimilation taking place.

In certain of its phases, marital adjustment may be measured by accommodation, the mode of living that minimizes conflict and promotes harmony. Many, perhaps the majority of, marriages remain on the level of accommodation.

From the standpoint of assimilation, adjustment is to be defined as the integration of the couple in a union in which the two personalities are not merely merged, or submerged, but interact to complement each other for mutual satisfaction and the achievement of common objectives. The emphasis is upon intercommunication, interstimulation, and participation in common activities.

A well-adjusted marriage from the point of view of this study may then be defined as a marriage in which the attitudes and acts of each of the partners produce an environment which is favorable to the functioning of the personality of each, particularly in the sphere of primary relationships.

Four corollaries follow from this definition:

1. The degree to which the above conditions are met would be the degree of adjustment realized.

2. Since personality differs from individual to individual, a particular combination of traits highly favorable to adjustment for one personality may be entirely unsuited to another.

3. Since a personality is a composite of role patterns, a marriage which is favorable to the functioning of one part of the personality may not be favorable to that of another part.

4. Since personalities are not static but are in the process of development, a combination favorable to the functioning of the personality at one time may not be so for a later period in that personality's development; and hence a period, or recurring periods, of unadjustment may provide conditions of "growth" until a relatively mature and stable level of personality organization is achieved.

Personality Interaction and Marital Adjustment

The personality relations in marriage are so complex and so little understood that it is as yet impossible to deal with them adequately. For purposes of this research it was found necessary to deal separately with five groups of factors that seemed to affect marriage relationships. These five groups may be named as follows:

1. Cultural-background factors.
2. Psychogenetic characteristics.
3. Characteristics associated with the social type.
4. Economic factors.
5. Response attitudes and patterns.

It must be remembered that these groups of factors do not operate separately but interact with one another to affect the marriage adjustment.

IMPRESS OF CULTURAL BACKGROUND Every person bears the impress of his cultural background. His socially inherited cultural patterns are those attitudes and traits which he possesses in common with the other members of his primary social groups.

The early cultural patterns particularly significant for marital adjustment appear to be those transmitted in the family, the play group, and the neighborhood; namely, those of nationality, of a particular section or region of the country, of economic and social class, and of religion. These are constituted by the body of memories, sentiments, and attitudes acquired in childhood that make an adult feel "more at home" with persons similarly reared and "more a stranger" with those of different cultural backgrounds. Some indices of the impress of cultural background upon the person are certain fundamental attitudes and values, pronunciation and idioms in language, manners and mannerisms, and food preferences.

In general, even in American society, marriage takes place within cultural groupings. There seems to be generally, on the part of the person and almost always on the part of his social group, more or less resistance to marriage with the outsider. But intermarriage does take place, particularly when a man and a woman are in a situation of isolation from others of their own race, nationality, religion, and social class. In these cases of intermarriage between persons of widely different cultural backgrounds, one or both of the spouses may be more or less irritated by behavior and attitudes which reflect differences in their early rearing.

It might therefore be assumed, *a priori*, that similarity of cultural background is favorable and that dissimilarity, if sufficiently great, is unfavorable to adjustment in marriage.

THE PSYCHOGENETIC PERSONALITY Edward Sapir has defined the psychiatric (psychogenetic) personality as an "essentially invariable reactive system."[11] By this he means not only the temperament of the individual but, in addition, certain psychically conditioned responses organized into a configuration which may be conceived as "a comparatively stable system of reactivity." This is the precultural personality formed on the basis of constitutional traits by prenatal and postnatal conditions in infancy and earliest childhood.

These reactive patterns are fixed neither by heredity nor by imitation but in the interaction of the infant and young child with mother and father, brother and sister. Some reactive patterns which may be significant for marital adjustment may include the following: extroversion, introversion, egocentricity, sociocentricity, emotional stability, emotional instability. Certain psychogenetic traits are aggressiveness and passivity, impulsiveness and deliberation, dominance and submission, control and feeble inhibition of temper, security and insecurity, sense of adequacy and inadequacy, and flexibility and rigidity.

With the passing of the well-defined traditional roles of husband and wife which, to some extent, controlled their relationship in the old American rural community, the adjustment of the psychogenetic personalities of the couple is becoming increasingly significant. In this study, therefore, an effort is made to determine whether or not and, if possible, to what extent marital adjustment is affected by the psychogenetic personalities of the husband and wife.

T H E   S O C I A L   T Y P E The social type of a person is the product of his roles as a member of different social groups. All these roles are derived from society, but they differ from the impress of cultural backgrounds in that the person appropriates them and makes them his own.

The roles to be considered in this study are the specific roles and patterns of behavior of given persons as they adjust to each other in courtship, engagement, and marriage.

Roles and expectations significant in marriage for the young man are, for example, his conception of himself as a husband and father, his ideal of a wife, his expectations of his career, his attitude toward a career for married women. These are related to his status as affected by his education, his religious identification and activity, and his participation in social life.

E C O N O M I C   S T A T U S By the "economic status" of a person we mean the different factors such as occupation, occupational prestige, income, and prospects of success that determine the conception which he and others have of his economic career.

According to American mores, marriage should be for love and not for money. In the great majority of marriages in the United States, direct economic considerations are probably subordinate to personal and affectional influences. But the economic status of the young people and of their families plays a part in courtship, engagement, and marriage. A man's occupation is often the chief organizing factor in his social personality and plays the leading part in orienting and controlling his behavior. He is rated as a "marital risk" largely upon calculations of his chances for occupational advancement. After marriage the economic factor would seem to become increasingly important. The status of the family is closely linked with the husband's occupation and with his rise in it. Upon his income, chiefly, the family's necessities and luxuries of life depend. The question of whether the wife is to work may be influenced to a large extent by the economic competence of the husband.

In the economic aspect of personality adjustment, the significant question to be investigated is to what extent marital happiness is a function of size or stability of family income.

RESPONSE PATTERNS   Two conceptions, not necessarily incompatible, dominate the attitudes of modern youth toward love and marriage. The first is that of romantic love with its notions of the ideal loved one, of love at first sight, of love transcending all else, and of supreme happiness in marriage. The second is that of affection developing out of companionship, mutual interests, and common activities. Besides these two major conceptions of love there are several specific reactions which affect adjustment in marriage. These include intensity of desire for demonstration of affection, gestural and verbal; the strength of the specifically sexual desires; the fixation in childhood of a particular response pattern; and aberrations of affectional and sexual responses.

In regard to response patterns the general question engaging our attention is: Which affords the more adequate basis for success in marriage—romantic love or affection developing out of companionship? The specific question will be: How are varying proportions of romance and companionship in the love relationship associated with adjustment in marriage?

Adjustment in marriage, it is now clear, involves a relation among several different aspects or characteristics of the two interacting personalities. Any study of marital accommodation and integration must accordingly take into account how the two persons interact with each other, both as persons with specific characteristics and as unified personalities.

The study reported in this volume is a pioneer and exploratory inquiry. It seeks, first, to define the problem of marriage adjustment; second, to find what factors present at the time of marriage are associated with marital success or failure; and third, to determine whether or not it is possible to devise a method of predicting before marriage its outcome in marital happiness or unhappiness.

Is it feasible to bring love and marriage within the purview of science, of prediction and control? Is it possible to increase our insight into and understanding of this realm of human life in which man's behavior seems governed least by his reason and most by his emotions and impulses? This study will attempt to give a preliminary answer to these questions.

9

FAMILY LIVING IN THE
LATER DECADES

ONLY RECENTLY has attention centered on the family life of the aging. Other aspects of changes with aging have been studied: physiological, psychological, economic, and social. But research on the status and problem of family living has been conspicuous by its absence.

Three recent events have called attention to the needs for research and to the importance of family living to persons in the later decades. In outlining the fields of study in his research planning report for the Social Science Research Council, Otto Pollak devoted a chapter to "The Family."[1] The First National Conference on Family Life held in Washington in 1948 called attention to family living in old age as the last stage of the family cycle. Finally, the First National Conference on Aging, held in Washington in 1950, included the subject of family living, living arrangements, and housing as one of its ten major divisions.

As yet, however, no systematic study of the social psychological aspects of family living in the later decades has been attempted. Within the last year two doctoral dissertations have made significant contributions to an understanding of the family relations of older persons, although not focused on this topic. They are *Isolation and Conduct in Later Life: A Study of Four Hundred Sixty-four Chicagoans of Ages Sixty to Ninety-five* by William H. Harlan[2] and *The Social Roles of Old People* by Ruth Albrecht.[3]

Reprinted from *The Annals of the American Academy of Political and Social Science* 279 (1952) : 106–14.

The findings of these two studies especially will be relied upon in discussing the majority of the following topics: basic facts relevant to family living, the last stage of the family cycle, the married couple in old age, living with in-laws, the widowed, and further research.

Facts about Family Living

There are a number of facts significant for understanding the family living of the aging that must be presented first. These are selected from three different sources.[4]

1. The proportion of older people is increasing. There are twice as many people in the United States today as in 1900, but nearly four times the number of persons 65 years and over.

2. The rural population is declining. Fifty years ago 60 per cent of the population was rural; at present only 41 per cent is. Of the rural population, those living on farms declined from 30 per cent in 1920 to an estimated 19 per cent in 1949.

3. The marital status of the population aged 65 and over is as follows: 66 per cent of the men are married, as compared with 37 per cent of the women; 54 per cent of the women are widowed, as compared with only 24 per cent of the men; the proportion that have remained single is the same for both sexes—8 per cent; 2 men and 1 woman per 100 of each sex are divorced.

4. The great majority of persons 65 years and over are living in families: 82 per cent of the men and 76 per cent of the women. Thirteen per cent of the males and 22 per cent of the females are living alone or with nonrelatives. Only 6 per cent of the men and 3 per cent of the women are living in institutions.

5. Low income is common among the aged. Nearly all persons receiving wages or salaries experience a sharp drop in their income at 60 or 65, which at present are the favored years for retirement. About one-fourth are receiving public assistance. The income distribution of older persons and the sources of income are given in detail in the article by Wilbur Cohen in this volume. The big drop in income of persons after age 65 is shown by the fact that their median income was only about $1,000 in 1948, compared

with around $3,000 for men in the age group 35 to 44 and approximately $2,400 for men of 55 to 64.

6. There is a decline of older men and an increase of older women in the labor force. The proportion of men 65 years of age and over who continue to work dropped from 68 per cent in 1890 to an estimated 45 per cent in 1950 while employment among older women increased from 5.7 per cent to 8.7 per cent. The changes and present situation are discussed in the article by Gertrude Bancroft.

7. There has been little increase in the life expectation of older persons. In fifty years the average life span has increased from less than 50 to more than 67 years in 1948. At the age of 65, however, the increase of life expectancy is only from 11.9 to 13.4 years. While more people live longer, those who have arrived at age 65 do not live much longer than they did a half-century ago.

8. Older persons average less schooling than those younger. Each age group in our society has had on the average more formal education than the next older group.

9. The amount of close companionship decreases with age. This is caused not only by the death of spouses but by the loss of intimate friends by death, change of residence, or other reasons.

10. Participation by older men and women decreases. This is shown by attendance at meetings, offices held, number of hobbies, and plans for the future.

11. There is an increased feeling of economic security in spite of lowered amount of income. The greatest economic insecurity seems to be in the 60's when the adjustment to loss of employment is necessary. In each succeeding decade the economic condition of the person becomes further stabilized.

12. Physical handicaps increase with age. Illness and nervousness are more frequent, and the feeling of satisfaction and health decreases.

13. Older citizens increase their religious activities and dependence upon religion. Frequency of church attendance drops in the 80's and 90's. Incapacity to go to church, however, is more than compensated for by listening to church services over the radio and by Bible reading.

14. Feelings of happiness, usefulness, zest tend to decrease with age, and lack of interest in life grows correspondingly.

15. Psychological tests show a lower median attitude score, indicating poorer adjustment. Attitude scores are representative of the way older people react to their experiences in the major areas of their life such as work, family, friends, recreation, leisure, and religion. They include also the subject's statements of attitudes on health, economic security, zest for life, and happiness.

The Family Cycle

The above statement of facts relevant to the family living of older adults presents a static picture. In actuality a longitudinal point of view is necessary for perspective and for the understanding of the problems of the aging.

Paul C. Glick, in an article on the family cycle, has indicated seven stages in the married life of individuals. The first four stages occur in youth and middle adulthood, the last three in the decades of the 50's, 60's, and 70's as determined by the median age of husband and wife. These stages are shown in Table 1.

The family cycle demonstrates that middle-aged and elderly people pass through different experiences. Therefore they may be

TABLE 1

MARITAL STATUS

Median Age of Husband and Wife at Each Stage of the Family Cycle
for the United States: 1940 and 1890

Stage of the Family Circle	Median Age of Husband		Median Age of Wife	
	1940	1890	1940	1890
A. First marriage	24.3	26.1	21.6	22.0
B. Birth of first child	25.3	27.1	22.6	23.0
C. Birth of last child	29.9	36.0	27.2	31.9
D. Marriage of first child	48.3	51.1	45.6	47.0
E. Marriage of last child	52.8	59.4	50.1	55.3
F. Death of husband or wife	63.6	57.4	60.9	53.3
G. Death of husband, if last	69.7	66.4	—	—
Death of wife, if last	—	—	73.5	67.7

Source: Paul C. Glick, "The Family Cycle," *American Sociological Review,* Vol. XII, No. 2, April 1947.

listed variously at different times as (1) parents living with single children, (2) parents living with married children, (3) parents living alone, (4) widow or widower living away from children, and (5) remarried aging persons.

One phase of the family cycle is change of residence. While there is no universal pattern, two variations may be hypothetically presented to indicate the series of residences in the life experience of older persons.

One urban pattern for middle-class persons presents the following residential cycle: (1) birth and rearing on the farm, in town, or in a small city; (2) attendance away from home at college or university, often in dormitories or rooming houses of a town or small city; (3) marriage before or shortly after graduation and living in furnished rooms or small apartment; (4) birth of first or second children and removal to a small single dwelling in the suburbs; (5) with growing family, purchase on time of larger residence in the suburbs; (6) after departure of children from the home and on retirement of husband, return of couple to city and rent of a small apartment; (7) after death of spouse removal of surviving member to hotel, furnished room, or kitchenette apartment.

Variations of the last two stages are moving to California or Florida to a small home and later to a small apartment or rooming house. Two other variations are having married children move in with parents, or taking up residence in the home of a married son or daughter.

Other patterns of residential change will occur to the reader. For example, when farmers retire they typically move into a smaller home in the nearby small town. Patterns of the residential cycle vary considerably with social class, ethnic group, and marital status of the older persons. Studies of certain trends in the mobility of older persons in a town of 6,000 persons are now being completed by Marian McLaughlin.

The Married Couple in Old Age

Of the population aged 65 and over, 35 per cent of the men and 18 per cent of the women constitute married couples living in their own homes apart from their children and other relatives. The great majority of these are first marriages, but they also include some remarriages of widowed or divorced persons.

Couples in this over-65 group comprise a high proportion who have been married for a long time and have been happily married. Most of them have celebrated silver weddings; some have had their golden wedding anniversaries. Husbands and wives have shared joys and sorrows. They have weathered crises. Their lives have become more or less closely intertwined. Now they are often living, perhaps more than ever before, in the lives and activities of their children.

The following personal document gives a picture of a successful married couple in Prairie City.

Mr. Royce is 68 and his wife is 62, but both look younger. Their four children, now married, live within a radius of 200 miles from the parental home. They are financially independent of their parents, have their own friends, and handle their own problems, but seem to enjoy visiting their parents and try to space their visits so one or two families visit every weekend. . . .

While the children were growing up the Royce family lived in a large eight-room house. . . . They attended school with other children of this upper-lower class neighborhood and had room to play and entertain their friends at home. When they finished school the boys went to work or joined the armed forces. There is no evidence that the break from home was overly difficult for either parent or the childen.

Mr. and Mrs. Royce sold the large house when the children left home and moved into the five-room cottage next door. It is more modern and comfortable, but Mrs. Royce says, "Sometimes we wish we still lived in the big house so all of the children and their families could visit us at the same time. The old house seemed so empty with all the children gone. Now they are all married and there are two in each family, and in one the family is four, so we don't have room for all of them at one time. . . ."

The Royces look forward to the children's visits. . . . Mrs. Royce keeps the guest bedroom ready at all times and has the baby beds set up for the grandchildren. They are proud of these grandchildren, have their pictures framed and prominently displayed.

Unhappy marriages in old age have not often been depicted in sociological studies. Waller, however, gives an account of an in-

compatible couple. He traces the process of alienation to its culmination in old age.

Conflict was constant and unremitting from morning until night,
from one week's end to the next; no intervals of peace relieved the tension [except] when one of the children was seriously ill. . . .

The initiative of these quarrels was almost wholly with the wife.
. . . The refusal of sex relations was one of her most potent weapons,
and she inflicted a terrible price upon her husband for any yielding.
She nagged constantly, complaining about every possible point. At
about the twelfth year of marriage, she developed a new technique,
that of constant whining, and for a time her husband objected stren-
uously to this, but soon it, too, was a part of the folkways of the marriage. She was an adept at dry, sarcastic humor; her genial wit and
humor made her highly popular outside her family, but when her jokes
were directed at her husband they always had a sharp edge.

. . . Throughout the long middle period of their marriage this pair
continued to live together in the manner described. . . . They made no
effort to get along; . . . The adjustment of the pair was conflict; conflict in its most inclusive and destructive forms. Every quarrel left each
member of the pair partly satisfied, but with new injuries to redress
and therefore ready to take up arms again. The pattern of association
was not one of distance, but one of extraordinary neurotic closeness.
Both suffered from these quarrels, but they also took pleasure in them.
In between times they prepared their statements, and when they managed to get off a telling shot, the triumphant expression on their faces
and the gloating tone of voice demonstrated their glee over their
success. . . .

When this marriage reached the period of devolution, it slowly but
steadily improved, although within very definite limits. . . . The two
never departed from their quarreling pattern. The wife never ceased
to fuss and whine and complain; the husband never ceased to be emotionally bound up in his conflict relation with her.[5]

Relatives

In Prairie City ties of kinship appear to be less strong than
in rural communities. Albrecht reports that only thirty-seven of
the group of one hundred persons who answered the questionnaire
claim one or more of the following: frequent social contact with

relatives, close family feeling, assistance during illness. Of the remainder, fifty have little or some contact, ten have little or no
interest or contact, and three have no living relatives. The actual
nature of association with relatives is shown by the following excerpts from two contrasting statements by people in their later
years:

We have all our relatives in this town or near enough to visit. We
have our car and go to visit them often. They come to see us all of the
time and there were six different visitors here yesterday. I came back
. . . here because my brother is here and when my husband died I came
back to the town where I grew up. I have lovely nieces and nephews,
their pictures are on the table, and I hear from them often and get a
chance to visit them once in a while. Our brothers and sisters are
scattered all around here and we see them often. I like to make pies and
make a lot of them for cousins. I have a brother in Denver and see him
ever so often. . . . We always kept up with our families and like to visit
them. Since we have no children of our own, we like to be with nieces
and nephews. On vacation we visit around with relatives.

. . . My brother is here but his wife is sick and we don't see each
other often. . . . I try to get to my sister's home about once in three
months and then I see other relatives but usually I am too busy for any
visiting.

In-laws

Among many primitive, ancient, and present-day Oriental
societies, the newlyweds take up their residence in the home of the
parents of either the bride or the bridegroom. When this occurs,
the young husband generally works for his father or father-in-law,
and the young wife carries on household duties under the direction of her mother or mother-in-law. The authority and power are
clearly in the hands of the aging parents. Old age is honored and
respected not only in the commuuity but also in the extended
kinship groups by the children and the grandchildren.

Under these conditions, conflicts and antagonisms no doubt
exist, as indicated by life histories and personal documents. In
general, however, manifestations of these attitudes are repressed

and controlled. Traditions, ceremony, and ritual regulate relationships, and the younger generation fits into the expected roles. Even with retirement from active physical labor of the aging parents, provision is made for their maintenance, and their position is secure.

In our own society, the norm is for the newly married couple to establish a home of their own. Nevertheless, through economic necessity, shortage of housing, or sense of responsibility, many older persons are living with their children, married or single. Statistics indicate that 32 per cent of all older men and 17 per cent of all older women are living with both their spouses and other relatives. These other relatives are not broken down in census reports, but undoubtedly include a considerable percentage of married couples. Among older persons who are not married (largely widowed, but also including the single and the divorced), 14 per cent of the men and 41 per cent of the women are living with relatives, the majority of whom undoubtedly are their own married and unmarried children.

The discussion of the relation of inlaws to their children will be taken up under three headings: (1) aging parents living with children; (2) aging parents residing apart from their children but maintaining satisfying relations with them; (3) aging parents living apart from children but in conflict with them.

Case studies of young married couples made by Burgess and Wallin[6] indicate conditions which make for satisfying or frustrating relations between aging parents and their married or unmarried children. These data are the basis of the discussion which follows.

LIVING WITH CHILDREN This situation may be a matter of choice or of necessity. Where both parents and children elect to live together, the arrangement may work out more or less satisfactorily. Where the wife is working, the mother-in-law often takes on the major charge of the household responsibilities. She may be very happy to function as a baby sitter when the young couple take a night off. Although there may be some disagreements these tend to be minor, and both generations report the relationship as satisfying.

Often, however, especially where the arrangement is one of necessity, difficulties arise. During the present housing shortage, many young couples have had to move in with either the husband's or the wife's parents. In these situations the wife generally gets on better with her mother than with her mother-in-law. Often the relationship may be satisfying to the aging parents, although a difficult one for the children. Sometimes the situation would be satisfactory except for the attitude of the young husband or wife.

LIVING APART FROM CHILDREN BUT HAVING SATISFYING RELATIONS   At the present time, the most satisfactory situation from the standpoint both of aging parents and of the married children is where the two generations have separate residences but maintain satisfying relations.

Mr. and Mrs. Brown have been a happy couple, independent of their children but with a close social relationship.

Mrs. Brown: I have four children, 19 grandchildren and 13 great-grandchildren. I see them often. They come in here a lot and sometimes bring the little ones for the day.

Mr. Brown: The grandchildren and their families come here and visit once or twice a week. It depends on whether I am working. We go with our children on long trips for vacations and one of our children always comes in and takes us to church.

The following case study illustrates a new type of attitude on the part of aging parents:

What do I think of children continuing to live with their parents after they are married? It is a fine idea and I am for it for everybody except myself. I have a twelve room house with two screened porches on a forty acre farm and I am always glad when my married son and his wife and children and my married daughter and her husband and children come for a visit. My wife and I are delighted to see them and the grandchildren, but after they have stayed two or three days, what a relief for both of us when they and the children all depart!

In her study, *The Social Roles in Old Age,* Ruth Albrecht concludes:

These old people are representative of other parents in roles they take and in their attitudes toward their children. Some parents like to be independent and want their children to allow them to remain so. Others appreciate the attention and care their children and other descendants offer unless they try to take too much responsibility away from them. Parents who have a good relationship to their children do not dwell on their own early lives but are happy in the present time.

Parents who are mutually independent of their children show the following characteristics:

1. They can accept or give favors or suggestions without feeling threatened. A basic security in loving and feeling loved removes the threat that could be present for either parent or adult-child.

2. They enjoy working or playing with the second generation.

3. They are proud of their children, like them and have not grown too far apart in interests and mode of life.

4. They accept in-laws as members of the family. Since they have interests outside of the family they are not threatened by the spouse of any second generation member.

LIVING APART FROM CHILDREN BUT IN CONFLICT   Not infrequently aging parents and their children are in conflict with each other. Typically, the antagonism tends to be between the mother-in-law and the daughter-in-law or son-in-law. The aging father or father-in-law seems to get on better with his son-in-law and daughter-in-law than does his spouse. Often there are differences in culture, particularly in religion, that make for chronic conflict. Where the aged parent or parents are dependent and do not live with the couple, the burden of financial support, although assumed by the son, may cause financial stress and even emotional difficulties on one or both sides.

More research is needed on the types of relation between aging parents and their children and the conditions under which they are emotionally satisfying or disturbing. Particularly significant is the hypothesis that the mutually satisfying relations are much more likely to be maintained where living with or away from parents is a matter of choice and not of necessity both for the elderly and for the younger couple.

The Widowed

Widows and widowers constitute a high proportion of persons 65 and over (54 per cent and 24 per cent respectively). They are persons who have experienced family life and are now deprived of it.

The higher proportion of widows as compared to widowers can be explained in three ways. First, the expectation of life is higher for women than for men. Second, brides on the average are younger than bridegrooms. Third, widowers who remarry select women on the average much younger than themselves.

The death of a husband or wife is a crisis forcing the person to make decisions important for family living. This crisis experience and its aftermath will be considered in two aspects: (1) bereavement, and (2) reasons for not remarrying. Interviews secured by William H. Harlan in his unpublished study *Isolation and Conduct in Later Life* provide the data for the following discussion.

The death of a spouse after a marriage of forty or more years does not terminate the association. The departed one, especially at first, may be recalled with a vividness that simulates actual presence. An eighty-year-old widower reports this experience, as well as the shock of his wife's sudden passing.

My wife died . . . sudden; got to feeling bad one night, so I called the doctor and he sent her to the hospital. The next night she died. I was lost for a time afterward; felt like it was the end of the world. For a while I went on thinking she was still there. I could imagine what she would be doing at a certain time, or what she would have said to something. Well, that went on for quite a while, but in the last few years I haven't thought about it so much. I guess in a few years more I won't remember it at all.

Another widower married for twenty-five years when his wife

died attempts to preserve his house as he thinks his wife would wish.

> I've tried to keep everything just as it was when she was alive. I've kept it just as I thought she would like it. I've always taken a great deal of pleasure in caring for the lawn and garden. Some men take up golf; my house has always been my recreation.

Reactions of widows to the deaths of their husbands are similar to those quoted from widowers. There is the disposition to reconstruct in memory and imagination the illusion of the departed.

Harlan summarizes the reasons widowers give for not remarrying, as

> a feeling that life purposes had been achieved in first marriage; feeling that remarriage would signify disloyalty to memory of wife or to her family group (and perhaps to children); and, an idealization of the first marriage. . . . Others quite obviously were not touched upon, such as necessity to support an invalid relative, devotion to career, unattractiveness, chronic illness and so forth.

Many of these reasons apply equally well to widows who do not remarry.

Problems a Challenge for Further Research

The materials presented indicate that aging in the later decades presents its particular problems of family living. Instead of their children being dependent economically and emotionally upon them, parents in old age often find they are dependent upon children for financial and emotional support. There arise new problems of relationships with their married children complicated by the attitudes and behavior of sons-in-law and daughters-in-law. These difficulties may be chronically disturbing if they are sharing the same living quarters, especially when this housing arrangement is a matter of necessity rather than of choice.

There are those deprived of family living—the widowed, the single, the separated, and the divorced. The problem of loneliness seems particularly prevalent and poignant among them, although some have made more or less satisfactory adjustments.

The many different patterns of family living among older persons and the various types of problems they encounter constitute a challenge for further research.

A quite complete outline for further research in the family relations of older persons is presented in Chapter 6 of Pollak's *Social Adjustment in Old Age*. Therefore only a few significant projects will be mentioned here.

1. Studies are desirable of the various patterns of family living of the aging by urban or rural residence, by region, by ethnic and occupational group, and by social class.

2. Particularly interesting studies could be made of patterns of family living according to the nature and degree of dominance exerted by the aging father over his wife and over his children, whether or not they are residing with him.

3. A significant study could compare the factors making for and against satisfying relations of the aging parent or parents with the children and grandchildren. Among those to be considered are temperamental and emotional compatibility or incompatibility, attitude toward marriage of children, acceptance or rejection of reciprocal roles, common or diverse interests, and adaptability or unadaptability.

4. A public opinion poll might provide interesting data on the approved patterns of family living for aging persons classified by the age of respondent, by region, by ethnic and occupational group, and by social class.

5. A valuable study could be made of couples who have celerated golden wedding anniversaries to discover the factors associated with the happy and with the unhappy unions.

6. The quasi family of older nonrelated persons is important for study, particularly from the standpoint of conditions and arrangements making for its successful or unsuccessful operation.

7. A study is feasible of the factors determining whether a widowed person does or does not remarry or does or does not wish to remarry.

8. Demonstration or experimental projects on preparation of the aging for retirement should include a section on planning for family living.

10

ECONOMIC, CULTURAL, AND SOCIAL FACTORS IN FAMILY BREAKDOWN

THE PUBLIC is greatly concerned with family breakdown. It is disturbed at the rising divorce rate. It is alarmed at reports of the increasing rate of juvenile delinquency. It is disposed to hold parents responsible for the delinquency of children and to blame the parents of young couples if their marriage disintegrates. It advocates legislation to punish parents for their children's delinquency.

This interdisciplinary organization, the American Orthopsychiatric Association, was founded to discover the causes of human behavior and to apply this knowledge in prevention and rehabilitation. Its members do not think of family breakdown in terms of assessing blame and punishment. By their training and experience they are looking for causative factors in the individual and in the community and for the best methods for the prevention and treatment of family breakdown. This paper will discuss three factors in family breakdown: the economic, the cultural, and the social.

No one can doubt that economic factors are related to family breakdown. The studies by Bradley Buell and his associates give eloquent proof of this relationship. Rates of nonsupport, desertion, divorce, mental disorder, infant mortality, and juvenile delinquency are highest in neighborhoods of the lowest income and of the worst housing.

Reprinted from *American Journal of Orthopsychiatry* 24 (1954) : 462–70. Paper read at the 1954 Annual Meeting in the opening session, "Family Breakdown." Copyright 1954 by the American Orthopsychiatric Association, Inc. Reproduced by permission.

But what is the nature of the relation between economic privation and family breakdown? It is seldom, if ever, direct. If it were, all families in poverty would experience family breakdown. Every social worker knows that this result does not follow. Studies show that well-integrated flexible families withstood our last depression where unintegrated unadaptable families failed to adjust.[1] Family breakdown results directly, as Dr. Lippman has emphasized, from the strains and conflicts in the interpersonal relationships of husbands and wives, parents and children.

If economic factors do not have a direct influence, in what way are they related to family breakdown?

One of my students made a significant study of two Italian neighborhoods, one in Blue Island, Illinois, with little or no juvenile delinquency and the other on the west side of Chicago with very high juvenile delinquency rates. What was the explanation for the difference? The economic status and, of course, the ethnic origin of the two groups were the same. But the Italians in Blue Island had settled in an orderly German-American community. At the same time the other Italian group settled in a deteriorating community on Chicago's West Side where delinquency rates were high. In Blue Island, the Italian newcomers fitted into a nondelinquent pattern of community life. On Chicago's West Side the Italian immigrant children were exposed to and adopted delinquent patterns of behavior.

Just as low economic conditions do not lead directly into family breakdown, high economic status does not prevent it. The most stable and happiest marriages seem to be in middle-class families with moderate stable incomes rather than among the very poor or the very rich.

Although indirect, rather than direct, the relation of economic conditions to family breakdown often is none the less real. Therefore, a minimum standard of living is a highly desirable aid in the prevention of family breakdown and in efforts for rehabilitation.

The relation of American culture to family breakdown needs to be understood as a precondition to any program of prevention and rehabilitation.

Our culture is something new under the sun. Certain of its

aspects seem to encourage rather than prevent family breakdown. Therefore it is highly important to understand our culture and its relation to family behavior.

First of all, American culture places a high value upon the individual, upon exploit (at least in the male), upon self-expression and upon personality development. At the same time, it devalues kinship ties, the subordination of the wife to the husband, and parental authority. For example, many young wives no longer, as in the horse and buggy days, seek advice from their mothers on how to raise their children. They consult a pediatrician, a psychiatrist, or join study classes on child psychology. The grandparents too often are relegated to the role of baby sitters.

In the second place, our American culture is highly competitive. This high value on competition is reflected and accentuated in family relationships. Psychiatrists in their probing into forgotten experiences in early childhood have discovered the tremendous role of rivalry among children for affection and attention from parents and the emotional disturbances arising from feelings of discrimination and rejection. Husbands and wives may be competitive to a degree that may wreck their union. At the same time, they may be without any adequate understanding of the motivations of their behavior which go back to sibling rivalry. The main contribution of Healy and Bronner's book on *New Light on Delinquency and Its Treatment* is not, I believe, recognized by readers of the book or by the authors. It is a dramatic demonstration of the factors operating to create a model child of one sibling and to push his rejected rival into juvenile delinquency.

Not only unconsciously but deliberately do parents foster competitive behavior in their children. Their overattention on good school grades, the father's ambition for the son to be a star athlete, and other projections of thwarted parental goals on son or daughter intensify competitive attitudes. Individual success becomes a goal of supreme significance, and other values become subordinate to it.

A third value of our society is that of democracy. Much of the history of the family in America could be written in terms of the progressive application of democracy, first achieved in the political field, to the relations of men and women, parents and children. There can be little doubt that the old-time family, dominated by the father and characterized by the subordination of the wife and children, was more stable than the modern family with its democratic structure of interpersonal relations. That it was externally more stable, the steadily increasing divorce rate for the past ninety years abundantly demonstrates.

Democracy in practice means increased freedom, both inside and outside the family, for its members to act on their own. Inside the family, children are not told what to do; rather their consent is sought. Instead of ordering the child of three or four to come indoors, the mother calls, "Come in now, O.K.?" Parental supervision of the social life of adolescents is reduced to an admonition to return home at a certain hour.

Family breakdown, at least as evidenced by statistics, seems to be related to our high evaluation of individualism, competition, and democracy. Our values stress the initiative, the independence, and the self-determination of the individual. When these values of the person conflict with those of the family, a breakdown is threatened. But is it inevitable that these values undermine the solidarity of the family? To answer this question we must turn to an examination of the society in which we live.

As Dr. Lippman has pointed out, the family is the basic social unit of society. The breakthrough of the family, therefore, is not only a menace to this age-long institution, but it also undermines the foundations of society.

Certain sociologists see in the increasing rates of family disintegration and juvenile delinquency the breaking up and atomizing of American society. Pitirim Sorokin and Carle Zimmerman are leading exponents of this point of view. Professor Sorokin writes:

The family as a sacred union of husband and wife, of parents and children, will continue to disintegrate. Divorces and separations will increase until any profound difference between socially sanctioned marriages and illicit sex-relationship disappears. Children will be separated earlier and earlier from their parents. The main socio-cultural functions of the family will further decrease until the family becomes a mere incidental cohabitation of male and female while the home will become a mere overnight parking place mainly for sex-relationship.[2]

Zimmerman, in *The Family and Civilization*, declares that the present American family is doomed unless it returns to what he calls the domestic type of our grandparents. "There is little left now," he warns, "within the family or the moral code to hold this family together."[3]

To meet the threatened dangers to society, these two sociologists have demanded a reinstitutionalization of the family, a return to something like the family of one hundred years ago with authority in the head of the family, with family objectives dominant, and with little or no divorce.[4]

In common with the great majority of sociologists engaged in research on the family, I reject both this interpretation of the situation and the recommendations.

Society and the family are not going to pieces. They are in a state of transition. Society is in process of change from a rural to an urban and industrial civilization. The chief aspects of this transition may be briefly enumerated: (1) the growth of cities and the "urban way of life"; (2) the decline in home enterprises not only of farming but of productive domestic activities; (3) the decrease of formal social controls and of religious sanctions on behavior; (4) the increasing freedom of women: occupational, educational, political, social, and personal; (5) the growing freedom of young people, especially in the association of the sexes; (6) the rise of a host of social welfare agencies, including family service, child guidance, marriage counseling, to meet the problems of an urbanized society.

All these changes, taken together, amount to a social revolution in the mores as profound as that of the industrial revolution. They are in part a resultant of the changes from agriculture to industry. They are in part a product of the application of democracy in the political field to social life. They are in part an effect of the influence of the new means of transportation and communication: the automobile, the airplane, the motion picture, the radio, and television.

Not only society, but the family, is in transition. The shift taking place is from the institutional to the companionship form. The institutional family was an adaptation to the rural situation of the past in which the interests of the individual were subordinated to those of the family. The companionship family is related to the urban way of life in which the central interest of the family is in the personality development of its members.

The characteristics of these two types of the family may now be contrasted:

Institutional	*Companionship*
Authority vested in husband and father; subordination of wife and children	All members share in decision-making; equality of wife
Conformity to law, customs, public opinion and convention	Affection, and emotional and intellectual stimulation
Duty	Personal happiness
Priority of family objectives	Personality development of members

The difference between the two types of family relationships can be made concrete by comparing the colonial with the modern family.

In the Puritan family, children were enjoined to honor and obey their parents. A son was taught to address his father as "Esteemed Sir." Today fathers are admonished to be "pals" with their sons. The same formality was observed by an engaged couple. Even as late as the Civil War a young man writing to a girl to whom he was to be married in three months addressed her formally as "Esteemed Friend, Miss Smith" and signed himself "Respectfully yours." Only in a postscript did he disclose any expression of intimacy when he added, "Good-night, Kate."

The cultural values of American society have been analyzed as those of individualism, competition, and democracy. They may now be discussed in the context of a society changing from rural to urban ways of living and of the family with declining institutional characteristics and with increasing companionship relations.

Individualism, democracy, and competition have undermined the old institutional family. They can, particularly if redefined, become cohesive factors making for the development of the companionship family.

Before dealing with the way in which individualism, democracy, and competition may contribute to family development let us consider three ways in which they are undermining the family.

1. The urban way of life has freed the adolescent from family control and from surveillance by the community. This emancipation gives youth the opportunity for choice of interests, of career, and of a mate. But too often the choice is impulsive, irrational, and no longer dominated by parents but by the adolescent group.

The explanation commonly given is that youth is immature, or as the sociologist would phrase it, not autonomous. A more complete interpretation would be in terms of the ambiguous role of the adolescent in our society. Youth is expected to be on his own, to make decisions, to act as if he were an adult. At the same time youth is not given adult status nor the means of achieving it. Juvenile delinquency is often an extreme manifestation of an abortive attempt at acting adult.

2. The urban way of life is characterized by great diversity as compared with the homogeneity of cultural backgrounds, interests, goals, and expectations of the old-time rural community. All these cultural, social, and personal differences make for increasing difficulties in mate selection and in decision-making in marriage. Three examples of conflict of expectations of husband and wife follow.

First, husband and wife may enter marriage with widely different expectations. The husband may hold to the institutional concept of the family where his is the voice of authority, and the wife may be imbued with the companionship conception of equality of the marriage partners. Such a case was that of a husband who called himself a "little Caesar" and who followed his mother's injunction to be the ruler of the home. He had forced his wife to give up her job, which she enjoyed, lest her economic independence be a basis for challenging his authority. The wife, although defeated in her attempts at equality in making decisions, was not yet beaten into submission. She was, in fact, contemplating divorce.

Second, marriages are entered into romantically on short or

superficial acquaintance. On better acquaintance, the couple may find themselves with conflicting expectations, with divergent interests, or with incompatible temperaments.

Third, expectations may change after marriage. The rising professional or business man finds that the girl who met his expectations when he was a college student does not meet adequately the new role he wishes her to fill.

3. Modern young people, faced with changing situations and problems unknown to their parents, seldom have the knowledge and skill to deal with them. The new knowledge derived from research is in the possession of specialists. Only recently, for example, has the knowledge gained from social science research on factors making for successful marriage become available to college students through courses, and to the general public through books and counseling centers.

There still remains the more difficult problem of the most effective dissemination of this new knowledge of human relations. General knowledge may be of little or no help in individual cases. Lectures are too didactic to have much influence on conduct. Discussion is more stimulating but it also is separated from action. Experimental procedures and projects are necessary if young and older people are to participate actively in setting up and achieving their goals.

The evidence is growing of the development of a new relation between the specialist and the layman in the field of interpersonal relations. It should be democratic, recognizing the capacity of people to share in knowledge. It should recognize the autonomy of persons, namely, the right to plan their lives. Competition should be friendly rivalry in increasing competence in personal relations. In this kind of competition everyone gains and no one loses.

Prevention and Rehabilitation

Child guidance clinics, marriage counseling centers, psychiatrists and clinical psychologists have a fine record of accomplishment in the treatment of behavior difficulties of children and adults. Their work should be strengthened and expanded. In addition, there is need for projects with groups of persons dealing specifically with community, cultural and social factors in family breakdown. Three projects in prevention and rehabilitation will be briefly presented. Two of these have centered their attention on juvenile delinquency, and one on marital relations. They all are examples of the cooperation of experts and laymen. They all are democratic in spirit and seek in constructive ways to aid the person in achieving autonomy and competence.

The Chicago Area Project aims to control the community factors that contribute to juvenile delinquency in the deteriorated neighborhoods of the city. These are also the low-income neighborhoods. The procedure is as follows:

1. A group of local citizens organize as a Community Committee.

2. This Community Committee takes full responsibility for a program of welfare activities for all the children in the neighborhood.

3. Subcommittees are appointed on various aspects of the program: recreation, education, juvenile delinquency, housing, neighborhood beautification, etc.

4. The Community Committee has the services of a trained person supplied by the Chicago Area Project as a consultant.

5. In work with delinquents and predelinquents the Community Committee relies on the volunteer services of members of the Committee and on the paid services of indigenous leaders.

These Community Committees, first organized in Chicago in 1932, now number twelve. Despite all the problems of low income and underprivileged neighborhoods they have been highly successful. They have demonstrated: (1) that community committees can be organized and function continuously in underprivileged urban neighborhoods over a long period of time, in one instance as long as twenty-two years; (2) that community committees can raise the major part of their budget from citizens in low-income neighborhoods; (3) that community committees can work successfully with the Juvenile Court, the police, the probation and parole officers and the Institute of Juvenile Research in a program of treatment of juvenile delinquency; (4) that over a sufficient period of time, juvenile delinquency rates can be reduced.

This project combines the services of the extent and the organized action of citizens in a program of child welfare in their own neighborhood. It seeks to release the capacities of residents, adult and juvenile, and increase their competence both as persons and as members of the community.

The Highfields Treatment Center was established in July 1950 in the State of New Jersey by the Department of Institutions and Corrections, Sanford Bates, Commissioner, and Lowell Bixby, Deputy Commissioner. Its purpose is to institute a new type of program of treatment for juvenile delinquents as a substitute for commitment to a reformatory. The features of the program are as follows:

1. Instead of committing certain boys to the reformatory, the Juvenile Court judge sends them to Highfields under probation status.

2. Residence at Highfields is normally for a maximum of four months.

3. Highfields is a residential, noncustodial center accommodating twenty boys.

4. The core of the program is constituted by the nightly sessions of guided group interaction, a special form of group therapy adapted to the rehabilitation of delinquent boys originally devised by J. Abrahams, a psychiatrist, and Lloyd W. McCorkle, a sociologist.[5] The purpose of the guided group interaction sessions is to stimulate the boys in a group situation to analyze the causes of their delinquent behavior.

The superintendent of the Center is the moderator of the sessions of each group of about ten boys, but he does not attempt to direct the discussion of their problems or to solve the problems for them. In nearly all the cases, the source of the boy's difficulty is a combination in varying degrees of two factors: (1) family breakdown, usually in the sense of conflict between parents and/or antagonism of the boy to the father which has become generalized into his rebellion against all authority, and (2) identification with the gang and subordination to it.

The following case indicates the way in which a teen-age boy finally analyzed the reasons why he was always picking a fight with other boys. As early as he could remember, his father had told him to fight for his rights against other boys. He now felt that his elation at his father's praise of his fighting was being reproduced in his response to the admiration of the boys for him as a "fighting man who wouldn't take anything from anybody." But the boy realized that there was another emotion experienced in his fighting besides the expectation of increased prestige. Finally he identified it as the same as his feeling of antagonism toward his mother. The release of this emotion in fighting was also satisfying.

Through this type of guided group interaction delinquent boys begin to look at their past and present behavior objectively and to devise new ways of future conduct in line with their changed attitudes. In other words, they emancipate themselves from their emotional antagonism to the family, free themselves from the tyranny of the gang, and achieve autonomy and competence in ordering their lives.

Participant experimentation is a new mode of group dynamics now being studied at the Family Study Center of the University of Chicago under the direction of Nelson N. Foote. It aims to develop competence in interpersonal relations, such as those of companionship and friendship, existing in the family and other intimate groups.

Three teams of two persons each are studying empathy, autonomy, and creativity in interpersonal relations. An assumption of the research is that the development of these skills not only would prevent many marital difficulties but would enhance the quality of family relations.

The method is participant experimentation. It is participant because the group provides an atmosphere of spontaneity for free expression of attitudes and opinions, for suggesting alternative solutions to problems, and for stimulating insight through self-examination and evaluation. It is experimental in using role playing in problem situations, in devising different strategies in meeting these problems, and in examining the success of these strategies in developing competence in interpersonal relations and in realizing the goals of the participants.

In summary, this paper has analyzed the role of three factors in family breakdown. Economic conditions were found to be underlying but not direct causes of juvenile delinquency and family disintegration. Outstanding values in American culture, namely, individualism, competition, and democracy, were perceived as emphasizing the development of the individual and weakening the institutional bonds of the family. The urban way of life characteristic of modern society appears to many to be an unfavorable environment for the family. Actually, the family is evolving into a new form—the companionship family. The factors that operate in dissolving the traditional family are the same ones that are binding in this evolving family. This new type of family has great potentialities for the personality development of its members, particularly in initiative, flexibility, and creativity. These characteristics also have high value for effective participation in our modern dynamic society. The family and its members, however, need the help which this and allied organizations can give for the successful cooperation of specialists and laymen in the prevention and treatment of family breakdown. This effort will succeed to the extent that it is democratic and aids individuals in achieving self-expression, autonomy, and competence in interpersonal relations.

III. Crime and Delinquency

Introduction

BY JAMES F. SHORT, JR.

JUVENILE DELINQUENCY and crime were early research preoccupations of Ernest W. Burgess, and their study remained of interest, if not as primary research concerns, throughout his life. In retrospect, Burgess's interest in the subject seems attributable to two abiding goals which characterized his sociological career, which is to say, in very large part, his life: (1) the amelioration of social ills, and (2) the development of sociology as a science. Crime and delinquency were important social ills, and social reaction to these phenomena provided data which could be used in pursuit of the second goal. Approaching both goals with a distinctly sociological perspective, Burgess, demonstrated integrity of purpose and continuity in their pursuit.

The two goals were closely related in Burgess's writings and in his life style. The title of his first published work implies both: "The Social Survey: A Field of Constructive Service by Departments of Sociology," appearing in the *American Journal of Sociology*, in January, 1916 (see this volume, chap. 16). That same month, his first article on juvenile delinquency appeared in the *Journal of Criminal Law and Criminology:* "Juvenile Delinquency in a Small City," based on a study conducted in Lawrence, Kansas. His life style involved "a remarkably long list of causes and campaigns—some professional, such as the American Sociological Society, the Social Science Research Council and the National Council on Family Relations, and others in the service of governmental or private efforts to solve social problems (see Philip M. Hauser, in *Ernest Watson Burgess, 1886–1966: Four Talks Given*

at a Memorial Service [University of Chicago, 1967], p. 28).
Everett Hughes recalls that Burgess "was always engaged in public
services of one kind or another; reforms I suppose one would call
them, but reforms that involved the understanding of social problems and the people whose behavior was thought to leave something to be desired" (ibid., p. 4). Burgess devoted countless hours
and untold financial support to these problems and to the relentless pursuit of knowledge about, and betterment of, the human
condition as he understood it. Much of this effort was unknown,
because anonymous, and much was unheralded, so unobtrusively
and selflessly was it given.

As is evident from his bibliography, by the mid-1920s Burgess's interests in family and community organization and interaction, as contexts within which the problems and processes of
social life are played out, had emerged as his major substantive
concerns. His interests were unusually (by today's standards)
broad, encompassing macro and micro perspectives, cutting across
disciplines, from biology and psychology to economics, probing
the sweep of history as well as the immediacy of events under observations. Thus, early contributions to human ecology were
coupled with a persisting interest in human personality and in
social organization. The "Old Green Bible," Park and Burgess's
Introduction to the Science of Sociology, was a compendium of
extremely broad scope. The range of "social problems" which engaged his attention was similarly comprehensive: in addition to
crime and delinquency, his published work includes analyses of
"family disorganization," "neighborhood work" (and note the
other half of the title of that 1924 article [see this volume, chap.
3], referring to a "scientific basis" for such work, a theme which
was to recur in other articles), "children's behavior problems,"
"adolescence and growing up" in general, "social planning,"
"gambling," "social breakdown," the effects on the family of the
Depression, and of war and its aftermath, "neuroticism" and
"mental disorders," and, finally, "aging and retirement." The appearance of the latter toward the end of Burgess's teaching career,
while an extension of his interests in family and community, entailed also an element of personal involvement. University of

Chicago students in the Department of Sociology during the late 1940s will recall the annual meeting of faculty and new graduate students which occurred each autumn, during which faculty talked briefly of their research interests. For me, this occasion took place in 1947. When it came his turn, Professor Burgess spoke chiefly of the fact that he and his colleagues were deeply involved in research concerning aging which, he noted with a twinkle in his eye, for "personal reasons" he preferred to call "later maturity."

None of these specific social problems, however, so preoccupied Burgess as did his career-long dedication to study of community and family. These he regarded as fundamental to social life, and to social problems—their understanding, and ultimately their control.

Despite the shift in his primary research efforts, however, Burgess's link to criminology remained strong throughout the decades of the twenties and thirties, and he spoke and wrote on developments in this field throughout his life. He was much involved in the work of Clifford R. Shaw, Henry D. McKay, and their associates at the Illinois Institute for Juvenile Research (known familiarly among criminologists as "IJR") and in the "action arm" of this effort, the Chicago Area Project (see the paper by Burgess, Joseph Lohman, and Clifford R. Shaw in the *National Probation Association Yearbook* for 1937, pp. 8–28). Landesco was Burgess's student while conducting the landmark study, *Organized Crime in Chicago* (University of Chicago Press, 1929; reprinted in 1968), as was Clark Tibbitts when he and Burgess joined forces to conduct the pioneering effort in prediction, "Factors Making for Success or Failure on Parole" (this volume, chap. 12).

The work at IJR gave Burgess the opportunity to pursue his interests in a wide range of sociological methodologies as well as substantive and theoretical concerns. *Delinquency Areas* (by Shaw, with the collaboration of Frederick M. Zorbaugh, Henry D. McKay, and Leonard S. Cottrell, Jr., University of Chicago Press, 1929) is widely known as the classic ecological study of juvenile delinquency, yet it also includes extensive case materials important both for illustration and interpretation. Shaw describes the study as "an initial phase of a situational approach" (p. ix) and as "an important first step in a cultural approach to the study of delinquent behavior among juveniles" (p. 1). He identifies the study, also, as representing "the sociological point of view" (p. 1). In his preface, Shaw acknowledges Burgess's contribution to the enterprise: "We are under particular obligation to Professor Ernest W. Burgess for his continued interest in the study and painstaking examination of the manuscript" (p. x). Five months later, in an editor's preface to Shaw's *The Jack-Roller* (University of Chicago Press, 1930), Burgess likened the life-history document to the biologist's microscope which "enabled the research worker to penetrate beneath the external surface of reality and to bring into clear relief hitherto hidden processes within the organism" (p. xi). The life-history document "enables [the student of personality] to see in the large and in detail the total interplay of mental processes and social relationships."

Earlier, in "The Study of the Delinquent as a Person" (this volume, chap. 11), Burgess had noted the primitive state of research efforts and measurement techniques in such study, in contrast with the burgeoning development of physical and psychological testing of the *individual.* Following Park's definition of the *person* as "an individual who has status," Burgess set out to systematize the study of persons, emphasizing the importance of social relationships, of roles assumed in such relationships, and of status within the group. While agreeing with William Healy's assessment that "statistics will never tell the whole story," Burgess nonetheless expressed the "hope of securing quantitative indexes." And he noted in conclusion that his article in fact "deals with the sociology of personality rather than of delinquency," but that after all, the criminal "is first of all a person, and second a criminal." (A 1972 study finds that professors in each of four disciplines sampled agree as to the continuing superiority—in these and other "scientific" respects—of the physical sciences, compared with sociology and political science. See Janice Beyer Lodahl and Gerald Gordon's article "The Structure of Scientific Fields and the Functioning of University Graduate Departments," *American Sociological Review* 37.)

Burgess remained much interested in the sociology of personality, as is evident from his family writings in particular. He did no original research in this area with respect to delinquents as criminals, but his commentaries on the intensive case studies published by Shaw and his associates provided a vehicle in this area. He was impressed by Edwin Sutherland's theoretical synthesis, the hypothesis of "differential association" (see Sutherland's *Principles of Criminology*, 3rd ed. [J. B. Lippincott Company, 1939]), and by the "important contribution" made by one of his own students, Daniel Glaser, in the theoretical statement of differential identification" (see this volume, chap. 14). Another of his students, Albert J. Reiss, Jr., carried forward Burgess's interest in the relation of sociological and psychiatric factors in delinquency ("Social Correlates of Psychological Types of Delinquency," *American Sociological Review* 17 [1952]:710–18).

Prediction of success and failure of prisoners on parole—as that of success or failure in marriage—also served the larger goal of scientific sociology. "For several years," Burgess wrote in 1929, "it has been . . . [my] conviction . . . that it would be possible to predict the future conduct of groups of persons on the basis of their past behavior" ("Is Prediction Feasible in Social Work: An Inquiry Based on a Sociological Study of Parole Records," *Social Forces* 7:534). The article begins: "Prediction is the aim of the social sciences as it is of the physical sciences." No index entry for "prediction" appears in the "Old Green Bible," but there is a good deal of discussion about "natural law," its prediction aims, and the prospects for sociology as "natural history" and as science.

The most significant prediction research in criminology with which Burgess was associated was the pioneering study of "Factors Making for Success or Failure on Parole" (this volume, chap. 12), which he directed as a member of the Committee on the Study of the Workings of the Indeterminate-Sentence Law and of Parole in the State of Illinois. The committee was appointed in 1927 by the presidents of the universities of Illinois and Chicago and Northwestern University, at the request of the chairman of the Parole Board of Illinois. It was a small committee, consisting of Judge Andrew A. Bruce of the Law School at Northwestern (Judge Bruce was president of the American Institute of Criminal Law and Criminology, a former Chief Justice of the North Dakota Supreme Court and member of that state's Board of Pardons and Paroles), Dean Albert J. Harno of the University of Illinois Law School, and Ernest W. Burgess. John Landesco, hired as a field worker, wrote one section of the committee's report (part 3: "Parole and Rehabilitation of the Criminal") and was recognized as a coauthor of the full report, "Indeterminate Sentence and Parole in the State of Illinois," *Journal of Criminal Law and Criminology* 19 (1928):239–86 (republished, with minor revisions, as "The Probation and Parole System," *Illinois Crime Survey* [Chicago, 1929], chap. 12). The collaboration between these distinguished lawyers and the two "working scientists" apparently was congenial. Its success is attested to by the fact that the report has been a classic. It was reprinted in full in 1968. (For an assessment some twenty years after Burgess's original work, see Lloyd E. Ohlin and Otis Dudley Duncan's article "The Efficiency of Prediction in Criminology," *American Journal of Sociology* 54 [1949]: 441–51). The report is best remembered, however, for the chapters authored by Burgess on parole prediction. A third "working scientist," Clark Tibbitts, is acknowledged "for his assistance . . . in the compilation and tabulation of the statistical data" for this chapter.

Detailed study of the records of one thousand men paroled from each of three "Illinois state penal and reformatory institutions" showed great variation in parole violation rates. Classifying these men into "offender" and "social" types, Burgess and his associates related these and a variety of background factors, personal characteristics, and experience in the criminal justice system to experience on parole. The results were dramatic, and Burgess argued that "expectancy rates" of parole violation and nonviolation "should be as useful in parole administration as similar rates have proved to be in insurance and in other fields where forecasting the future is necessary." He warned, however, that expectancy rates derived from his study were "illustrative of the possibilities of the method and not in any sense . . . adapted for immediate use." He urged further refinement and application to more cases for each institution "in order to obtain an adequate statistical basis for the accurate working of satisfactory expectancy tables" (p. 248).

It was typical of Burgess that he perceived his scientific interests as having practical consequence. Parole expectancy rates could not only be an aid with respect to parole board decisions, but "they will be equally valuable in organizing the work of supervision. For if the probabilities of violation are even it does not necessarily mean that the prisoner would be confined to the penitentiary until his maximum was served, but that usual precautions would be taken in placing him and in supervising his conduct. Less of the attention of the parole officers need in the future be directed toward those who will succeed without attention and more may be given to those in need of assistance" (p. 248). Burgess was mindful always of the twin objectives of the criminal justice system: protection of the public and rehabilitation of the criminal. A 1936 address before the American Prison Association (this volume, chap. 13) makes this point forcefully. The paper also speaks to the "conditions essential for parole to reach a high level of efficiency in protecting the public," why this is difficult ["All the mistakes of the other phases of criminal justice come to a head in parole") and to public concern and popular misconceptions.

Burgess shared with Park a strong sense of the sociological importance of public opinion. The opening paragraph of this 1936 paper is illustrative: "In a democracy the final test of any public policy is that of public opinion. Parole and in fact our whole system of criminal justice must constantly be prepared to face trial in the court of public opinion."

Like Park, Burgess was sensitive to the role played by the mass media in shaping public opinion. "As a sociologist," he approved "the lively interest of newspapers and of their readers in parole," and felt it should be "utilized in the correction and improvement of the parole system." He concluded the paper with an "appeal to statistics" as an antidote to the publication of a few sensational parole failures, and the suggestion that newspapers might introduce "a weekly or perhaps even a daily column on 'Crime and Its Treatment.' "

Alas, no such systematic attempt to "cover" crime has been

made by the media. We still rely upon the sensational and dramatic case, the human interest story, and the entrepreneural ingenuity of those who prepare materials for the media, and those who seek their attention.

A final Burgess inquiry into prediction in the general area of criminology is represented by his 1955 address to the (Illinois) Governor's Conference on Youth and Community Service, "Can Potential Delinquents be Identified Scientifically?" Burgess had retired from the University of Chicago some four years earlier, but he remained active in several research and community affairs in emeritus status. After briefly reviewing the diffuse official definition of delinquency, the early "self-reported" delinquency studies, and early attempts to understand crime, Burgess dealt in detail with the findings of the then most recent large-scale study of delinquents and matched controls, *Unravelling Juvenile Delinquency*, by Sheldon and Eleanor T. Glueck (The Commonwealth Fund, 1950). With a touch of irony, he used their own data to suggest that "association with delinquents" was a far more predictive factor with respect to delinquency than were the family relations and psychological characteristics stressed by the Gluecks. Burgess was mindful of his audience, consisting in large part of persons associated with the Chicago Area Project and similar community organizational efforts in other parts of the state. He closed with a suggestion for "spotting potential delinquents by incipient association and identification."

The argument concerning the importance of differential association and identification and other processes related to delinquency continues. New theoretical formulations have been introduced, and new data, but Burgess is still worth reading.[12] It is regrettable that he cannot still be a part of the debate.

In the final analysis, then, Burgess came to view community and family organization—and socialization within these contexts —as fundamental to the causation and the amelioration of social ills, including the earliest "social problem" to draw his scholarly attention, juvenile delinquency, and the last, problems of the aged. In between, he studied a considerable variety of social forms, families, and communities, adolescence, immigrants, and communication, "the" depression, social planning and social policy, mental health, personality development, war and sex, and the discipline of sociology, its problems and prospects, its scholars, methods, and status in the scientific community. For one so bland in appearance and manner, he led us all on a lively search for facts and ideas, which could make a difference in the human condition. Were he alive today one suspects he would be sending his students out to study the newer forms and styles of community and family life, and their social implications, e.g., communal living, child adoption by "singles," and current "unisex" styles of teenagers. Burgess saw clearly the necessity for sociologists to be attuned to social change. In one of his last published works ("Our Dynamic Society and Sociological Research," *Midwest Sociologist, winter* 1955) he noted, "It is not that some changes occur in a context of stability; the entire context as well as the phenomena found in it are changing."

THE DELINQUENT AS A PERSON

THE STUDY of the delinquent as an individual was introduced by the epochmaking volume, *The Individual Delinquent*, by an American psychiatrist, William Healy.

Before Healy, the delinquent was studied statistically or was made the subject of general observation. Lombroso, Tarde, Bonger, and Ferri, to mention certain European criminologists,[1] organized general theories of crime and of the criminal upon the basis of observation, speculation, and statistical data.

The general theories of crime, although imposing and apparently substantial when considered separately, tended, when compared, to undermine and weaken each other, and thus to imperil the entire structure of the European style of interpretation. In effect, this has been the outcome. A brief examination of the theories of Lombroso, Tarde, Bonger, and Ferri is all that is necessary to show how they tend to destroy each other.

General Theories of Criminology

The systems of criminology of Lombroso and Tarde are at logical extremes; they stand in absolute and final contradiction to each other. To Lombroso the criminal was a biological variety; to Tarde he was a social product. The main points in the criminology of Lombroso in its latest form have been concisely analyzed by Näcke,[2] a German criminologist:

Reprinted from the *American Journal of Sociology* 28 (1923) : 657–80.

The real criminal, that is, the habitual criminal

(*a*) is a "born" criminal;
(*b*) is the same as the moral insane;
(*c*) has an epileptic basis;
(*d*) is to be explained chiefly by atavism; and
(*e*) constitutes a biological and anatomical criminal type.

The criminal man of Lombroso, with his stigmata of degeneracy, i.e., low forehead, outstanding ears, powerful, prognathous jaw, receding chin, etc., if reconstructed pictorially would resemble quite closely the primordial human being, Pithecanthropus, or Neanderthal Man in Well's *Outline of History*. Lombroso had no doubt that the criminal as a subspecies of the human race was actually the persistence of, or reversion to, a savage type, as irresistably and innately impelled under conditions in modern society to criminalism as is the epileptic to epileptic seizures.[3]

Tarde held that the criminal was not born but made. He challenged at every point the conclusions of Lombroso. To Tarde the criminal was not a madman, nor a savage, nor a degenerate, nor an epileptic, nor a combination of all these, but a professional type created by society partly as the result of his own crime and partly as an outcome of criminal justice.[4] The principle of imitation, Tarde held, provided a complete explanation of crime as of all social phenomena.[5] Crime conformed to the laws of fashion. As crimes and vices were formerly propagated from the nobles to the people, so now they spread from the great cities to the country.

Bonger's theory of criminality as a result of economic conditions may be classified as a special type under theories of social causation such as Tarde's. The explanation by economic determinism shows also how readily general observation and statistical data may be manipulated to construct a comprehensible and systematic theory of delinquency even upon a narrow and particularistic basis. Bonger, a Dutch socialist, sought to explain crime in terms of Marxian economics. He massed statistics to prove that in the capitalistic organization of society, members of the proletariat were forced into crime, either as victims of the economic and political order or as rebels against it.[6]

Ferri, writing before Bonger, is mentioned last because his system of criminology is eclectic. Avoiding the biological extreme of Lombroso and the social extreme of Tarde, Ferri took a middle-of-the-road poistion. Instead of constructing his system of thought upon the narrow basis of one cause, he sought rather the broad foundation of many causes. Harmonizing, then, at least by inclusion in a more general system the narrower points of view of Lombroso and Tarde, he formulated a comprehensive classification of causes of crime and types of criminals. The following excerpt gives a statement of Ferri's theory in his own words:

Crime is the result of manifold causes, which although found always linked into an intricate network, can be detected, however, by means of careful study. The factors of crime can be divided into individual or anthropological, physical or natural, and social. The anthropological factors comprise age, sex, profession, domicile, social rank, instruction, education, and the organic and psychic constitution. The physical factors are: race, climate, the fertility and disposition of the soil, the relative length of day and night, the seasons, meteoric condition, temperature. The social factors comprise the density of population, emigration, public opinion, customs and religion, public order, economic and industrial conditions, agricultural and industrial production, public administration of public safety, public instruction and education, public beneficence, and, in general, civic and penal legislation. . . . . All criminals can be classified under five groups which I have called (*a*) criminal lunatics, (*b*) criminals born incorrigibles, (*c*) habitual criminals or criminals from acquired habit, (*d*) occasional criminals, and (*e*) emotional criminals.[7]

Ferri's eclectic theory of criminology may be taken as illustrating the net result of the method of general observation and statistical data. Avoiding the extreme generalizations of Lombroso and Tarde, he had the good sense to substitute a pluralistic for a single explanation of criminal behavior. But assigning many causes to crime, he devised no way of gauging the weight of the different factors involved. Indeed, the omnibus inclusion of all possible factors of delinquency into a system of explanation with no fundamental point of view and no method of determining relative signficance tended to confusion more than to explanation. So while

Ferri's theory corresponds closely with what common sense would expect, it went little beyond the findings of common sense.

The Delinquent as an Individual

General theories of crime, whether generalizations of extreme standpoints, like those of Lombroso and Tarde, or elaborations of common sense, like Ferri's, proved to be of little or no practical value in the treatment of the individual and in the understanding of his behavior. Healy states his own experience:

It is quite fair to speak of most previous works on this subject as theoretical, for their marshallings of statistical and individual facts often may be likened to the gathering of building stones for an edifice of opinions already designed. Not only have many theories been published at great length, but volumes have, in turn, been written in review of them. Our experience is simply that we found the facts too much for the theories. Through the detailed study of cases, under good conditions for getting at the essentials, the path of preconceived etiology and classification was seen beset with difficulties. The intricacies of causations appeared manifold. It was then that the plan of making straight for the facts, all the facts available, showed itself of significant worth to us. It was clearly evident that classification by crimes leads only in special instances to knowledge of the criminal; that statistics of seasons, and races, and head-measurements, and alcoholism, and so on, mean almost nothing for the fundamental understanding of the individual case; that epileptic and atavistic theories could not be substantiated by case histories; that refinements of psycho-physical measurements sometimes used on criminals need a tremendous amount of overhauling before they can be regarded as valid for conclusions; that the elders, who spoke so glibly of "the criminal" as a born type, had not the means of investigating whether he was not rather a born defective, and a criminal through accident of environment.[8]

Brushing aside the general theories of crime, Healy emphasized the necessity of intensive study of the individual case. He says:

The dynamic center of the whole problem of delinquency and crime will ever be the individual offender. Nothing is shown by our data more convincingly than the predictable inadequacy of social measures built upon statistics and theories which neglect the fundamental fact of the complexity of causation, determinable through study of the individual case. Studies of individual cases, and final summary analysis of these cases, form the only way of arriving at the truth. Most serviceable to us is the conception of the individual as the product of conditions and forces which have been actively forming him from the earliest moment of unicellular life. To know him completely would be to know accurately these conditions and forces; to know him as well as is possible, all of his genetic background that is ascertainable should be known. The interpretations that may be derived from acquaintance with the facts of ancestry, ante-natal life, childhood development, illness and injuries, social experiences, and the vast field of mental life, lead to invaluable understandings of the individual and to some idea of that wonderful complex of results which we term "personality."[9]

Thus Healy set up for himself the ideal of the complete study of the delinquent. In place of the method of general observation, theoretical speculation and the amassing of available statistical data he substituted the method of case study. This new technique wrought a revolution in criminology. The study of behavior was now placed upon an empirical, inductive basis.

Healy's research, based upon the investigation of a group of youthful recidivists, brought out one significant point, namely, that the study of the criminal is a study of human behavior, and not the study of a special biological variety of the human race as Lombroso held, nor of a separate social class, as Tarde maintained.

Healy conceived his task to be a search for all the influences, factors, and forces which determine behavior. That he was more successful in analyzing the criminal as an individual than as a person was only natural. His own special training was in psychiatry and psychology. Accordingly his technique was highly developed in the individual aspects of the behavior of the delinquent, namely, in the physical examination, anthropometric measurements, and mental tests. With no sociological training, indeed with little that was pertinent in sociological literature aside from the suggestive viewpoint of Cooley,[10] we may rather wonder that Healy gave as much attention as he did to social influences. The explanation however, is simple. First of all, he found the modified form of psychoanalysis which he employed of distinct worth in arriving at the explanation and control of delinquent behavior. His search for the concrete materials of the mental life of the individual led necessarily to some appreciation of social influences. Secondly, through the use of the case-study method he could not if he would ignore the play of social forces. Healy quite naturally recognized the value of the experience of the social worker in securing facts about the family history and social environment, but apparently perceived no place for the technique of the sociologist and of sociological research. His appreciation of the rôle of social factors went little farther than common sense. In other words, his actual procedure was the study of the delinquent primarily as an individual instead of as a person.[11]

The Delinquent as a Person

In sociology the distinction is now clear between the individual and the person. The study of the individual, of the reaction of the organism to its environment, falls in the fields of psychiatry and psychology. The study of the person, the product of social interaction with his fellows, lies in the domain of sociology. Park thus defines the person:

The person is an individual who has status. We come into the world as individuals. We acquire status, and become persons. Status means position in society. The individual inevitably has some status in every social group of which he is a member. In a given group the status of every member is determined by his relation to every other member of that group. Every smaller group, likewise, has a status in some larger group of which it is a part and this is determined by its relation to all the other members of the larger group.[12]

The significance of this distinction between the individual and the person for the study of behavior is indicated by the following case.[13] Here the individual handicap, a special defect in mathematical ability, gets its meaning in its effect upon the status of the boy in his social group.

CASE I

George, a boy of fourteen years, is the eldest of three children, all of whom are living. The other children are girls—one twelve, in grade 7B; the other ten, in grade 5B. Both girls are bright-eyed, alert, keenly interested children. George can do seventh-grade work in all subjects but arithmetic. For this reason, he was placed in the subnormal room in one of the city schools. He at once became truant, disobedient, and much given to fighting.

George is a tall, well-built boy; looks his age, and "holds his own" physically among boys of the same age. He is not interested in school, nor in anything that goes with it, and was very anxious to quit school when I first saw him. He told me rather scornfully that he hated the school and the teachers. "They put me in the feeble-minded room," he said, "and I ain't feeble-minded; I just can't do fractions."

His mother is an intelligent woman; she was a school teacher before marriage. She is keenly alive to George's need for careful supervision at this particular time. She recently passed a civil service examination, and is now employed at the post-office. As a girl she was always good in all subjects but arithmetic; she managed, however, to do the work required. The children's father died five years ago of heart trouble. His only living relative, a brother, is a minister with a small church.

George, since he was ten years old, has sold papers after school and on Saturday. He recently won a prize for selling the second highest number of copies.

When I talked with him about fighting, he said, "O, you don't understand, I've got to fight. I don't want to, but you see, these here boys say I'm feeble-minded, and I'm going to fight 'em 'til they quit saying it."

George worked manfully with me to bridge the gap between fractions and seventh-grade arithmetic. He made rapid progress at first, due both to interest as well as to the novelty of having a tutor; but as the work became more difficult, his progress was slower. One day he came to me with a badly battered face, and acknowledged that he had been "licked," but felt confident that he would "lick the whole school tomorrow." "But why waste your energy that way, George?" I asked him, "why not put it on arithmetic?" He had never thought of that; but he didn't think it would work; those boys had not only to "be shown," they had to "be beat." He struggled and perspired and accomplished very little that day.

Now, after three months of hard "digging," he is beginning to feel rather hopeful. The teacher says he may leave the subnormal room at the end of the year, and if his progress continues, he may make his grade next year. His truancy has become negligible, and his fighting has perceptibly diminished. He declares he has "come near licking the whole school, single-handed, and they are beginning to think I ain't feeble-minded after all."

In this case the distinction between a diagnosis of behavior from the standpoints of psychiatry and sociology is clear. As an individual the boy had a special defect in mathematical ability; as a person he had suffered a degradation in status in his group. Although from superficial observation he had charged against him the delinquencies of truancy and fighting, actually he was putting up a desperate struggle to maintain his status.

Among the types of mutation in status, the simplest example is perhaps that caused by movement, as by change of residence. Moving from one group to another in order to acquire a new status is a familiar fact. A person who has lost status in his home town by failure, misconduct, or crime, may take refuge in a distant community "to make a fresh start" or "to begin life over again." Healy found, in cases of delinquent children, that a change of neighborhood by the family was correlated with a high ratio of success in reformation.[14]

The person, as previously defined, is the individual with status. Personality may then be regarded as the sum and co-ordination of those traits which determine the rôle and the status of the individual in the social group. Certain traits of the individual—as his physique, mentality, and temperament—definitely affect his social standing. Primarily, however, his position in the group will be determined by personal relations such as his group participation, his character, his personal behavior pattern, and his social type. The following outline offers a scheme for studying behavior in terms of individual and personal traits.

The technique for the study of the individual is naturally much further developed than the technique for the study of the person. The physical examination now represents a diagnosis based upon the latest researches of medical science. Since 1905–11 when Binet

OUTLINE FOR THE STUDY OF INDIVIDUAL AND PERSONAL TRAITS

I. STUDY OF THE INDIVIDUAL

1. Physical examination
2. Mental tests
3. Affectivity score
4. Will profile
5. Temperamental type

II. STUDY OF THE PERSON

1. Participation
    (*a*) Extent of membership in groups
    (*b*) Intimacy of membership (social world)
    (*c*) Rôle in groups
2. Character
    (*a*) Stabilized
    (*b*) Unstabilized
3. Personal behavior pattern
    (*a*) Objective or direct
        (1) equable, (2) enthusiastic, (3) frank, (4) aggressive
    (*b*) Introspective or indirect
        (1) imaginative, (2) secretive, (3) sensitive,
        (4) inhibited
    (*c*) Psychopathic or perverse
        (1) eccentric, (2) egocentric, (3) emotionally unstable,
        (4) psychic inferior
4. Social type
    (*a*) Practical or philistine
    (*b*) Liberal or bohemian
    (*c*) Idealistic or religious
5. Philosophy of life.

and Simon devised a scale for the measurement of intelligence, mental tests have been undergoing a process of constant revision and standardization. Pressy's affectivity test may be noted as one of the attempts to gauge emotional reactions. Dr. June Downey on the basis of handwriting material has worked out what promises to be a valuable method of measuring will reactions. For example, her tests differentiate twelve volitional traits, namely: volitional perseveration, co-ordination of impulses, interest in detail, motor inhibition, finality of judgment, resistance, reaction to contradiction, motor impulsion, speed of decision, flexibility, freedom from load, speed of movement. Attempts to determine or measure experimentally temperamental types are still in the tentative stage. Shand, Jastrow, and others have, however, at least restated the problem. The tendency seems to be to accept the classic names for different temperaments—the choleric, the sanguine, the melancholic, and the phlegmatic—and to redefine these permanent moods in terms susceptible of measurement.

The outline suggested for the study of the person includes aspects of behavior for which no standardized technique of measurement has been accepted. It may be that the description of factors like participation in groups, character, personal behavior patterns, and social types will always remain primarily a matter of qualitative definition. Our investigation here is too recent, however, to abandon at the start the hope of securing quantitative indices. For illustration, the extent of membership in groups may be stated as the ratio of the groups with which the person is affiliated to the total number of the groups in which membership lies open to him. Or the degree of intimacy of membership in one group may possibly be expressed by the fraction of his total leisure time devoted to the life of this particular group. The classification of character in terms of stability is obviously relative to the social norms of particular groups or to the social standards common to all forms of group life.

The threefold division of personal behavior patterns into objective or direct, introspective or indirect, psychopathic or perverse, is one made tentatively by the writer of this article.[15] These differential types of behavior are not personality, and are not even the spontaneous expressions of temperament or other traits of human nature. They seem to be what the general term personal behavior patterns implies, namely, characteristic types of the behavior of the person fixed in the matrix of social relations in infancy and childhood. Naturally original differences in mentality, in temperament, and in volition enter into the determination of the form of personal behavior patterns, but their organization and fixation occur in social interaction.

Mentality, affectivity, temperament, and will are not uninfluenced by social experience. They are all more or less profoundly modified by education and social contacts. But personal behavior patterns like egocentrism, instability, and secretiveness take form and become fixed in the social interactions of the family and of the play group. These personal patterns of behavior are not biologically transmitted as temperament seems to be. Nor are they derived by imitation of others as is the social type or the philosophy of life of the person. (The personal reaction of the individual to his social world is the resultant of the play of social forces in infancy and early childhood.) Whether the fixed responses of the person to his social environment will be in the main (*a*) direct, (*b*) indirect, or (*c*) perverse are apparently determined by the rôle which he assumes, or which is forced upon him in his earliest social interactions. In the molding of a social type of personality and in the acceptance of a philosophy of life the influence of the group is definitely exerted. At the same time, the social copies which the person takes for models appear to him to be but the realization of his most ardent wishes.

The operation of social processes in the formation and development of personal behavior patterns is partially revealed in the following two cases. Unfavorable comparison by others, which results in the sense of inferiority and the mechanism of withdrawal, may create the imaginative introspective type of personality.

CASE II

Mary was more or less the "ugly duckling" of her rather good-looking family. Her two sisters and two brothers, pretty children that they were, received more attention both from their parents and the world outside. Plain Mary was usually completely ignored—her pug nose and freckled face were made the butt of many a family joke. Consequently, Mary withdrew somewhat from her family and their interests and developed about herself a shell—a wall difficult to penetrate. Perhaps this wall of isolation would have not been so hard and so fast had not a certain incident occurred. One day when Mary was eleven years old, she and her two sisters attended a birthday party. When it came time to choose partners for the supper every girl was provided for except Mary. The hostess said to the odd little boy (the rest were already paired off), "Now, Jimmy, there's Mary here, take her." Jimmy sullenly replied, "That homely old pug-nosed thing? I guess not." Mary's dreams were shattered—her little ship had gone on the rocks. She was hurt, terribly wounded. Needless to say, that was the last party she ever attended. Her two sisters laughed at the incident, and made fun of her at home. This aggravated her still more.

Mary made few friends; she felt herself odd, out of the group. She developed a taste for reading, and built about herself a world of her own, in which she and the "nice" characters in the books lived in an atmosphere of rosy pleasantness. She would have little to do with her family—they received none of her confidences—and she made no friends. This sensitive little girl withdrew into a world of her own making and there found the happiness which she longed for.

The egocentric behavior of the "only" or of the "favorite" child, empirically recognized by common sense, forms a chapter in the literature of psychoanalysis. There may be, who knows, an inherited predisposition to egocentrism. Unquestionably, however, a condition of its development as a personal behavior pattern, is the complex of family sentiments and attitudes centering around the "only" or the "favorite" child.

CASE III

Marietta lived in the prettiest brick home in the block. "Six rooms and bath, hardwood floors, electric lights and even laundry tubs in the basement," the ambitious real estate agent might describe it. Her father was just one of a large group of ordinary men who might be seen running for his train any morning, and her mother was just one of the many women of the suburb who delighted in displaying shiny windows and highly polished floors. But the significant fact about Marietta was that she had no brothers and sisters. She was one of the army of "only" children.

Marietta's father and mother had been married seven years when she was born—hence they were well established, well prepared and anxious to care for her more or less indulgently. From babyhood on she was decidedly spoilt: for the first seven months of her life she was very ill, often hovering between life and death. Each little cry, every slightest whim and whimper, was carefully watched and analyzed. Once on the road to recovery, conditions did not change. If things did not go exactly as she liked them to, she let out a terrifying yell and scream; so her wishes were always respected.

At the age of three she began to show signs of all the characteristics which she later exhibited more fully. She was decidely selfish, high-tempered, jealous, vain, impulsive, emotional, and at times peculiarly kind-hearted. She developed a rebellious mechanism, revolting against all forms of control. Often while in a high temper, angry at her father or mother, Marietta would bite them fiercely, and then, in an impulsive act of regret, kiss them passionately. She was never severely punished—a few good spankings might have aided in changing here—but the casual reprimands, to use the vernacular, "went in one ear and out the other," they made no permanent impression. At times when she had accidentally broken some choice curio or some valuable bit of china she would lie to her mother and tell her that she had not broken it. Her father, in order to shield her, would often take the blame upon himself.

Every spare penny was used to make Marietta attractive. Her little coats and frocks were the best that could be bought, luxuries for the middle-class family. Her mother devoted a certain amount of time each day curling her hair. Marietta could not help but feel her superiority over the other children. I remember an incident which occurred when Marietta was four; she was visiting a family with her parents, radiantly bedecked in a flowing red accordion pleated dress, and little red shoes to match. Marietta remarked to the other little girl, "Oh, *you* haven't a pretty dress like mine, *I* won't play with you!" and turning up her nose scornfully, walked away. No amount of strategy, coaxing, or commanding could make Marietta play with the little girl.

Marietta loved friends and playmates as long as they carried out her commands. She would bring all the little girls up to her playroom, and once there, they would have to do as she authorized, or she would order the offenders to go "right straight home!" She had the most and the prettiest toys of any little girl in the block. All the children loved to play with them; so rather than go home they would do as Marietta bid them. Marietta's grandfather, who lived near by, also aided in spoiling her. In the rare cases when her parents refused to do as she wished, her grandfather would pet and fondle her.

At school Marietta proved herself an apt pupil: she learned quickly and well, and found herself as she climbed from grade to grade always at the head of the class. She could not help but assume a superior air, the "I know it all and more than you, anyway" attitude. She became a teacher's "pet" quite naturally, of course, for the teachers always prefer the brightest pupil. At school, just as at home, her selfishness and her vanity developed.

At the age of thirteen, with Marietta just beginning high school, her mother died. This changed entirely the course of Marietta's life. She might have developed normally and have grown up a selfish and rather arrogant person, without any further difficulty. But an unforeseen crisis occurred.

For a few months after her mother's death, Marietta and her father were together constantly, the best "pals" in the world. But her father soon began to realize the burden of keeping up a house with an inefficient housekeeper. He realized as the only solution of the problem that he must remarry. He talked it over with Marietta, now fourteen, but she simply exploded in a fit of anger. For once in his life her father did not heed her words; her will was crossed.

Marietta became jealous of her father. All her life she had been more or less jealous; her father had never dared to kiss her mother without kissing Marietta too. Marietta quieted down and realized that there was nothing she could do but obey. Her father remained the same kind, indulgent father, satisfying her every whim. The woman he married was very kind to Marietta, and sought to win her confidence. Marietta had a serious conflict with her father before she would call her stepmother "mother."

The hardest part for Marietta was telling her friends that her father was married (her high school friends did not live near her home; so they knew nothing of it). Day after day she made up her mind to tell them, but just as surely it was put off from one day to the next. She became bitter, irritable, and extremely unhappy. She was frightfully jealous of her father. His remarriage meant giving up the dear old comradeship she so loved; there was always, for Marietta, the third undesirable person to be considered. Yet she could not exactly hate her stepmother and be mean to her face, as the latter seemed always anxious to be helpful to Marietta.

Marietta became more restless. At about this stage she began to steal although she had a good-sized weekly allowance of her own, and had no need for more money. At times it was only nickels, dimes, or quarters from her father's pockets. Then, as time went on, it developed into more serious thefts. The climax was reached one day when at a friend's house a valuable ring was found missing and traced to Marietta. She could give no particular reason for her theft. She "just took it, that's all."

But Marietta's father was a far-sighted man and he did not punish her. Instead, he tried to discover the cause and the case was analyzed. Marietta's father moved to the opposite side of the city, sent her to a new school to make entirely new friends, and in the course of time the situation became adjusted. Marietta gradually became adapted to her home life, which on the whole was not unhappy, for her father was still the same overindulgent parent, and her stepmother tended to follow in the father's footsteps.

While both individual and personal traits enter into the organization of personality, its essential mark is to be found in social relationships, that is, in the status and rôle of the person in the social group. In an article in the *Journal of Abnormal Psychology and Social Psychology*, the Allports, Floyd H. and Gordon W., give explicit recognition of this fact.

The true criterion of personality is without doubt to be found in the field of social interaction. We are incapable of giving a complete popular description of personality without indicating the manner in which the personality in question stimulates or influences other human beings and the manner in which the behavior of other human beings produces adjustments or responses in the personality in question. In describing this personality we inevitably take the viewpoint of those "other human beings."

Robinson Crusoe, alone on a desert island, undoubtedly displayed a very measurable degree of intelligence in his adaptation to his environment. It was only with the advent of Friday, however, that his personality could be said to stand forth in its full significance. Not only is the language of personality a social one, but the problems arising from the interaction of various personalities are in the truest sense social problems. They include every form of social maladjustment—from the whims of the eccentric to the worst deeds of the criminal. In general it may be said that the aim of personality measurements is the establishing of adjustments between an individual and his fellows which are a benefit to both.[16]

Compensation as a Mechanism to Maintain Status

The status of the person in the social group is in the last analysis a matter of social attitudes: (*a*) the individual's conception of his own rôle, and what is even of greater significance (*b*) the attitudes toward him of the fellows in his group, of the community and of society.

This complex of the attitudes of others toward one is subject to change. These changes may be gradual or abrupt. Gain or loss of status is naturally of absorbing interest to the person. Since all of us begin life as infants, and since in some one trait at least, if not in many, every one of us is surpassed by his fellows, it is inevitable that consciousness of inferiority is a universal experience. The inferiority complex tends to become organized about deficiency in a characteristic that has a value in the group which constitutes the social world of the person. The possession of this trait gives superior status in the group. Adler in the *Neurotic Constitution* analyzes the phenomenon of compensation in instances of constitutional or psychic inferiority.

The following case indicates how a Negro lad through the mechanism of compensation for physical and mental inferiority organized a personal behavior pattern that secured for him leadership and a superior status in his social world of the gang.

CASE IV

Harry M. is a colored lad, fourteen years old, and forty-nine inches tall. He is perceptibly stunted in growth, and slightly deformed in his legs, not enough, however, to interfere with walking. He is "knock-kneed," walks with a swaying gait, and is sensitive of his difference from the physique of normal boys. Both his two brothers, ages twelve and seventeen, are well developed. Harry dresses mannishly, and assumes a studied air of self-composure. He does not talk freely even in play. His behavior suggests an attempt to conceal his physical weakness and deformity with the prestige which his unexpressed thoughts and *possible* strength might inspire.

Between Harry and his elder brother there has been rivalry for leadership in their common group. Harry carries a scar on his head as a result of a former dispute.

On his father's side there are indications of alcoholism. His parents have been separated for a number of years. One of his early recollections is of appearing in Court with his mother and father when divorce proceedings were in progress. He remembers distinctly that his parents were debating who should keep the children, each with emphasis on a preference to be relieved of the responsibility. It was finally decided that two of the boys should stay with the grandmother. He doesn't believe his grandmother had a husband. He dislikes his father, whom he accused of "staying drunk a lot and cussing," and is moderately fond of his mother although he sees very little of her, living as she does at another address in the city.

Harry has only reached the third grade in school. He thinks his teachers like to "peck" on him. His teachers declare him dull and slow, and devoid of interest. He has a very shallow knowledge of arithmetic, and reasons poorly. For example, he says that a horse weighing 400 pounds standing on four legs, weighs 300 pounds standing on three legs.

His grandmother works out during the day and he and his brother are left to their own devices. The family lives in the section of the Negro community that produces the largest number of delinquent colored children. The boy has never been in the Juvenile Court, but a number of his chums have. His manual training instructor asserts that he is a gang leader, although the smallest in the bunch. On several occasions he has been tempted to leave home, "to go to work somewhere," he "reckoned." This feeling came over him usually while he was chafing under the injuries done him by his father and larger brother.

His grandmother has drilled into him an assortment of moral precepts and practices like saying his prayers and grace before meals. He has a good sense of judgment between right and wrong, but when he plays he "forgets sometimes." One complaint of his grandmother is that he has a mind of his own, going out when he feels like it, and acting generally as he pleases. Incorrigibility, fighting, truancy, and lying are his principal delinquencies. His success in fighting is due largely to the fact that he can induce his pals to do his fighting for him. The boy has a remarkable influence with his "bunch," and can take an interest in useful as well as destructive activities. A test of this came recently when his instructor made him squad leader to shovel snow. Mental conflicts appear to have resulted from his dislike for his father and his rivalry with his brother. This perhaps accounts for his impulse to run away from home.

Although he seems to have compensated for his physical disability through his power over the gang, his school record could be improved by striking his interests and perhaps by placing him in a school with male teachers, since women teachers "make him sick."

Behavior tendencies in this case are clearly in the direction of juvenile delinquency. Although the boy has been able to secure a superior status in his play group he remains in a position of irritating inferiority in the family with no compensation through success in the academic subjects of the school. Mental conflicts, as this case indicates, are significant in their relation to status. Tendencies to delinquency, as running away from home, would undoubtedly be prevented if certain obvious adjustments were made in the social situation.

The Social World of the Person

Status, as has been indicated, is to be studied from the standpoint of social attitudes, social forces, and social processes. Wholesome conditions of normal social development require a congenial social world in which the wishes of the person find expression. The attempt at absolute suppression of the wishes tends to their expression in perverted form. The technique of social work devised from the common-sense observation of a situation has too often lacked the refinement requisite for adaptation to differences in folkways and mores, for detection of subtle personal attitudes, or for appreciation of the surging and changing wishes of the person. The kind of sympathetic insight which literature gives into the manifold expressions of human nature so perplexing in their multitudinous superficial variations, so alike in their fundamental simple patterns does not come from the typical training in the narrow routine of the principles of case-work. Too often the "blame" is placed by the social agency upon the refusal of the person or of the family to co-operate in spite of the many "good chances" offered. In the case of a delinquent girl who was said by a welfare agency to have had as many "chances to reform" as any girl in its history, a sympathetic analysis clearly proved that not a single one of the alleged "good chances" afforded a real opportunity for reformation. The following case is a telling illustration of the difference between the surface and the reality of a so-called "good" environment for a delinquent girl:

CASE V

I walked down the avenue looking for the house number, wondering how the poor little waif whose sordid history I had just read could have come from such a neighborhood. "This is scarcely the setting I expected to find. Truly," thought I, "the child is a degenerate." By that time I had come to my number. Before me was a little frame cottage, set in the midst of a soft, green lawn, shaded by big old trees, a veritable haven from the hot July sun.

My knock—there was no door bell—was answered by a gray-haired woman. "Mrs. Brown," said I, "I am Miss James. I have come to talk to you about Elsa." I had been given the information that Mrs. Brown was the grandmother, but it did not seem possible that she could be a relative. She was in fact not the grandmother, but the foster mother. She greeted me warmly. "How is little Elsa? Where is she? My dear, come right in." I walked into a house of a generation ago, and through my mind flashed, "Turn back the universe and give me yesterday." "What a delightful home," I exclaimed. "Yes, it is, and just as it was when we came here thirty years ago. And this was little Elsa's room. My home and my heart are so empty without that child." I answered her eager questions, told her that Elsa was in the industrial school, that I was investigating home conditions so as to ascertain if she should be returned to her old environment, asked her what kind of a woman Elsa's mother was, what sort of home the child had. She broke in, "That home! In that home there was no washing day, no ironing day, no mending day, no cleaning day, no baking day, no Saturday, no God's day. How could a girl be good?"

She told me in her own way, which I should like to quote, but which would make too long a story, of the mother's being left a widow when Elsa was four years old; of the mother's poor health, their struggle with poverty, the mother doing what work she could with her little strength, the child at times almost starved, her lips bloodless. Then, when Elsa was eleven, of the mother's second marriage to a "drunken brute," of the two small crowded rooms in which they lived, of Elsa's "seeing too much," and her subsequent delinquency; of the mother, frantic with anxiety, walking the streets at night looking for her child, of her trying in her own way to amuse the daughter, taking her to picture shows—any place where there was excitement—taking the worst way to reform her, giving her no healthy interest to take the place of the unhealthy ones she had; of her misdemeanors and punishment at school, and of her committal to an institution; of her mother's grief and of the daughter's desire to commit suicide. Then how she, Mrs. Brown, with legal aid, had gotten the girl out of the institution, had taken her into her home and kept her seven weeks, teaching her to cook and serve meals, to wash and iron and clean, to say her prayers, to stay at home in the evenings, with no playmate but a pup.

Then abruptly she led me to the back porch. "Recite the Twenty-third Psalm," she said, and to humor her I began, "The Lord is my Shepherd; I shall not want. He maketh me to lie down in green pastures." "Here is the green pasture," and I looked at the soft green grass with its border of old-fashioned flowers. "Go on," she said, and I continued, "He leadeth me beside the still waters." She pointed toward the lake, very quiet and blue in the afternoon sun. "How could little Elsa run away? How could she be unhappy? I can't imagine it." But I could imagine it. I could imagine little Elsa sitting on the back porch, depressed by the monotony of the quiet of it all, and thinking, "Be good and you'll be happy—but you won't have any fun," for Elsa is of the class for which this expression originated—and weighing against this comfortable home with its cleanliness, order, and restrictions; her mother's home, with its dirt, its squalor, its freedom and fun. No more satisfying and sufficing to a child of fourteen are interests of good housekeeping and cooking, exclusively, than those of running around with strange boys, sleeping in hallways for the sake of adventure. If there could have been a mixture of the two, the good home of Mrs. Brown with its practical training, with some of the mother love to soften, some playmates, some amusements, some diversion, perhaps Elsa could have developed into a moral and industrious young woman. But Elsa ran away to her mother. Mrs. Brown got her to come back, but the seed had been sown. Elsa was discontented and impudent. Mrs. Brown would keep her no longer and returned her to the court.

By this time her mother had degenerated, followed her husband and had taken to drinking, had become, not immoral, but "lower than a nigger," and taught Elsa to steal. She would take Elsa to the grocery stores during rush hours and while the mother was making a small purchase, the daughter would pick up any packages which had been tied up for other shoppers.

"I want Elsa when she is out of school," said Mrs. Brown as I was leaving. "There is good in that girl, and I can bring it out." I promised to call again if I could find time, or at least to write her regarding Elsa's progress at school.

Judged by conventional standards the foster home was an ideal social environment. From the standpoint of the wishes of even the normal girl, not to consider Elsa with her delinquent career already begun, it was nothing other than a prison house.

The poolroom has often been indicted, not without reason, as "a breeding place of crime." A discerning analysis of the pool hall from the standpoint of the social attitudes and the wishes of youth reveals it as the young man's social world. The life-history of Jerry discloses how the poolroom attracted him, gave expression to his wishes and determined and fixed his philosophy of life.

CASE VI

Jerry is a bright, energetic Irish boy who got into trouble because of his emotional temperament, lack of home control, and bad associates. He has been arrested for fighting, gambling, and petty stealing two or three times, but he has not yet been sent to any reformatory institutions.

Jerry's parents do not appear to have any great interest in him and there is a marked lack of respect on Jerry's part toward them. His father is to him "the old man" and his mother "the old lady." He comes and goes just about as he pleases; if the front door is locked when he comes home he goes through the window into his own room. There is little religious life in the home. Grace is said at meals when company is present, and on Sunday afternoons Jerry's sister plays hymns on the piano while his mother sings. Jerry quit going to Sunday school when he was fourteen, two weeks after he learned to play pool. He now spends most of his spare time in the local poolroom, playing when he has money and lounging around when he is "broke." In his early life Jerry was frequently whipped by his father; but when he grew too large for this sort of control no other form was devised, and now he goes unpunished.

He left high school in his second year to go to work, but he only works two or three months in one place. When he has accumulated a little money, he quits and loafs around until it is spent. Mentally he is bright, and being a good talker he has little trouble getting work. In the poolroom where he has made most of his friends he is popular;

but he is a follower, not a leader. He is quick-tempered and quarrel-some, but his anger disappears almost as quickly as it flares up. He acts on the spur of the moment and has never shown much foresight or ability to plan. He has much physical courage, and is usually good-natured and agreeable.

Jerry is not ambitious. He used to envy the firemen, who sit around all day in armchairs and talk and play cards. At other times he wanted to be a life guard on the beach or a rich man's chauffeur.

Jerry's misconduct and failure in life are not due to a "bad" char-acter or low ideals but rather to his lack of character and his aimless drifting nature. Lack of home discipline and the free and easy pool-room life have kept him from advancing.

Social analysis of the case reveals conversion, in the socio-logical sense of a sudden mutation of attitudes, here from the Sun-day school to the poolroom. The poolroom is discerned as a social world with its peculiar canons and codes of conduct satisfying the wishes of the person. For example, in the poolroom there is par-ticipation and response in the good fellowship of the fellows, of recognition in success at the game, of new experience in the dare-devil and sometimes dangerous exploits of the gang. And finally Jerry's philosophy of life was fixed in "sliding through" existence in the easiest way, in the "softest snap of a job" he could find.

The Collapse of a Person's Social World

A final case deals with a situation which becomes signifi-cant when the career of a delinquent is considered as a person and not as an individual. Sudden loss of status or "the collapse of one's social world" is perhaps the greatest catastrophe in the life of the person. Few persons ever recover, or in slang parlance "come back," after a complete loss of status. The following case is an il-luminating example of a life "wrecked" through an assault upon the standing of the person among his fellows.

CASE VII

This is the case of a young man about twenty years of age whose character has been very much affected by unusual home conditions. He bids fair in spite of excellent qualities to develop an anti-social attitude. All of his family with the exception of his mother have the reputation for exceedingly irregular moral behavior. The father is a notorious gambler and a man who has always gone with "loose" women openly. He is a man of fine presence, large, powerful, bold, with a straightforward "devil-may-care" attitude. He spent several adventurous years in South Africa and acquired a courage and strength of will that make him feared and admired. He is a most agreeable and friendly man, but has a violent quick temper. An older son and daughter have also both been sexually irregular, but the conduct of the younger son as a high-school boy had been irreproachable.

Difficulties arose because the young man has naturally made friends with boys of respectable families and associated with them down town, but was seldom asked to their homes. In the last five years he has become more and more bitter. The older brother had poor physique and all of his father's bad habits with none of his good ones. This young man is a youthful image of his father, has vigorous health, is strikingly good looking, and as for intelligence was able to keep near the head of his class all through high school without doing much work. He has such a frank, honest, sportsmanlike way with him that he makes friends everywhere he goes. But he is proud as Lucifer, more so than his father. Generosity with money is one of his outstanding qualities. He went to college with some of his high school friends and was greatly enraged, humiliated, and deeply hurt because their parents did everything in their power to prevent the boys going to the same college with him.

This incident brought to a head all the long series of little snubs and cuts that had not made so much difference when the boy was younger. I saw him the day before he left and it was evident that nothing in his life had ever affected him so deeply. He seemed to feel that some tragedy had occurred from which he could never recover. He was furiously bitter about the whole affair. He had some reason to feel resentment, for his own conduct had been almost beyond reproach. The only possible bad habits of which he could be accused were smoking and gambling. He did not practice either to excess. None of his family were drinkers and he seemed to be free from their common disposition to sexual irregularities.

He did excellent work in college but he could not get over the injury to his pride. He became morose and would not accompany his friends to social functions, although, of course, he was far away from all slanderous tongues. His friends almost unconsciously, perhaps, were not as cordial and intimate with him as before. At any rate, on his part, or on theirs, a change in attitudes had taken place. He began to frequent gambling and disorderly places. But he was too clever to lose money. However, it got him into trouble. Although his college work was more than satisfactory he was called before the officials because he had been present at a time when the police raided a place. His pent-up rage burst on the dean and other faculty men who were present. His natural courage served him well and in a torrent of profane and abusive language he told them that nobody could tell him with whom he could or could not associate. He denounced them with all the curses he could lay his tongue to, blindly abusing them for all his misery. There were papers lying on the table relative to his case. He snatched them up and tore them into pieces, swore they couldn't expel him because he was going to leave.

He came home and secured a first-class position very soon, and has held it ever since. But he is going rapidly on the downward path. He has taken to drinking heavily, frequents disorderly resorts constantly, and is badly diseased. He is not able to do as his father has done—defy the world's standard of morality and enjoy life in his own way.

The Sociology of Delinquency

Sociology is now undergoing a transformation like that which has almost completely changed psychology from metaphysics to an experimental science. From a philosophy of society sociology is emerging into a science of society. Consequently the interest of the new sociology is now turned to defining the experimental point of view, to classifying problems for investigation, and to developing a technique of research.

Not only criminality, but all social problems, indeed the entire area of group behavior and social life, is being subjected to sociological description and analysis. The person is conceived in his interrelations with the social organization, with the family, the neighborhood, the community, and society. Explanations of his behavior are found in terms of human wishes and social attitudes, mobility and unrest, intimacy and status, social contacts and social interaction, conflict, accommodation and assimilation.[17]

The study of the delinquent as a person opens up a fertile field.

Materials in the form of case-records, personal documents, and life-histories, are now available for analysis. Psychiatry and psychology in attacking the problem of the criminal from the standpoint of individual behavior have made contributions of high value, which have prepared the way for sociological research. The psychiatric, psychological, and sociological methods of investigation are not in conflict with each other but rather complementary and interdependent. The sociologist will continue to rely upon the findings of these other sciences of behavior for a knowledge of individual differences in mentality and temperament, while they in turn will be disposed to look for sociology for light upon the adjustment of the person in the social organization.

In conclusion, the point may be raised that this article deals with the sociology of personality rather than of delinquency. The criminal, however, is first of all a person, and second a criminal. Therefore, it is well to study him primarily as a person and secondarily as an offender against the laws of organized society. The basic fact to an understanding and control of the behavior of the criminal seems to be that the lawbreaker is a person, that is, an individual with the wishes common to all human beings and with a conception of his rôle in group life.

12

FACTORS MAKING FOR SUCCESS
OR FAILURE ON PAROLE

IS IT POSSIBLE to find out the factors that make for success
or failure on parole? The members of the Parole Board, the super-
intendents and the staff of the different institutions, and the parole
officers all are convinced from their experience that differences in
personality of the men and differences in factors in their background are related to the success or failure of the man to abide by
his parole agreement.

The Committee, therefore, undertook to find out:

1. What specific facts about the man and his past history as
stated in the record could be related to the fact that he had, or had
not, violated parole.

2. What, if any, additional facts significant in the light of his
record on parole might also be secured.

At the time this study was undertaken all the paroled men had
been released from confinement in the State Penitentiaries at Joliet
and Menard and the State Reformatory at Pontiac for at least two
and one-half years, and in a considerable proportion of cases for as
many as four or five years. Consequently, more than sufficient time
had elapsed to determine their record on parole.

The observation or violation of parole was compared with the
following twenty-two facts as entered in the materials in the records (1) nature of offense; (2) number of associates in com-

Reprinted from *The Journal of Criminal Law and Criminology* 19, part 2
(1928) : 239–306, by special permission of *The Journal of Criminal Law,
Criminology and Police Science*. Copyright © 1928 by Northwestern University School of Law.

mitting offense for which convicted; (3) nationality of the
inmate's father; (4) parental status, including broken homes; (5)
marital status of the inmate; (6) type of criminal, as first offender,
occasional offender, habitual offender, professional criminal; (7)
social type, as ne'er-do-well, gangster, hobo; (8) county from
which committed; (9) size of community; (10) type of neighborhood; (11) resident or transient in community when arrested;
(12) statement of trial judge and prosecuting attorney with reference to recommendation for or against leniency; (13) whether or
not commitment was upon acceptance of lesser plea; (14) nature
and length of sentence imposed; (15) months of sentence actually
served before parole; (16) previous criminal record of the prisoner; (17) his previous work record; (18) his punishment record
in the institution; (19) his age at time of parole; (20) his mental
age according to psychiatric examination; (21) his personality
type according to psychiatric examination; and (22) psychiatric
prognosis.

Offense Named in the Indictment

The general public is inclined to the belief that certain offenses are indicative of more vicious tendencies in the criminal and
would, by their very nature, forecast failure upon parole. Murder
and certain sex offenses, for example, arouse the most intense feelings of abhorrence and are charged with the most severe penalties.
The tabulation of offenses in relation to record on parole give the
astonishing results shown in Table 1.

At all these institutions men convicted of sex offenses, murder,
and manslaughter show a relatively low rate for violation of parole
while those convicted of fraud, forgery, and (except for Pontiac)
burglary have disproportionately high rates for violation. This
seems to indicate either that some groups of offenders are given
unusually careful parole supervision or else that they are more
susceptible to reformation than those prone to other forms of delinquency.

Each of the general types of offenses may be subdivided and
analyzed with reference to violation on parole. For example, those

TABLE 1

<small>PAROLE VIOLATIONS IN RELATION TO GENERAL TYPE OF OFFENSE</small>

General Type of Offenses	Violation Rate by Institutions		
	Pontiac	Joliet	Menard
All offenses	22.1%	28.4%	26.5%
Larcency	23.2	29.3	24.7
Robbery	12.6	29.7	20.5
Burglary	26.3	36.2	33.0
Fraud and forgery	24.2	42.4	38.3
Sex offenses	11.1	18.3	14.8
Murder and manslaughter	27.3	9.0	15.6
All other offenses	20.0	11.1	7.4

charged with grand larceny are one-half as likely to violate parole as those charged with petit larceny. It is apparent that other factors have a bearing upon success or failure under parole rather than the type of crime for which the person was charged and convicted.

Number of Associates in Crime Resulting in Conviction

In a large proportion of cases the crime for which the man was convicted was not committed by one man but two or more men. In Pontiac, out of one thousand cases, the delinquent has no comrade in his crime in 368 cases, one comrade in 375 cases, two comrades in 169 cases, three comrades in 63 cases, four comrades in 13 cases, and five or more comrades in 12 cases. In Menard out of one thousand cases, the offender had no associate in his crime in 659 cases, one associate in 181 cases, two associates in 117 cases, three associates in 25 cases, four associates in 13 cases, and five or more associates in 5 cases. In Joliet out of one thousand cases, the convict had no confederate in 558 cases, one confederate in 226 cases, two confederates in 120 cases, three confederates in 43 cases, four confederates in 22 cases, and five or more confederates in 31 cases.

The most significant finding from a consideration of the relation of parole violation to number of associates was the high violation rate (except for Menard) where the offender had no associate, and the surprisingly low violation rate for all three institutions when the convict had three or more associates. For example, where the delinquent had four or more associates the violation rate is only 4.0 per cent for Pontiac, 11.1 per cent for Menard, and 13.2 per cent for Joliet, as compared with 31.3 per cent for Pontiac, 28.1 per cent for Menard and 32.1 per cent for Joliet when the offender is a "lone wolf." The Pontiac figures showing that 632 out of 1,000 cases involved one or more persons indicate the rôle of the groups, or gang, in the delinquency of youth. These facts indicate the importance of the study of the criminal not only as an individual but also in his gang and other group relationships.

National or Racial Origin

For each of the three institutions, violation of parole was compared with the national or racial origin of the prisoner as determined by the country of birth or race of his father. The largest single group was that of the native white of native parents, or 527 at Pontiac, 643 at Menard, and 350 at Joliet. The group second in size was the Negro with 152 at Pontiac, 216 at Menard, and 201 at Joliet. The remainder were distributed among the other nationalities and races with 321 at Pontiac, 141 at Menard, and 449 at Joliet. All institutions seemed to show the tendency to find the smallest ratio of violations among more recent immigrants like the Italian, Polish, and Lithuanian, and to disclose the highest rate of violation among the older immigrants like the Irish, British, and German.

Parental Status and Marital State

The records at the different institutions were very unsatisfactory upon the relations of the prisoner to his parents and upon the type of home in which he was reared. At all institutions there was a large number varying from about one hundred at Joliet to over two hundred at Pontiac upon which all information seemed to be lacking in regard to the relation of the inmate and his family. The records of 823 men at Menard give 504 from disrupted homes and only 10 from stable, well-organized families. Of the

894 men at Joliet, 524 left home at an early age to make their way in the world; an additional 342 came from broken homes; and only 17 had had an experience of the average wholesome American family, as far as could be inferred from the records. There is real need of securing additional data upon family relationships. The percentages of violations of men coming from "broken homes" was higher than the average, while that of those coming from the better type of home was significantly lower.

At all institutions the single men constituted the largest individual group. At Pontiac their numbers were overwhelming, constituting 851 to 127 married men, 21 divorced or separated, and 1 widower. At Menard the single men have a plurality instead of a majority with 420 representatives, the married men are nearly as large a group with 397, those divorced or separated number 113, while the widowers total 69. Joliet reports 478 single men, 392 married men, 70 men divorced or separated, and 59 widowers. Both Menard and Joliet show a violation rate higher than the average for single men, and lower than the average for married men. At Pontiac, on the contrary, the married youths exhibit a slightly higher rate of parole violation than the average.

Type of Offender

The four main types of criminals have already been differentiated. This violation rate is much lower for the first and occasional offender than for the habitual and professional criminal, and considerably below that of the occasional offender.

The run of the figures clinches the point that the first offender

TABLE 2

TYPE OF CRIMINAL IN RELATION TO PAROLE VIOLATION

Type of Criminal	Violation Rate by Institutions		
	Pontiac	Menard	Joliet
All criminals	22.1%	26.5%	28.4%
First offender	15.8	21.4	17.0
Occasional offender	24.2	32.5	36.0
Habitual offender	39.1	51.4	48.9
Professional criminal	52.4	....	41.7

is a "better risk" than the occasional offender, and the occasional offender is a "better risk" than either the habitual or professional criminal. Moreover the larger half of the first and occasional offenders are technical and minor violators of parole, while the great majority of violations among habitual and professional criminals are the result of detection in new crimes. Table 3, parole violators from Joliet, will illustrate this significant point.

TABLE 3

PERCENTAGE OF MINOR AND MAJOR VIOLATIONS OF PAROLE FROM JOLIET

Type of Criminal	Per Cent of Violators		
	Minor	Major	Total
All offenders	11.2	17.2	28.4
First offenders	9.3	7.7	17.0
Occasional offenders	14.5	21.5	36.0
Habitual offenders	11.0	37.9	48.9
Professional criminals	4.2	37.5	41.7

It is evident from Table 3 that the proportion of serious violation of parole is five times as great among habitual and professional criminals as among first offenders, while the percentage of minor violations among professional criminals is less than half that of first offenders. In other words, the professional criminal tends to obey the technicalities of parole agreement much better than the first offender, but he is five times as liable to continue in the criminal career.

The Criminal as a Social Type

The attempt was made to determine the social type into which each person would fall as gangster, farm boy, recently arrived immigrant, drunkard. This was not a classification appearing on the records, but was derived from the history of the man and his offense as contained in the record. This method of differentiating social types gave some highly significant comparisons.

When criminals are classified by social type, wide differences in the rate of parole violation occur. The farm boy and the newly arrived immigrant both seem disposed to make satisfactory adjust-

TABLE 4

SOCIAL TYPE IN RELATION TO PAROLE VIOLATION

Social Type	Violation Rate by Institutions		
	Pontiac	Menard	Joliet
All persons	22.1%	26.5%	28.4%
Hobo	14.3	46.8	70.5
Ne'er-do-well	32.8	25.6	63.0
Mean citizen	....	30.0	9.5
Drunkard	37.5	38.9	22.7
Gangster	22.7	23.2	24.1
Recent immigrant	36.8	16.7	4.0
Farm boy	11.0	10.2	16.7
Drug addict	4.3	66.7	83.3

ments under parole. But the hobo, the ne'er-do-well from the city (Joliet statistics), and the older drug addict, all are liable to become parole violators. The gangster, interestingly enough, has a parole violation rate a little under that of the average. This fact suggests that special effort directed toward persons of this type might not be so unavailing as is popularly believed.

Place of Residence

Of the 1,000 youths in Pontiac, 430 were temporary or permanent residents of Cook County and 570 of the remaining counties of Illinois at the time of their commitment. At Menard inmates had been committed for the most part from the southern part of the State. Of the 1,000 Joliet cases, 609 had been sentenced in Cook County and the remainder in general from the other northern counties. In classifying the 3,000 paroled men by the size of the community in which they had lived before commitment to the institution, no significant variation from the average in percentage of violation was discovered except a uniformly low rate for those whose homes had been in the open country. For those with homes on the farm only 12.5 per cent from Pontiac, 14.6 per cent from Menard, and 9.3 per cent from Joliet became parole defaulters.

About one-fourth of the 1,000 men from each institution (222 from Pontiac, 272 from Menard, and 253 from Joliet) were transients in the community in which the crime resulting in their conviction took place. The parole defaulter rate was smaller than the average for actual residents of the community, being 14.1 per cent for Pontiac, 19.0 per cent for Menard, and 23.7 per cent for Joliet, but much larger for transients convicted of crime, or 24.3 per cent for Pontiac, 46.0 per cent for Menard, and 41.1 for Joliet.

The material in the records was not so satisfactory for determining the type of neighborhood where the man lived at the time of his arrest. It did seem important to find out, however, whether an inmate of a prison whose last place of residence was a residential neighborhood would be a "better risk" under parole supervision than one whose last dwelling place in civil life had been in the criminal underworld or along the "Main Stem" of Hobohemia.

TABLE 5

TYPE OF NEIGHBORHOOD IN RELATION TO PERCENTAGES OF PAROLE VIOLATORS

Type of Neighborhood in Which Prisoners Reside	Violation Rate by Institutions		
	Pontiac	Menard	Joliet
All neighborhoods	22.1%	26.5%	28.4%
Criminal underworld	42.3	45.5	38.1
Hobohemia	21.4	48.4	52.9
Rooming house district	45.8	34.6	38.7
Furnished apartments	28.6	....	20.0
Immigrant areas	25.0	26.1	25.9
Residential district	17.8	14.2	22.3

It is apparent from this table that the neighborhood of last residence previous to commitment is an important index on whether or not a man will make good or fail when put on parole. The experiences that are associated with life in Hobohemia and the criminal underworld do not, it seems, fit a man to take his place as a law-abiding member of organized society.

Factors Involved in the Trial and the Sentence

The statute requires that the trial judge and state's attorney shall file with the Parole Board a written statement concerning the circumstances of the crime and the character and associates of the convicted criminal. In more than half of the cases of men committed to Menard and in over three-fourths of the cases sent to Joliet and Pontiac, the statement of the trial judge and the state's attorney is purely factual; in the remainder they either enter a recommendation for leniency in the granting of parole or protest against it. That this statement should be given consideration by the Parole Board may be seen by comparing the violation rate of recommendations and protests as 16.9 per cent compared with 46.7 per cent for Pontiac; 23.7 per cent as compared with 27.6 per cent for Menard, and 16.4 per cent as compared with 31.2 per cent for Joliet.

In cases where the trial judge and the state's attorney accepted pleas for less than the offense originally named in the indictment there seemed to be no appreciably higher rate of violation than where the paroled man had been convicted on the original charge.

Except for certain crimes where the law provides a flat sentence as in treason, murder, rape, and kidnapping, the sentence is indeterminate and provides for a minimum and a maximum period of imprisonment. But whether the sentence is for a definite or indeterminate period, the parole law applies and it is therefore possible to compare the rate of violation under different types of sentences.

The striking conclusion to be drawn from Table 6 is the low violation rate for flat sentences and (except at Pontiac) for the

TABLE 6

The Relation of the Type of Sentence to Parole Violation

Type of Sentence	Violation Rate by Institutions		
	Pontiac	Menard	Joliet
All sentences	22.1%	26.5%	28.4%
Flat sentence	16.7	13.0	4.8
From 1 to 5 years	31.6	25.9	33.3
From 1 to 10 years	24.0	26.3	29.8
From 1 to 14 years	20.0	30.7	33.8
From 1 to 20 years	24.2	31.3	34.6
From 3 to 20 years	14.3	20.0	24.1
From 1 year to life	....	2.4	18.2

heavier penalties of three to twenty years and of one year to life. These findings correspond to the other surprising discovery that murderers and sex offenders, who receive flat sentences, have only a small proportion of their number among the parole violators.

More significant, perhaps, than the sentence imposed is the sentence served. Since all the men included in this study of 3,000 cases had been released on parole, it was possible to compare the actual time served in prison or reformatory with the percentage violating the parole agreement.

TABLE 7

THE RELATION BETWEEN TIME SERVED IN PRISON TO PAROLE VIOLATION

Number of Years Served	Violation Rate by Institutions		
	Pontiac	Menard	Joliet
All periods of years served	22.1%	26.5%	28.4%
Under 1 year	10.7	21.3	14.5
1 year but under 2 years	22.0	23.2	20.8
2 years but under 3 years	20.1	27.9	25.2
3 years but under 4 years	32.1	29.4	37.9
4 years but under 5 years	43.5	37.5	37.6
5 years but under 8 years	46.2	43.0	37.3
8 years and over	....	25.0	39.5

In general, the finding to be derived from Table 7 is that the longer the period served the higher the violation rate. A larger proportion of habitual and professional criminals serve longer terms than do first and occasional offenders, according to a special analysis of figures giving this comparison which was made for those released from Joliet. Nevertheless, it would seem to be a good policy for the Parole Board in fixing the length of sentence for the first and occasional offender to keep in mind the relation of the duration of the sentence to making good on parole.

Previous Criminal Record and Parole Violation

How far does a man's past record enable us to predict his future conduct? Does the fact that a prisoner has a criminal and penal record before the commission of the offense for which he has been committed make him more or less likely to obey or to disregard his parole agreement with the State?

Facts upon the man's previous criminal history were available in the records. They were derived from the statement of the trial judge and the state's attorney, from information furnished by the prisoner to the recorder and the psychiatrist at the institution, and from reports furnished the recorder from local and federal bureaus of identification. Out of the 1,000 men at each institution, there was no report of a past criminal history in 541 cases at Pontiac, 666 cases at Menard, and 490 cases at Joliet. The past criminal history of the others varied from the slight offenses that might lead to commitment to a boys' industrial school or to being fined or placed on probation or even sentenced to local workhouse, to those more serious offenses that brought with them a term in a reformatory or a penitentiary.

TABLE 8

PREVIOUS CRIMINAL RECORD IN RELATION TO PAROLE VIOLATION

Previous Record	Violation Rate by Institutions		
	Pontiac	Menard	Joliet
All persons	22.1%	26.5%	28.4%
No criminal record	16.3	21.2	15.9
Industrial school record, only	37.0	46.2	27.8
Fine or probation, only	16.2	12.5	24.1
Workhouse or jail record, only	31.0	25.6	46.5
Reformatory record	34.1	37.9	39.0
Penitentiary record	....	39.4	37.8

It should be stated here that each individual was classified in our tabulation under his most serious previous offense, so that while a man with a penitentiary record might also have an industrial school and a reformatory record he would not be classified there but only under "penitentiary record." At both Menard and Joliet a previous reformatory and penitentiary record show high rates of parole violation, while the lack of a criminal record exhibits a lower violation rate.

Previous Work Record

One question on the face sheet was "Working When Arrested?" The returns from the penitentiary give 21.8 per cent working and 34.2 per cent not working at the time of arrest in the Menard group; while Joliet records state that 25.3 were working and 30.8 per cent were not working at the time the crime was committed.

Of more significance than the fact of working is the general character and regularity of the work. The records were not complete and accurate enough to permit any detailed analysis, but in most cases they contained sufficient information to allow the classification into "no work record," "casual work," "irregular work," and "regular work." Under casual work was entered the intermittent labor of unskilled workers. In the majority of cases irregular work is that of skilled workers who were not steadily employed. Regular work record referred to those who were reported to have a history of steady employment.

TABLE 9

WORK RECORD IN RELATION TO PAROLE VIOLATION

Previous Work Record	Violation Rate by Institutions		
	Pontiac	Menard	Joliet
All persons	22.1%	26.5%	28.4%
No previous work record	28.0	25.0	44.4
Record of casual work	27.5	31.4	30.3
Record of irregular work	15.8	21.3	24.3
Record of regular work	8.8	5.2	12.2

The very low percentages of parole violation for men with a record of regular employment is eloquent in its testimony to regular habits of work as a factor in rehabilitation. This fact gives new emphasis to the recommendations in Part III for the reorganization of the penal and reformatory institutions in order to promote the training of their inmates in trades which they may pursue after their release, and that the record of their work progress be considered in granting or refusing parole. Under the Parole Law as amended, the Parole Board has the necessary authority to obtain information of this type.

Punishment Record in Prison

Although the work record before and during imprisonment has not had much weight in determining fitness for parole, the punishment record in the institution has always received great attention. Punishment of an inmate for serious offenses may lead to demotion in grade and the loss of so-called "good time." Accordingly his stay in the prison is prolonged beyond that of the person who has had no punishment record and so has regularly advanced from grade C to grade B and from grade B to grade A, and so is entitled to a hearing before the Parole Board when the minimum of the sentence expires. The relation of the punishment record in prison to reaction to the conditions of parole is, therefore, a subject of vital interest to all concerned with the theory and practice of penology.

TABLE 10

PUNISHMENT RECORD IN RELATION TO PAROLE VIOLATION

Punishment Record	Violation Rate by Institutions		
	Pontiac	Menard	Joliet
All inmates	22.1%	26.5%	28.4%
No punishment recorded	17.0	20.0	18.6
Demerit	*	....	30.4
Solitary confinement	....	41.9	52.4
One or two demotions	27.2	34.3	35.9
More than two demotions (or in Pontiac and Joliet to Grade E)	33.1	33.3	47.1

* Only two cases, insufficient for calculation of percentage.

At both penitentiaries the inmates who were punished by solitary confinement had an unusually high violation rate, particularly in comparison with the low violation rates of those without recorded punishments. The figures do not, of course, give a final answer to the question whether the violation of parole is a manifestation of the same antagonistic attitude toward rules and regulations as against prison discipline, or whether the recipient of severe punishment within the institution, embittered, is thereby animated with a deeper enmity against society.

Age When Paroled

What is the relation of the age of the paroled man to the probabilities of his violating or observing his parole agreement? Where do youth, middle age, and old age stand as factors favorable or unfavorable to success on parole?

The prison population as a body is a group of young men. Even when paroled the average age of our 1,000 Joliet men was only 34.7 years, of our 1,000 Menard men only 33.9 years, and of our 1,000 Pontiac youths only 21.6 years. The ages ranged, however,

TABLE 11

AGE AT PAROLE IN RELATION TO PAROLE VIOLATION

Age When Paroled	Violation Rate by Institutions		
	Pontiac	Menard	Joliet
All ages	22.1%	26.5%	28.4%
Under 21 years	17.7	25.0	16.7
21 to 24 years	23.1	23.3	23.3
25 to 29 years	31.2*	30.7	28.9
30 to 39 years	....	28.4	33.2
40 to 49 years	....	22.1	23.2
50 years and over	....	23.1	22.0

* The 154 cases on which this per cent figure is based contain two cases 30 years of age and over.

at time of parole from 17 to 32 years at Pontiac, from 19 to 86 years at Menard, and from 17 to 81 years at Joliet. It was desirable, therefore, to arrange the men in age groups in order to determine the relation of age to parole violation.

The youngest and the oldest have the lowest violation rates according to this analysis. This finding bears out the double contention first, that the youth who has impulsively embarked on a career of crime is more amenable to supervision than the more experienced criminal of twenty-five and thirty years, and second, that the older man of forty and over is beginning at last to learn the lesson "that crime does not pay."

Intelligence and Personality as Factors

Illinois enjoys the honor of having been the first state in the Union to establish the position of state criminologist. Under his direction the mental health officer at Pontiac, Menard, and Joliet gives the mental and psychiatric examination of the inmates. A diagnostic summary of this examination together with a statement by the mental health officer of the probabilities of success or failure of the inmate upon a return to the community is entered in the material that comes to the Parole Board for consideration. From these records it was possible to correlate the findings on general intelligence, personality type, and the psychiatric prognosis with the rate of violation of parole.

It was through the work of Dr. Herman M. Adler, State Criminologist, in an examination of the population of Illinois penal and reformatory institutions, that the first conclusive demonstration was made that the proportion of those of inferior intelligence in the criminal and delinquent group is no larger than in the general population. Indeed the percentage of youth of inferior intelligence in Pontiac from Cook County was found to be lower than the percentage of inferior intelligence among men from Cook County examined in army camps during the World War. So, while inferior mentality can no longer be given as one of the major causes of crime, it is of interest to determine how men of different intelligence levels react to supervision upon parole.

The most significant finding from this analysis is, probably, the indication that those of inferior intelligence are as likely, perhaps more likely, to observe their parole agreement than are those of average and superior intelligence. In a study, *Comparison of the Parole Cases, Parole Violators and Prison Population of the Illinois State Penitentiary during the Year 1921*, Dr. David P. Phillips, mental health officer, called attention to the fact that although those of inferior intelligence constitute 28.6 per cent of the prison

TABLE 12

INTELLIGENCE IN RELATION TO RATE OF PAROLE VIOLATION

Intelligence Rating	Violation Rate by Institutions		
	Pontiac	Menard	Joliet
All persons	22.1%	26.5%	28.4%
Very inferior intelligence	24.3	25.0	21.3
Inferior intelligence	14.7	27.1	23.4
Low average intelligence	22.4	23.2	31.4
Average intelligence	17.1	23.5	32.0
High average intelligence	19.8	40.0	24.1
Superior intelligence	26.8	34.8	16.7
Very superior intelligence	9.5	40.0	23.8

population at Joliet, they comprise only 15.6 per cent of those paroled and likewise only 15.5 per cent of the parole violators. He adds: "It is interesting to note that the intelligence level has such a marked influence when the subject of parole is considered, and those cases which rate in the inferior group are not released in the same ratio as in the other groups." Since these two independent studies give the same result, namely, that parole violation is no more frequent—if as frequent—among those of inferior than among those of higher intelligence, it would seem that inferior mentality should no longer constitute a barrier to the granting of parole.

From this table there seems to be some evidence of a higher ratio of parole violation in certain groups of higher intelligence. In the study of the intelligence of the reformatory and penal population of Illinois already referred to, Dr. Adler found that recidivists, or repeaters, in these institutions had, on the average, a higher intelligence rating than had first offenders.

Although less and less emphasis is being given to inferior mentality as a cause of delinquency and crime, more and more attention is being paid to the study of the personality of the individual offender. Herein lies the interest in the classification of personality type by the mental health officer.

The figures from Joliet, and to a lesser degree from Pontiac, seem to indicate that the paroled man with egocentric personality pattern faces the great difficulty in social readjustment. Curiously

TABLE 13

PSYCHIATRIC PERSONALITY TYPE IN RELATION TO PAROLE VIOLATION

Personality Type	Violation Rate by Institutions		
	Pontiac	Menard	Joliet
All persons	22.1%	26.5%	28.4%
Egocentric	24.3	23.5	38.0
Socially inadequate	20.0	24.7	22.6
Emotionally unstable	8.9	*	16.6

* Number of cases insufficient for calculating percentage.

enough, the emotionally unstable seem to have the least difficulty of keeping a clean record under supervision.

From the results of these examinations and from other data, the psychiatrist makes a prognosis as to whether or not in his judgment a man is likely to succeed or to fail upon his return to civil society. His recommendation wherever feasible was classified under the terms "favorable," "doubtful" or "unfavorable" as to the outcome. It should be added that in only one-half the cases in Menard and Joliet and two-thirds of the cases in Pontiac was a definite prognosis found in the record. In the remainder of the cases only the intelligence rating and the personality classification was given. In a small proportion of the cases the records contained no report from the mental health officer.

For Pontiac and Joliet, the psychiatric prognosis gives highly satisfactory results. Compare the low percentage of violation where a favorable outcome had been predicted, 14.8 per cent at Pontiac and 20.5 per cent at Joliet, with the high rate of violation where an unfavorable outcome had been indicated, as 30.5 per cent at Pon-

TABLE 14

PSYCHIATRIC PROGNOSIS OF OUTCOME ON PAROLE

Psychiatric Prognosis	Violation Rate by Institutions		
	Pontiac	Menard	Joliet
All persons	22.1%	26.5%	28.4%
Favorable outcome	14.8	21.4	20.5
Doubtful outcome	17.6	28.1	51.4
Unfavorable outcome	30.5	33.8	49.2

tiac and 49.2 per cent at Joliet. The explanation for the poorer correlation of expectation and actual findings at Menard is in all probability due to the fact that the Southern Illinois Penitentiary has only the part-time services of a psychiatrist, and that therefore the individual examinations must be hurried. Since at present the mental health officer is the only person at the prisons and reformatory making a scientific study of behavior, it is certainly a minimum program that each institution be provided with the full-time services of a psychiatrist.

Religion as a Factor

In this study no attempt was made to correlate religion with parole violation. In the first place it is well known that the church preferences given by prisoners do not greatly vary from that of the general population, or at any rate from that of those economic and social groups from which criminals come. In the second place, the visits of the members of the Committee to the different institutions uncovered evidence that only a small fraction of the inmates had been regular in church attendance prior to commitment to these institutions. Reverend J. H. Ryan, the Protestant chaplain at Pontiac, in an interesting and detailed study found that of a group of 1,000 youths questioned only 90 had been attending regular religious services until the time of arrest, 75 had never attended religious services, 689 had once attended but had left the church and that the others numbering 146 had been very irregular in attendance.

Conclusion

This survey of the records of our penal and reformatory institutions reveals what a mass of detailed information is available about their inmates. It has indicated also what a real bearing this record of facts has upon the question whether or not a man will succeed on parole. Some of these data are not as complete and as accurate as they might be, particularly those dealing with family, group, and neighborhood relationships. Provision should be made for rounding out this material into a complete picture of the man in his social setting.

There is new and pertinent material to be secured. The record of work and the school progress of the inmate within the institution may well receive the same careful attention that is now given to the punishment record. A program of industrial education when introduced will bear directly upon fitness for parole. Then, too, the report of a careful investigation of the situation in which a man is to be placed under parole supervision will give added indication of the probabilities of a successful outcome.

Finally, there can be no doubt of the feasibility of determining the factors governing the success or the failure of the man on parole. Human behavior seems to be subject to some degree of predictability. Are these recorded facts the basis on which a prisoner receives his parole? Or does the Parole Board depend on the impressions favorable or unfavorable which the man makes upon its members at the time of the hearing? Or does influence, political or otherwise, enter into the decision?

13

PROTECTING THE PUBLIC BY PAROLE AND BY PAROLE PREDICTION

In a democracy the final test of any public policy is that of public opinion. Parole, and in fact our whole system of criminal justice, must constantly be prepared to face trial in the court of public opinion.

And what is the attitude of the public to parole? To get the answer one has but to ask one's neighbor, to read letters from readers in the voice of the people, to peruse news columns and editorials in our daily papers. The so-called "average man" is doubtful, critical, hostile to parole. His opinion can be summed up in one sentence: "Why should the police go to all the trouble to arrest a criminal, the state's attorney to prosecute, the judge and jury to convict and sentence him and then have the Parole Board turn him loose on the streets to resume his criminal activities?"

What is the explanation for this attitude of the public?

As we all know, it runs directly opposite to the considered judgment of the great majority of criminologists and of practically all laymen who have given time and study to parole. Criminologists, jurists, representative citizens interested in penology are almost unanimous in favor of parole as an essential and valuable part of the system of criminal justice.

They point out that parole is "the conditional release under

Reprinted from *The Journal of Criminal Law and Criminology* 27 (1936) : 491–502, by special permission of *The Journal of Criminal Law, Criminology and Police Science*. Copyright © by Northwestern University School of Law. Address delivered before the American Prison Association, 15 September 1936.

supervision of a person from institutional confinement before the expiration of his sentence." They emphasize the fact that it is the period during which the offender against society is being aided in making his adjustments to the community. They stress the principle that parole is a period of testing his willingness and ability to keep the parole regulations and to become a law-abiding member of society. And finally they call attention to the fact that release from prison upon parole is much better than release without parole, because release without parole gives no opportunity of supervision and leaves the confirmed offender free to resume unhampered his criminal operations. In proof of this point they call as witness the professional criminal who is everywhere and always a bitter enemy of parole.

Some persons place the blame for the unfavorable attitude of the public to parole upon the newspapers. They maintain that the press presents only the failures of parole and never the successes.

There is some basis of fact, it must be admitted, to this charge. When a man on parole commits a crime, or is arrested as a suspect, the newspapers invariably feature the fact that he is a paroled man. Editorials are almost certain to appear critical of parole. The titles of a few characteristic editorials from Chicago papers during the past year illustrate this attitude: "The Busy Parolee," "Sloppy Parolee," "Abolish the Parole Board?" "Reform Parole or Abolish It." The first mentioned editorial after enumerating five crimes by paroled convicts in three days concludes:

"The news in this record of three days is that there is no news in it: just the old story of criminals turned loose to carry on. But a growing number of citizens are wondering why they are paying taxes to maintain the parole system as it is."

It is, of course, well-known to all of us that parole failures make newspaper headlines while parole successses never see their names in print. Violation of parole is news, and it is news because of its significance to newspaper readers.

As a sociologist, I would be the last person to disapprove of the lively interest of newspapers and of their readers in parole. It is basically sound because it represents a concern of citizens in all walks of life with the problem of crime and its treatment. This interest and concern of press and public in parole should not be condemned. It should rather be recommended and utilized in the correction and improvement of the parole system.

And speaking now as a Chicagoan may I not add that the people of Chicago are proud of the record of our city in its fight against crime. So far as I know never in its history have its newspapers attempted to protect the reputation of the city at the expense of concealing conditions of crime and vice. Almost alone of the large cities of the United States, Chicago made open war on organized crime during the period of national prohibition even at the risk of being unfairly called the crime center of the country.

Today, Chicago is reaping the rewards of this valiant fight against organized crime and its alliance with politics. The year 1935 shows the lowest figures in years for major crimes known to the police and the year 1936 promises still lower numbers. All the different factors responsible for this result cannot be determined and exactly equated. The Chicago Crime Commission gives credit to the reorganization of the police department and its efficient administration by the present police commissioner; to the state's attorney for his effective investigation and prosecution of cases; and to the judges of the Municipal Court and of the Criminal Court. Especially significant has been the coordination of the operations of all these branches of criminal justice in the breaking up of organized crime and its relation to politics.

But back of this fine achievement of the agencies of criminal justice has been the solid, undramatic, continuous and cumulative work of the Chicago Crime Commission and the publishing of the facts upon crime and criminal justice by the Chicago daily papers. Publicity, often pitiless publicity, has been the weapon relied upon by the representative citizens and the press of this community to win the war on crime.

It is, therefore, quite understandable why citizens and newspapers alike look with a critical eye upon parole as the one part of the machinery of criminal justice which may undo all that has been achieved by the police, the prosecuting attorney, the judge and jury, and penal confinement. In short, the citizen feels that he is being protected from the criminal by the police, the state's attorney, the court and the prison. He mistrusts parole, because he feels that it does not provide him security. He is fearful that through parole criminals are being turned loose to prey upon the public. He may sincerely believe that parole is a menace rather than a service to society.

But how can this public attitude against parole be changed?

Only, I am convinced, by demonstrating to the public that parole is an instrument for protecting the public. This task is not, in my judgment, an easy one. The basic reason for this is that parole work is the most difficult, as it is from the standpoint of social protection the most important, part of the procedure of criminal justice. It is most difficult because it is concerned with the actual work of the rehabilitation of the offender.

In crime, as with disease, prevention is much easier, less costly and more certain than cure.

Parole work is the most difficult phase of criminal justice for another significant reason. All the mistakes of the other phases of criminal justice come to a head in parole. If a judge fails to give probation to a worthy case of a first offender and thus causes him in confinement to associate with hardened criminals and come under their influence, this mistake will show up in parole. If a so-called reformatory or prison fails to provide its inmates with work and industrial training to fit them for employment upon leaving the institution, this defect will also show up in parole. The parole system may, therefore, often be charged with failures for which it is not entirely responsible. The failures of our entire system of criminal justice, to repeat, accumulate and become evident in parole.

This means, then, that parole must be considered as an integral part of the entire system of criminal justice. It also means that the success or failure of men on parole measures the efficiency and the degree of coordination of our entire system of criminal justice.

Parole in particular and our system of criminal justice in general have two main objectives: first, and foremost, the protection of society from the criminal; second, and equally important, the rehabilitation of the criminal.

These two objectives are not in conflict with each other, they are, in fact, mutually inter-dependent. In the first place the best way to protect society from the criminal is to rehabilitate him, that is to say, to restore him to society as a law-abiding citizen. In the second place, if the protection of society is held as the actual guiding principle of prison administration and parole, the work of reforming the criminal and of crime prevention will be markedly advanced.

These two interrelated objectives, the protection of society and the reformation of the criminal, are indispensable to the successful workings of our prison and parole system. If these two goals are kept steadily before us we may be saved from the two extreme points of view which prison and parole officials as well as the public are too often prone to adopt. At the one extreme is the policy of severity and repression or as it is commonly called "treat the criminal rough." At the other extreme is the policy of leniency sometimes termed "coddling the criminal."

Both of these policies fail in protecting the public and in reforming the criminal. It is difficult to decide which is the more harmful policy. Experience has demonstrated again and again that undue severity increases criminality and so fails to protect the public. Likewise, the policy of leniency has been proven by repeated trials to fail in reforming the criminal and to endanger public safety.

The problem, then, is one of demonstrating to the public that parole can be organized and administered for its protection which, as we have seen, includes the rehabilitation of the criminal.

In my judgment there are six conditions essential for parole to reach a high level of efficiency in protecting the public:

1. The further development of adult probation so that the majority of actual first offenders who are found to have no confirmed criminal tendency be given the opportunity of reformation in the community under adequate supervision. In this way, society will be protected against the determined influence of their association in correctional and penal institutions with experienced criminals.

2. The introduction of a system of classification of inmates of penal institutions on the basis of which the men would be segre-

gated according to the probability of their reformation and a program of individualized treatment be worked out for each inmate. This should include among other points correction of physical defects, additional school training whenever advisable, industrial education and appropriate work assignment within the institution.

3. The planning of a program of work and other activities within correctional and penal institutions, to utilize the inmates' time and to fit them for re-entering society. Because a job is the best single method yet known for getting men to "go straight" I would stress here the importance of providing in every correctional and penal institution the opportunities for work and industrial education which will fit men to get and hold jobs when they are released upon parole.

4. Preparing men for parole should begin as soon as they enter the institution. The prisoners should be informed that evidence of reformation such as good conduct, school progress, satisfactory work record, mastery of trade and industrial skills will be taken into consideration in granting parole. Friends and relatives should be informed that it is to the best interests of the prisoner to wait until he is prepared to return to the community and until the best possible plan has been worked out between the prisoner, his family and his parole adviser for his readjustment to society. It is evident that parole officers should be sufficient in number and qualified by personality, experience, and training to give effective assistance to the paroled man in making satisfactory adjustments to his family, to his work and to his neighborhood.

5. Of central importance are high qualifications for the members of the Parole Board. In 1928 the committee which made its report on "The Workings of the Indeterminate-Sentence Law and the Parole System in Illinois" recommended that:

The Parole Board should be taken out of politics as nearly as possible under our form of government. The members appointed should hold office for definite terms which should expire at different times and in such a manner as to free the Board from the pressure of political influence. The Parole Board should enjoy the standing and independence of the Supreme Court of Illinois in order to discharge fully its equally great responsibility, and the compensation of its members should be the same as that of the judges of the Supreme Court in order to attract and to hold men and women of the highest qualifications.

Colonel Henry Barrett Chamberlain of the Chicago Crime Commission in his recent report upon parole to Governor Henry Horner makes a more detailed and even stronger recommendation:[1]

An administrative Board with definite tenure of office to supersede the present Parole Board, its personnel to consist of five persons appointed by the Governor and selected for their particular fitness without reference to politics, religion, nationality, fraternal or other affiliations. Each member selected to be not less than thirty years of age, with the equivalent of a university education and preferably a member of one of the learned professions. No person to be selected who has held elective or appointive office within five years prior to such appointment. Any appointee of the Board to be disqualified for holding an elective or appointive office for a period of at least three years after leaving the Board. The members of the first Board to be appointed for terms of three, six, nine, twelve and fifteen years respectively. Thereafter, one member to be appointed every third year for a period of fifteen years. The pay to be sufficient to attract competent persons. No member of the board to have other occupation, but to devote his entire time to the work. The idea here is to prevent a change in the personnel of the Board at the will of each incoming governor and to assure the services of men who are willing to make careers of this type of work. In other words, to provide for career men; men who will take pride in their work, who become trained for it and who possess the requisites for success for service to the commonwealth. Some provision should be made for retirement and pension and in the event of incompetency or corruption, action for impeachment and removal of any member should be provided, preferably by some original action in the Supreme Court of Illinois.

These are high standards, but none too high when measured against the magnitude and difficulty of the parole problem and the significance of the effective administration of parole for public protection.

6. The prediction of the probable success or failure of men

when released on parole is a new instrument which if wisely and cautiously used will be of assistance in protecting the public against the habitual and professional criminal.

In Illinois especially during the past four years greater or less progress has been made in achieving all these six conditions to the effective operation of parole. No progress, so far as Cook County is concerned, has been made in the field of adult probation. Adult probation is now the weakest part of our machinery of criminal justice not only in Illinois but in many other states. The public will sooner or later realize that the denial of supervised probation to a youth who merits it is often the same as pushing him into a criminal career at public expense both in taxes and safety.

A classification plan has been introduced into Illinois with diagnostic depots at Joliet and Menard under the direction of the State Criminologist, Dr. Paul L. Schroeder. Each man upon being sentenced by a judge goes first of all to one of these diagnostic depots where he is examined by specialists. On the basis of a careful study of his physical condition, mentality, family and community background, work record, past criminal experience and probabilities of reformation he is assigned to one of the four state institutions with a recommendation for individual treatment.

Progress has been made, although more at some institutions than at others, in reducing the number of idle inmates. At present the best opportunities for industrial and general education are at Pontiac, the institution set aside for the first offender with good prospects for reformation.

Distinct advance has been made in the program of preparing men for parole. Pre-parole classes have been organized and an attractive manual of useful information for the paroled man has been prepared. At the present time a parole study is in progress under the general direction of George J. Scully, chief parole supervisor.

The present Board of Pardons and Paroles was carefully selected by Governor Horner and with less consideration for politics than in the past. This is evidenced by the fact that the chairman is a holdover from the previous administration and that another member, a man who has devoted his life to the study of criminology, was appointed upon the endorsement of a non-political group of citizens.

In 1933 Illinois introduced prediction technique as an aid in parole work. In this new advance it has the distinction of being the leader as in several other noteworthy developments in the field of criminology as witness the first Juvenile Court, the first institute for the study of juvenile delinquents, the first state criminologist, the first Crime Commission.

What is parole prediction and in what ways may it be of use in protecting the public against crime and criminals?

Parole prediction may be defined as a method of determining what are the chances that a man will succeed or fail when released upon parole. In other words, it is a way of giving every man who is being considered for parole a risk rating, as a "No. 1 risk," a "No. 2 risk," a "No. 5 risk," and even as low as a "No. 18 risk."

There is, at present, a growing body of literature upon different methods of parole prediction. Notable contributions to the theory and practice of parole prediction have been made by many research workers including Hornell Hart, S. B. Warner, Sheldon and Eleanor Glueck, Clark Tibbitts, John Landesco, George B. Vold, S. A. Stouffer, Jerome Davis, Ferris F. Laune and his office, C. C. Van Vechten and Sam Daykin. Now under way is a nationwide study of parole prediction included in the Attorney General's Survey of Release Procedures and directed by Barkev S. Sanders.

This is not the time or place to weary you with the technical details of these studies. In spite of their many differences they are all based upon the following simple principles:

1. Certain factors are selected like previous criminal record, previous work record, whether married or single, conduct in the institution and so forth.

2. A large number of cases are studied to find out if these factors are or are not related to violation of parole. For example, it has been found as might be expected that men with previous criminal records are poor risks on parole, while men with no previous criminal records are good risks; men with regular work record before arrest are good risks; those with irregular work record, poor risks; married men are good risks; single men, poor risks; those

who observe prison regulations are good risks and those that violate them, poor risks. In almost every case statistics justify common sense observations.

3. The next step is to get a sum total of the probabilities of success or failure in each case studied. For example it is now evident that a man who has no previous criminal record, who worked regularly in the past, who was married and who observes prison regulations is, or should be, a much better risk on parole than a man with a previous criminal record, who has only worked irregularly at casual labor, who is single, and who has been a persistent violator of prison rules.

4. The final step is the construction of what is called an experience table which shows actually what was the violation rate for each group ranging from the group with the lowest expectancy of parole violation to the group with the highest expectancy of violation.

Three expectancy tables are now in use in Illinois institutions. The one at Joliet, based on 1,000 cases, consists of nine groups with the proportion violating parole ranging from 1½ per cent to 76 per cent. The one at Pontiac, based on 3,000 cases, of twelve groups with the proportion violating parole ranging from 1 per cent to 99 per cent. The table in use at Menard, based on 2,772 cases, consists of 18 groups with violation rates ranging from 1 to 99 per cent.

Whenever a case is considered for parole by the Parole Board a statement is furnished by the sociologist and actuary of the statistical probability of violation of parole. The final summary of the report might be for example that inmate A is classified in the group where only 1½ per cent are likely to violate parole, B in the group with a violation rate of 30%, and C in the group with a violation rate of 85%.

The question is, of course, still open whether or not inmate A, appearing before the Board, will fall in the 1½ per cent who violate or the 98½% who will observe parole, whether inmate B is likely to be one of the 30% who violate or of the 70% who observe parole, and whether inmate C is likely to be one of the 85% who fail or the 15% who make good on parole.

In all these cases the members of the Parole Board must use their own best judgment because the statement of parole expectancy does not serve its purpose if it is used too mechanically. In Illinois the members of the Parole Board have other data which they take into account, the report of the psychiatrist, the detailed report upon past criminal history of Chicago cases by the Chicago Crime Committee, the report by the parole officer about arrangements for a job and about adjustment to home and neighborhood situations, and last but by no means least a hearing of the prisoner himself. Then above and beyond these data the Parole Board must always, in granting parole, give attention to the public, especially in paroling those individuals where community feeling runs high against them.

Prediction tables are useful, not only to the Parole Board, but for parole supervision. In Illinois copies of the probabilities of parole violation are supplied to the Division of Parole Supervision. In this way, the parole officer knows in advance what are the probabilities of parole violation in each case. His job then becomes that of preventing the prediction of failure from becoming an actuality.

Illinois has now had three years of experience with parole prediction in actual use. What have been the results? Do prediction tables actually work out in practice? Does parole prediction provide added protection to the public?

First of all, expectancy tables have worked out in practice. A careful and detailed statistical study shortly to be published by Mr. Sam Daykin, assistant sociologist and actuary of the Illinois State Penitentiary shows how closely for 18 different groups the actual outcome in experience is to the statistical expectancy.

In the second place, this study and the data from the other two institutions show that since the introduction of parole prediction methods three years ago there has been a marked decline in parole violation.

The figures are interesting. One institution shows a violation rate in over 1,000 cases paroled under the present Parole Board that is 24.4 per cent less than expectation. This result is probably due in part to the care of the Parole Board in selecting good risks. It is also partly the result, in all probability, of the more effective work of parole supervision during this period.

Figures from another institution made possible an even more detailed analysis. The expectancy table called for a certain violation rate; the actual number of failures upon parole was 40 per cent less than expected. A careful study of the distribution of cases by different risks, however, showed that this result had been achieved, in part, by a selection of cases from the groups with low violation rates. When the expectancy table was corrected for this factor, the actual violation rate, even then, was 18.8 per cent less than expected. In the case of poor and bad risks the decline in violation rates was even greater, or 34.2 per cent.

These findings re-emphasize the value of parole prediction of the practice of the Parole Board in selecting good risks and of more effective parole supervision. These figures probably also reflect the effect upon crime reduction, including parole violation, of the greater efficiency of our whole system of criminal justice.

What then are we to conclude in regard to the relation of parole and of parole prediction to the protection of the public?

The available statistics seem to indicate that people of Illinois, as measured by the decrease in violations, have had better protection from its parole system in the last three years than at any time during the past twelve years.

But this is contrary to what the public has been led to believe. The explanation for this is not difficult. The publication of a few cases of parole failures, particularly if they have dramatic or sensational features, will be sufficient to arouse public apprehension that all is not well with parole.

The only way I know to meet this natural public reaction to the dramatic case is by the appeal to statistics.

Seven years ago a committee composed of the late Judge Bruce of Northwestern University, Dean A. J. Harno of the University of Illinois, John Landesco, now a member of the Illinois Board of Pardons and Paroles, and myself recommended to the Parole Board not only the adoption of parole prediction but also the annual publication of statistics upon the workings of parole, statistics which had been analyzed and audited by a statistical expert or competent committee.

Only by some such means will even effective parole work gain and keep the confidence of the public.

The newspapers can, and I believe they will, be of increasing service in our common objective of protecting the public by all the instrumentalities of criminal justice including parole. They will, of course, continue to publish cases where paroled men commit crimes because that is news, but they will also print parole statistics because they also are news.

Before concluding this paper I would like to offer a suggestion for the purpose of securing your reaction. For some time I have been intrigued with the idea that one of our great daily newspapers might make an outstanding contribution to the solution of the problems of crime and criminal justice by introducing a weekly or perhaps even a daily column on "Crime and Its Treatment."

This column should, I think, be patterned somewhat upon the "Health Columns" which have been so successful in advancing the cause of public health. It should present its material in interesting and non-technical language, avoiding cant, sentimentality and propaganda for any "ism." In other words the column would aim to give the public factual, significant and authentic information upon crime and its causes, the workings of the machinery of criminal justice and the new and promising developments in the study, the prevention and the treatment of the criminal. The public, because of its growing concern and interest in the crime problem, would welcome such a column.

In conclusion, there can be no doubt of the rising tide of demand by the press and by citizens that parole be administered for the best possible protection of the public. The public will demand in parole, as in all aspects of criminal justice and crime prevention the utilization of every resource of science and of technical skill. More and more the public will ask that the results of parole be subjected to accurate measurement. For these reasons, the experience of Illinois in the field of parole prediction may have a nationwide significance.

14

CAN POTENTIAL DELINQUENTS BE IDENTIFIED SCIENTIFICALLY?

To SIMPLIFY my problem in this paper I am arbitrarily going to deal with only one-half the problem. At the risk of being charged with unfairness to the fair sex I am going to leave out of consideration the potential female delinquent and be concerned only with the potential male delinquent. I am not implying that the question is essentially different with female offenders. I believe it is practically the same, but there happen to be more research findings available on male than on female delinquents.

The answer to the question, "Can potential delinquents be identified scientifically?" depends on the definition of two phrases, "potential delinquent" and "identified scientifically."

By "delinquent" might be meant anyone who commits an act defined by the law as a delinquency. The Illinois statutes define the juvenile delinquent as

any male child who while under the age of seventeen years . . . violates any law of this State or is incorrigible, or knowingly associates with thieves, vicious or immoral persons, or without just cause and without consent of its parents, guardian, or custodian absents itself from its home or place of abode, or is growing up in idleness and crime; or knowingly frequents a house of ill-repute; or knowingly frequents any policy shop or place where any gaming device is operated; or frequents any saloon or dram shop where intoxicating liquors are sold; or patronizes or visits any public pool room or bucket shop; or

Reprinted from *Twenty-Fourth Annual Governor's Conference on Youth and Community Service* (Springfield, Ill.: Illinois Youth Commission, 1955), pp. 33–39.

wanders about the streets in the night without being on any lawful business or occupation; or habitually wanders about any railroad yards or tracks or jumps or attempts to jump onto any moving train; or enters any car or engine without lawful authority; or uses vile, obscene, vulgar, profane or indecent language in any public place or about any school house; or is guilty of indecent exposure; any child committing any of these acts herein mentioned shall be deemed a delinquent child.

Under this definition practically every male baby at birth can be defined as a "potential delinquent" since nearly everyone will commit an act designated under the Illinois statutes as juvenile delinquency.

Certainly a much narrower definition of "delinquent" is required, such as an adolescent who commits a serious crime—for example, a felony rather than a misdemeanor.

The criterion of seriousness of the offense has been called into question by the published study of Professor Austin Porterfield and by an unpublished study of Professor Paul Wallin. Porterfield obtained anonymous schedules from college students and Wallin secured confidential life histories from male students in his classes on their history of delinquent acts. A high proportion of men admitted felonies including robbery, burglar, assault, and attempted rape. Yet these young men were not delinquents or criminals. At least, they did not so consider themselves and were not so thought of by others. In general they were respected as gentlemen, at worst as "wayward" or "wild."

We are forced, then, to define "delinquent" or "criminal" not as having committed a delinquent or criminal act but as having the stigma of being a delinquent or criminal placed upon the individual by conventional society and by the person accepting this role and identifying himself as a delinquent or criminal.

Gabriel Tarde made this point clearly and forceably when he stated: "There are two factors that go into making a person a criminal. The first is his delinquent act, the second is the way in which society treats that act."

There are stages in the delinquency-making process by which the boy and youth become more and more deeply confirmed as delinquent and criminal: being arrested as over against no arrest; brought into juvenile court rather than being released to parents without court appearance; placed on probation by the judge as contrasted with being discharged; sent to a state training school for boys rather than having no institutional experience; commitment to a reformatory as against no stay in a reformatory.

The process might be carried on through to prison experience, solitary confinement, and repeated incarceration. The point is that each step in the process deepens the stigma upon the delinquent, further alienates him from conventional society, and fixes more firmly upon the person his identification as a delinquent.

The second phrase in my subject is "identified scientifically."

It has long been a major objective of criminologists to identify "potential delinquents." Historically, the majority of those who have attempted the scientific identification of criminals have conceived this as meaning a differentiation of the delinquent and criminal from the non-delinquent and law-abiding by some biological characteristic or characteristics.

Lombroso, the father of modern criminology, thought he had found the answer in stigmata of criminality, or physical characteristics that differentiated the criminal from the non-criminal. The criminal was to be identified by such features as asymmetrical cranium, long lower jaw, flattened nose, scanty beard, low sensitivity to pain. If an individual has five or more such stigmata, he is to be identified as the complete criminal type.

The Englishman, Charles Goring, by introducing a control group, demolished the Lombrosian explanation but did not discourage others from seeking a constitutional basis for scientifically identifying criminals.

The late Professor E. A. Hooten, physical anthropologist, conducted an elaborate study in which he compared criminal with a control non-criminal group composed of Boston out-patients, militia men, bathing beach habituees, and Nashville, "jolly fat firemen," to use Hooten's own descriptive characterization. With this uniquely selected control group he did find small differences in physical characteristics, most of which were significantly non-significant. He found 9 physical characteristics that seemed to differentiate robbers from other types of criminals, but when he ran all his criminal group through these 9 criteria he was able to sort out only one robber out of 414 in his total sample. He expressed his disappointment at this futile finding.

Sheldon discarded the notion of differences in unit physical characteristics and substituted the theory of differences in body type and the corresponding type of temperament as a method of differentiating delinquents and criminals from law-abiding individuals.

The Gluecks have been interested in finding constitutional characteristics that would identify scientifically the delinquent. In *Unraveling Juvenile Delinquency* they report the findings of anthropological measurement of the Sheldon type. Small differences were found showing that "the delinquents are superior in gross bodily size to the non-delinquents, this superiority being expressed especially in the shoulders, chest, waist, and upper extremities, and outlining the picture of the masculine physical type with tapering torso, heavy arms, small face, strong neck and wide shoulders."[1] In other words, the delinquent is a more athletic type. It would, however, hardly be feasible to identify potential delinquents by selecting children of the athletic build.

If the potential delinquent and criminal cannot be identified biologically by physical stigmata or other biological characteristics, can he be identified psychologically?

Two of the chief attempts to identify the delinquent by emotional reactions will be discussed. The first of these was reported on by William Healy and Augusta Bronner in their book, *New Light on Delinquency and Its Treatment*. Their subjects were delinquents and a control group of non-delinquent siblings. By this method they apparently ruled out the influences of different economic conditions, family environment, and neighborhood influences. They found one marked factor in the delinquent group that was almost unrepresented in the control group, namely, major emotional disturbance due to feelings of rejection in affectional relations, frustration, inferiority, jealousy, internal mental conflict, and feelings of guilt, or family disharmony of parents. Emotional disturbances were present in 91 per cent of delinquents and in only 13 per cent of non-delinquent brothers and sisters.[2]

These findings would be most convincing if the children had been interviewed before they became delinquent. Unfortunately, from the scientific standpoint, they were interviewed after they were delinquent. It cannot therefore be determined whether the emotional disturbance caused them to become delinquent or whether their emotional disturbance was the result of having become delinquent. We know from observation that all emotionally disturbed children do not become delinquent. Therefore, emotional disturbance cannot be used to identify the potential delinquent.

In *Roots of Crime*, Alexander and Healy, two psychiatrists, psychoanalyzed eleven persons with criminal records.[3] They concluded that their subjects were all neurotic. However, they did not claim that being neurotic was the cause of their criminality. They were not able to do so because the patients of psychoanalysts manifested the same symptoms and were not criminals. They therefore concluded that the reasons why some neurotics did not become criminals must be due to some constitutional difference. They did not attempt, however, even to speculate on what this difference might be.

The second and much more comprehensive attempt to find a psychological basis for predicting juvenile delinquency was made by the Gluecks in their book, *Unraveling Juvenile Delinquency*. On the basis of their findings they prepared three prediction tables: one on family relations, one on character traits from the Rorschach test, and the third on psychiatric personality traits.

Let us examine the categories in each of these three tables and see if we can determine whether they can be considered as *causes* or *effects* of juvenile delinquency, since all cases of delinquents were studied after they had been admitted to two state correctional schools. First, the items in the family relations table.[4]

Family Relations Factors	*Weighted Failure Score*
1. Discipline of boy by father	
Overstrict or erratic	71.8
Lax	59.8
Firm but kindly	9.3

Family Relations Factors	*Weighted Failure Score*
2. Supervision of boy by mother	
Unsuitable	83.2
Fair	57.5
Suitable	9.9
3. Affection of father for boy	
Indifferent or hostile	75.9
Warm (including overprotective) .	33.8
4. Affection of mother for boy	
Indifferent or hostile	86.2
Warm (including overprotective) .	43.1
5. Cohesiveness of family	
Unintegrated	96.9
Some elements of cohesion	61.3
Cohesive	20.6

Were the father and mother "overstrict and erratic" or "unsuitable" in discipline, "hostile" or "indifferent" as a result of the delinquency of the son or did these attitudes cause the boy to become delinquent? Certainly the designation of the family as "unintegrated" could likewise be a subject of debate on this point.

The character traits as determined by the Rorschach test may be similarly examined.[5]

Rorschach Character Traits	*Weighted Failure Score*
1. Social assertion	
Marked	75.9
Slight or suggestive	63.8
Absent	39.7
2. Defiance	
Marked	91.0
Slight or suggestive	76.7
Absent	34.9
3. Suspicion	
Marked	67.3
Slight or suggestive	47.3

Rorschach Character Traits	Weighted Failure Score
Absent	37.5
4. Destructiveness	
Marked	77.7
Slight or suggestive	69.9
Absent	35.7
5. Impulsiveness	
Marked	75.2
Slight or suggestive	65.0
Absent	40.0

The characteristics assigned to the delinquent as compared with the non-delinquent as exhibiting "marked assertion," "marked defiance," "marked suspicion," "marked destructiveness," and "marked impulsiveness," are all traits which are associated with acts of delinquency. They are not necessarily traits which led the boy into delinquency. They are particular ways of action that develop in residents in a custodial institution.

The third table presents the personality traits of the boy as derived in an interview of an hour or less by a psychiatrist who knew, of course, whether or not he was examining a delinquent or a non-delinquent. The items in the table are as follows.[6]

Psychiatric Personality Traits	Weighted Failure Score
1. Adventurous	
Present in marked degree	75.3
Not prominent or noticeably lacking	35.4
2. Extroverted in action	
Present in marked degree	66.5
Not prominent or noticeably lacking	37.8
3. Suggestible	
Present in marked degree	69.4
Not prominent or noticeably lacking	35.5
4. Stubborn	
Present in marked degree	83.4
Not prominent or noticeably lacking	39.0

Psychiatric Personality Traits	Weighted Failure Score
5. Emotionally unstable	
Prominent in marked degree	62.0
Not prominent or noticeably lacking .	26.5

The traits which characterized the delinquents much more than the non-delinquents in marked degree are "adventurous," "extroverted in action," "suggestible," "stubborn," "emotionally unstable." Here again the tantalizing question arises: "Would the psychiatrist have designated these boys as having these traits in marked degree at the age of six or are they rather traits that develop in the process of becoming delinquent and in confinement in a correctional school?"

The Gluecks stated that if the boy's chances of delinquency are "high in accordance with either or both the Rorschach and psychiatric prediction tables, it should indicate to the therapist that he may be dealing with a very recalcitrant individual, the prevention of whose delinquent career might be extremely difficult and involve nothing short of a basic reorganization of his character structure and temperamental constitution. Here it is probable that the difficulties are deeply rooted, perhaps genetically, in the very first years of the parent-child emotional interchange."[7]

The Gluecks believe that personality traits do not change or change with the greatest difficulty. They think they are inborn or deeply rooted in the first few years of the parent-child emotional interaction.

The success, however, of juvenile delinquency prevention and rehabilitation program in which you are engaged demonstrates that delinquency can be prevented and delinquents rehabilitated without changing the basic personality structure of individuals or without changing family relations except so far as they change as a result of the son's ceasing to be delinquent.

The conclusion is inevitable that the Gluecks have not demonstrated the feasibility of prediction from their tables. The only way to have proof of their assumptions and conclusions would be to have examinations of children by their methods at the age of six years and determine at the age of 11 to 17 what characteristics are related to those that did and those that did not become delinquent.

Must we now conclude that there is no way of identifying potential delinquents scientifically?

There is a way, but it is so simple that you may not want to call it "scientific."

It is a method which might have been suggested to the Gluecks by their study but one they rejected outright. The one item they found in their research most closely correlated with delinquency was *association with delinquents*. They found that 98.4 per cent of delinquent boys chummed largely with delinquents while, despite the fact that the non-delinquents lived in similar neighborhoods, only 7.4 per cent of them had intimates who were delinquents.

The Gluecks found several closely related items. For example, on play spaces the corresponding percentages for delinquents and non-delinquents are:[8]

	Delinquents	Non-delinquents
Distant neighborhoods	86.8	14.2
Street corner	95.2	58.4
At home	41.6	93.2
Playgrounds	29.4	61.0
They also learned the following:		
Belonging to a gang	56.0	0.6
Regular church attendance ...	39.3	67.1

The difference between delinquents and non-delinquents on places of play, gang membership, and church attendance are as great or greater than appear in any of the three prediction tables.

Why then is not *incipient delinquency*, as best indicated by beginning intimate association with delinquents, the simplest and the most efficient predictive device for identifying those who may become serious delinquents? According to the Gluecks' statistics this procedure would identify all but nine of the 500 delinquents and include only 30 non-delinquents. By contrast their three tables would show the following results:

Table	Delinquents		Non-delinquents	
	Total No.	No. not Identified	Total No.	No. not Identified
Family relations	451	162	439	102
Rorschach traits	255	100	281	35
Psychiatric personality traits .	470	108	467	75

As compared with identifying delinquents by the incipient de-linquency method, the three prediction tables of the Gluecks are wasteful since they do not identify from 13.4 to 37.5 per cent of the delinquents and would identify 15 to 23 per cent of non-delin-quents as delinquents.

This method of determining potential delinquents by associa-tion has strong support in studies of delinquents and criminals. Clifford R. Shaw found that 90 per cent of male delinquents charged with offenses against property committed the delinquent acts which brought them into the juvenile court with one or more associates. He has also traced by court records the network of contract and communication of one delinquent with another over a considerable time period. Through his intensive case studies he has shown that almost always delinquency is learned behavior, the previous non-delinquent boy learning from more experienced friends. Only seldom is delinquency an expression of a basic per-sonality structure, as assumed by the Gluecks.

The late professor E. H. Sutherland has convincingly presented the theory of differential association to explain the development of delinquency and crime. Professor Daniel Glaser has in my judgment made an important contribution based on a study of criminal inmates by the concept of criminal identification which sharpens the essential meaning of differential association and an-swers objections to the earlier formulation.

But would the method of spotting potential delinquents by in-cipient association and identification work in practice?

One way, but evidently not the only way, would be to select in every neighborhood a sympathetic observer whose business it would be to keep in touch with boys and girls of the area. It would not be difficult for him to identify groups of boys who are not incorporated in the conventional organization and activities of the area and who are wandering off into other neighborhoods.

Such a plan of identification may not be regarded by some as scientific. It does not have the aura of science that seems to attach to psychiatric interviews, psychological examinations, and Rorschach tests.

But the test of scientific method ultimately is whether or not its use gives understanding and control over behavior by a procedure which can be repeated and verified by others. By this criterion this proposed plan of identification must be accepted as scientific.

One further and conclusive test may be given to demonstrate the validity of this plan. The concepts of differential association and differential identification have implications for practical application in the prevention of juvenile delinquency. Accordingly, the procedure of identifying potential delinquents should be a part of a program of delinquency prevention and treatment.

DISCUSSION OF
"THE JACK-ROLLER"

THE CASE of Stanley is, and is not, typical of juvenile delinquency in Chicago. No single case could be representative of all
the many variations of personality, of the permutations of situations and the diversity of experiences of the hundreds of boys who
year by year have entered the Cook County Juvenile Court.

Why This Case Is Typical

There can, however, be no doubt that this case is typical, in
the sense that it has aspects that are common to a statistically high
proportion of cases. For example:

1. Stanley grew up in a delinquency area. In 1926, 85.4 per
cent of all the boys arrested by the police came from homes in
delinquency areas.[1]

2. He lived in a "broken home." Of all boys brought into
Juvenile Court in the year Stanley was first committed, 36.1 per
cent came from "broken homes."

3. He began his delinquent career even before he started to
school. Authorities in this field agree on the large proportion
among criminals of those who are early initiated into delinquency.

4. He had institutional experiences in rapid succession: the
Detention Home, the Chicago Parental School, St. Charles Training School, the Illinois State Reformatory at Pontiac, the House

---

Reprinted from Clifford R. Shaw, *The Jack-Roller* (Chicago: University of
Chicago Press, 1930), pp. 184–97.

of Correction, but the treatement at these correctional, reformatory, and penal institutions failed to check his delinquent career. Healy and Bronner found in an intensive study of 116 cases of male juvenile delinquents committed to the Parental School that 68 per cent failed to make good on their return to the community, and in a similar study of 158 boys who had been inmates of St. Charles 72 per cent continued in their delinquent career.[2] Of boys with experience in the Parental School 39 per cent like Stanley were later inmates of St. Charles.[3] Of the boys who failed to make good after leaving St. Charles, one-half were later committed either to the State Reformatory or the House of Correction, or like Stanley himself to both.

5. He was a "jack-roller," and his experiences are typical of the jack-roller. A large proportion of all jack-rollers, as an examination of scores of cases of this type indicates, are "runaway" boys. Boys who run away from home in Chicago, as well as "runaway" boys from other cities, drift naturally into West Madison Street. All invariably come into contact with homosexuals in the hobo group and among those who submit to their advances a large proportion, like Stanley, become jack-rollers, exploiters of homosexuals and of drunkards. Stanley in his personality traits appears to be a fairly representative jack-roller.

Judged by these external characteristics, the experiences of Stanley may be assumed to be roughly similar to those of a large proportion of other juvenile delinquents. If this assumption is proved correct, then an intensive study of this case and of other cases may enable the student of human behavior to probe beneath the surface of delinquent acts and to take a firm grasp upon the underlying motives of conduct.

The point is sure to be made. Why study one case so intensively? Why not make an extensive study of one thousand cases on the basis of which conclusions may be arrived at which will be backed up with mass data?

A sufficient answer, perhaps, is that such studies have been made. Indeed, the findings recently published by Mr. Shaw and his associates, *Delinquency Areas*, constitute one of the most telling of the statistical studies which have yet appeared in this field.

But the fact remains as succinctly stated by William Healy with reference to his quantitative examination of his own data, "Statistics will never tell the whole story."[4]

This one autobiography of a delinquent career is a concrete and dramatic exemplification of what a case-study may reveal about the causes and treatment of delinquency that can never be arrived at by more formal techniques like statistics, which must depend very largely upon external data.

The case of Stanley appears also to be typical in a more real sense than can be verified by any statistical calculation. It is typical (i.e., belonging to the type) in the same way that every case is representative of its kind or species. This case is a member of the *criminal* species, and so of necessity must bear the impress of the characteristics and experiences of the criminal. It may not be the best specimen, perhaps only a good specimen or even a poor specimen. There can be no doubt that any case, good, bad, or indifferent, is a specimen of the species to which it belongs.

The individual person is more intrinsically a specimen of any group of which he is a member than is a plant or animal of its biological species. The plant or animal is a specimen of botanical or zoölogical species, because through heredity there is transmitted to it a uniform morphological and physiological pattern. The human being as a member of a social group is a specimen of it, not primarily, if at all, because of his physique and temperament but by reason of his participation in its purposes and activities. Through communication and interaction the person acquires the language, tradition, standards, and practices of his group. Therefore, the relation of the person to his group is organic and hence representative upon a cultural rather than upon a biological level.

This point is dramatically put by William Bolitho in referring to Mr. Shaw's study of neighborhood tradition as a factor in delinquency:

Mr. Shaw, and his patient investigators into the connection of area with juvenile delinquency, have shown conclusively the district tradition, which each new immigrant family into a slum area takes over with the occupancy of the house. This area tradition, as it were impregnated into the very houses themselves, like the patina of soot that has eaten into the stones, can only be compared with the tradition of a great old school, of an ancient regiment, even of a monastery. The place is stuffed with history and example, handed down by boy to boy, until the house wreckers come.[5]

This intimate relation of the person to his group and neighborhood makes each person not so much a replica of a pattern as an intrinsic part of an ongoing process. Hence the study of the experiences of one person at the same time reveals the life-activities of his group.

This is why the experiences of any individual person reflect group opinion; why habit in the individual is an expression of custom in society; and why mental conflict in the person may always be explained in terms of the conflict of divergent cultures.

In the career of Stanley it is strikingly evident how he absorbs and expresses the attitudes, philosophy of life, and standards of the criminal world. It is also apparent that his reformation is quite as much or more a matter of changing his social groups as of effecting a change of attitudes or purposes. Actually, of course, the shift in group identification and the permutation of attitudes takes place simultaneously.

In analyzing any case as a specimen of the other cases of its kind, it is desirable and perhaps necessary always to make comparisons with other cases, both those which are like and unlike it. The following generalizations are derived, not alone from this autobiography, but from other documents of similar and dissimilar experiences.

The Boy's Own Story

First, this document, and others like it, indicate the value for scientific purposes of materials in the first person. The "boy's own story," the narratives of parents, the verbatim family interview are objective data. Much of the material on personality now extant, including the case records of social agencies, is vitiated for full use for research purposes by the fact that they are subjective records, that is, translations by the visitor of the language, emotional expressions, and attitudes of the person interviewed. A great advance in the study of personality has been achieved by the development of the record in the first person.

Those who have read this life-history in manuscript have all been astounded at its vivid and dramatic style. There is, of course, ample convincing evidence in contemporary books and articles of the literary ability of several ex-convicts. So far as the writer can judge, Stanley's style is not markedly superior to the run of present and former delinquents and criminals. Because of the enforced leisure of confinement, convicts read quite as much as any other group in our population, with the possible exception of teachers, clergymen, and writers.[6] Besides it seems to be universally true that one can talk or write best upon the subjects with which he is most familiar. Every person, we have been told, has the ability to write at least one book, his autobiography.

Astonishment at the literary excellence of a personal document is often followed by skepticism of its authenticity. In the personal interview or in the narrative, how is it possible to check the validity and reliability of statements?

The formal procedure to establish the validity of a document is to check up on the significant points, particularly upon apparently dubious ones. In the case of Stanley there was the court record, the work record, and by good fortune the report by Dr. William Healy. Other points not confirmed by these official records were tested by independent inquiry. The net result was the substantiation of the objective facts as given by Stanley, but quite often widely different interpretations of these facts. Stanley, in telling the truth as it appears to him, unwittingly reveals what we want most to know, namely, his personality reactions and his own interpretation of his experiences.

How does it come about that Stanley and other hardened young criminals tell the truth frankly and freely? Parents, teachers, and officers of the law are in unanimous agreement that nearly all "bad" children and on occasion "good" children are liars because they have discovered them in falsehoods. The answer to this paradox seems to be found in the fact that the lie is a response to a specific stimulus. The adequate stimulus for the lie response appears to be the punishment situation. Physicians, psychiatrists, and sociologists, whose attitude is that of scientific research into the solution of personal problems, elicit, not falsehood, but truth. Dr. William Healy once reported that in his experience with thousands of cases of problem boys and girls he found only a negligible percentage of deception.

The best guaranty, perhaps, of the reliability of a document is the degree of spontaneity, freedom, and release which a person enjoys in writing or in telling his own story. That is the essential superiority of a life-history like Stanley's to the usual formal record obtained by asking a series of "cut-and-dried" questions. To the extent that a person tells his own in his own way, so that the narrative takes on the character of a chronicle, a defense, a confession, or a self-analysis, to that extent it is revealing and definitely and clearly manifests its internal consistency. The more a man tells, as all criminal investigators know, the more he is certain to entangle himself in inconsistencies and contradictions, if he is attempting to deceive. The lie persisted in and elaborated builds up ultimately a huge structure of falsehoods that collapses of its own weight. On the other hand, a document like that of Stanley's shows more unity and consistency with increasing detail. It stands up under the test of internal coherence.

Granted that Stanley has told the truth about himself as he sees it, the reader will have still a further question, What were the facts as they are about Stanley's stepmother, about the Parental School, St. Charles, Pontiac, and the House of Correction, about the prostitute who "befriended" him, the boy companion with whom he broke? The absolute truth about these or other points cannot be secured by the life-history and probably cannot be obtained by any other known method. But in human affairs it is not the absolute truth about an event that concerns us but the way in which persons react to that event. So in the case of Stanley, it is his reaction to the events of his experience that interests us, because they give us the materials by which we can interpret his attitudes and values, his conduct and his personality.

The life-history of Stanley in a dramatic and challenging manner introduces the reader to an intimate understanding of the social factors which condition the beginnings and persistence of a criminal career. "Broken homes," "poverty," "bad housing," "bad companions," "destructive neighborhood influences," and other common-sense terms are quite inadequate to define the dynamic relationship between the personality of Stanley and his varied and stimulating experiences. His career is a series of acts in response to changing social situations; the discrimination of his stepmother against him in favor of her children; the freedom and release of exploration in a disorganized immigrants' area; the patterns of stealing presented by the neighborhood tradition; the lures of West Madison Street; the repression of treatment in the correctional and reformatory institution; the fellowship and code of an oppressed group and the education in crime freely offered to him by his associates in these institutions; the thrill of adventures in crime; the easy money quickly obtained and spent; the dullness and monotony of the chances to reform offered him. These are factors common to the actual experiences of thousands of youthful bandits and gangsters.

Personality Formation

An intimate and revealing life-history like Stanley's permits penetration beneath the surface, not only of the social factors, but also of personality traits. In seeing Stanley as he sees himself and his career, the reader is enabled to define and to analyze the processes of personality formation and of the creation of the criminal rôle.

In examining several hundred life-histories and in studying many of them intensively, the writer concludes that the manner of writing the document reveals at least four different personality types. There is the person who writes a chronicle of his life, putting down in order the external events of his career without explanation, or with only conventional explanations. He might be called the Chronicler. Then there is the individual like Stanley who writes a justification of his whole career. He may be termed the Self-defender. There are others who reveal what hitherto he has sedulously concealed of the drama upon the stage of his own thoughts. The writer of this document may be called the Confessant. A fourth fairly discernible type is the person who in his life-history dissects his every act and motive. The denomination of Self-analyst may be applied to him.

The personality traits of Stanley, which taken together indicate the self-defender document, may be concretely inventoried as follows:

1. Early rise and persistence of a sense of injustice
2. Self-pity
3. Hypercritical of others
4. Always right; never takes blame but readily blames others
5. Readily makes friends and as easily breaks with them
6. Excessive interest in attention
7. Lacks insight into his own motives and those of others
8. Suspicious toward others without sufficient cause
9. Ideas of persecution.
10. Substitutes rationalization for insight
11. Builds up rational system of explanation
12. Absorbed in his own ideas and plans and relatively immune to suggestions from others
13. Resentment of correction and resistance to direction
14. Tendency to escape from unpleasant situations by the method of protest
15. Tendency to moralize
16. Speed of decision and strength of reaction

The foregoing traits are, it seems, the characteristic attributes of the personality pattern of the individual who is able even under adverse circumstances to maintain his ego against an unfriendly and even hostile social world. Indeed, it may well be that the development of this type of individualistic personality is the one way in which certain human beings are able to meet the failures and disappointments of life.

The study of life-history documents has led the writer to accept, at least tentatively, the hypothesis that the main outlines of the personality pattern are fixed in the early years of the child's social experience and are subject to only minor modifications in youth and manhood.

A brief analysis of these traits of Stanley will, perhaps, clarify this point. The early rise and persistence of *a sense of injustice* may be taken as the key trait of which the others are natural outcomes. A situation in which a sense of injustice arises is one in which the stepmother discriminates against him as a stepson in favor of her own children. Stanley and his brother and sister refused to accept this situation and persisted in running away. Stanley, in his struggle with his stepmother, is sustained by the feeling of his own worth and her unfairness. Toward himself he early manifests the *feeling of self-pity* which protects his ego under later adverse situations. Toward his stepmother he continues to be *hypercritical* in attitude; this develops into unsparing criticism of the institutions of which he is an inmate and of persons whom he dislikes. It follows that in his unequal struggle against Fate (to use his own term) he tends to take the position of being *always right*. In this document he is disposed never to take blame, but to blame others or Fate.

It is significant to note that he *readily makes friends and as readily breaks with them*. While other persons are necessary to his existence, he is not a good group member. He seems to adjust better with older persons, especially those whom he admires, than with those of his own age. He is too much an individualist to feel strongly the claims of loyalty and affection in friendship. He cannot "roll drunks" without a comrade, but the relationship is one of utility rather than of sentiment. He is not devoid of sympathy and sentiment, but they are stronger when closely personal than when directed to others. He shows *an excessive interest in attention* and develops ingenious techniques to secure it.

His *lack of insight into his own motives and those of others* is a characteristic trait of the self-centered person. This arises from the inability to look at one's self in a given situation with something of the detachment of the point of view of another person. Stanley has imagination, but he is not introspective, although he has his moments of introversion (pp. 63 and 103). The *suspicion of others* without adequate reason and *ideas of persecution* develop naturally from the tendency to substitute *rationalization for insight*. Consequently, the person builds up a *rational system of explanation*. Stanley's system is that of Fate and lucky and unlucky "breaks"; this is the philosophy, in general, of the underworld; it is a philosophy that steels the resistance of individuals against the untoward events of life. The *absorption* of the person *in his own ideas and plans* results in *relative immunity to suggestions from others.*

Stanley exhibits in an unusually accentuated degree the traits of *resentment of correction* and *resistance to direction* which characterize persons of strong "ego" feeling. Since he is unable to maintain his ego by holding jobs, he tends to substitute *the protest method of escape* from the humiliating situation of being fired.

Finally, two remaining traits complete the clinical picture of the egocentric personality. He has the inveterate tendency to conceive his behavior and the behavior of others around him in *moralistic terms* of right or wrong. His behavior is impulsive, being marked by *speed of decision and strength of reactions.*

Stanley, no more than anyone else, is neither to be praised nor blamed for his personality traits. They were formed for him before he gained conscious control of his destiny. The point to be grasped is that the formation of the personality pattern is a natural product of forces in the constitution of the individual and in his childhood situation. Once this conception of behavior is clearly understood, we will learn to accept people as they are and work with, rather than against, the basic set of their personality.

Mr. Shaw once made the comment that personalities of Stanley's type may be unadjusted or maladjusted but they are not disorganized; in fact, they are if anything too highly organized. The traits of the egocentric person are those of an overorganized personality, one that is so rigidly set that it finds difficulty in making the usual normal adjustments to other personalities or to changing situations.

Permutations of Social Type

In analyzing this and other life-histories, a basic distinction must be made between personality pattern and social type. So far we have been describing the personality pattern which may be

defined as the sum and integration of those traits which characterize the typical reactions of one person toward other persons. The
personality pattern, according to our tentative hypothesis, is
formed in infancy and early childhood through a conjunction of
constitutional and experiential factors and persists with some
modification and elaboration as a relatively constant factor
through later childhood, youth, and maturity. It is determined, it
should be noted, in the interaction between persons, but not by
imitation.

The term "social type" does not refer to the mechanisms of personality reactions but to attitudes, values, and philosophy of life
derived from copies presented by society. The rôle which a person assumes and to which he is assigned by society creates the
social type. With Stanley, becoming "a professional runaway," "a
delinquent," "a criminal," was taking on a rôle. His acceptance
of the criminal code and the orientation of his ambitions to succeed in a criminal career have to do with attitudes and values and
are elements that enter into the creation of a social type.

The so-called permutations of personality are the abrupt and
often revolutionary changes in social type, not in basic personality patterns. The transformation of Stanley from a criminal to a
law-abiding citizen was a change in social type; his personality
pattern remained the same. All similar conversions as from sinner
to saint, radical to conservative, Democrat to Republican, dry to
wet, or vice versa, are changes in social type, not in personality
patterns. Our hypothesis is that personality patterns, since they are
fixed in infancy and in early childhood, are likewise susceptible
to reconditioning only in this same period. The conditioning of
social types takes place in later experiences and may accordingly
be reconditioned in youth and maturity.

Experimenting with a New
Technique of Treatment

Ultimately the value of all scientific discoveries in human
as well as in physical behavior must submit to the test of their significance for purposes of practical control. In the field of per-

sonality study there are many indications that hypotheses on the causes of behavior problems may perhaps best be tested through actual experiments in treatment.

The brilliant success of the treatment processes set into operation by Mr. Shaw cannot be attributed to the accidental favorable outcome of a single case. In fact, this is only one of a series studied and treated intensively and experimentally with equally striking results. Accordingly the analysis of the treatment that follows will be based upon my knowledge of Mr. Shaw's general procedure as well as upon the special methods employed in this case.

The first step in the course of treatment is the approach to the boy, not by sympathy, but by empathy. Through his life-history his counselor is enabled to see his life as the boy conceived it rather than as an adult might imagine it. Empathy means entering into the experience of another person by the human and democratic method of sharing experiences. In this and other ways rapport is established. Sympathy is the attempt through imagination to put one's self in another person's place with all the fallacies which are almost necessarily involved.

The telling or writing one's life-story is itself part of the treatment. The very act of pouring out one's experiences not only has a cathartic effect, particularly where tensions and inhibitions are released, but also gives the subject perspective upon his life. This gaining of perspective upon one's experience is the chief way in which persons achieve control over their impulses and motives and work out their destiny toward some challenging goal.

Mr. Shaw does not use the methods of the psychoanalyst, he is not dealing with the materials of the unconscious, but with the memories, wishes, plans, and ambitions of the conscious mind. Working with these, he devises an experimental plan of treatment that attempts to take into account the personality pattern, the attitudes, interests, talents, and plans of the boy himself.

But more than any other student of delinquency and problem behavior, Mr. Shaw pays attention to the powerful factors of group and neighborhood influence. He recognized, as had Dr. Healy earlier, that, although Stanley could not live in the emotional tension of his home, one of his chief needs was the response and intimate appreciation which only wholesome home life can give. It was a case for transplantation. The environment was to be changed so that the powerful influence of the social situation would work for, rather than against, reformation. Lodging was secured for Stanley in a home which provided not only sympathetic maternal interest but also intimate contact with higher cultural standards. There was naturally enough a period of conflict between the old neighborhood gang life and the new life opening up before him. The decisive influence in this time of indecision was undoubtedly the continued contact with Mr. Shaw, the daily influence of his landlady, and the new associations he was forming at work and at night school.

Interestingly enough, the personality traits which enabled Stanley to break so completely with his criminal past and the gang were the chief obstacles to his vocational adjustment.

The treatment of obtaining employment where the employer would take a special interest in his employee's progress, which had worked well in other cases with similar personality patterns, failed with Stanley. His extreme resentment against correction and his deep-seated aversion to taking orders seemed to make all attempts at vocational placement futile. Mr. Shaw's final choice of the occupation of commercial salesman showed his ingenuity in adapting treatment to the traits of personality. As a salesman in the field, he took orders only from himself and was not liable to correction from others. His personality traits of attractive manners, his forcible and logical presentation of points, and his ability to make friends were positive assets in his new vocation.

The life-history of Stanley, taken in conjunction with the facts on the concentration of delinquency presented in *Delinquency Areas* and the analyses of boy gang life and organization in Thrasher's *The Gang*, provide a foundation for new modes of attack upon the problem of the delinquent and the criminal. Attention has largely been centered upon case work with the individual, but that is only a partial approach. An all-round program will require, in addition, research upon the social factors in delinquency and the development of techniques of group and community treatment. This volume is a notable pioneer contribution to that end.

To many readers the chief value of this document will not consist in its contribution to an understanding of the personality of Stanley and other delinquents or of the methods of treatment of similar cases. To them its far-reaching significance will inhere in the illumination it throws on the causation, under conditions of modern city life, of criminal careers and upon the social psychology of the new type of criminal youth.

To them this autobiography will point the way to a basic attack on the conditions of boy life in deteriorating neighborhoods in Chicago. They will become convinced that the problem of the gangster and the gunman will be to get back to first causes in the neighborhood where traditions teach delinquency and where crime is the most interesting play of children. They will demand a thoroughgoing program of community prevention in place of the present emphasis upon institutional correction, the futility of which is so clearly shown by this volume.

To the writer the permanent significance of the case of Stanley lies in its contribution to the fund of scientific knowledge. It represents a distinct advance in research both in method and in fundamental conceptions.

The contribution in method inheres in the perfecting of the technique of the boy's own story, specifically for the field of delinquency but generally applicable to all personality study. This and other documents secured by Mr. Shaw provide objective data to all students of personality because they present the person's own story uncolored by translation into the language of the investigator. While he offers his own interpretations, the materials stand on their own footing and may be interpreted variously by other students.

For the first time in the field of delinquency this volume provides adequate material for description and analysis from the standpoint of explanation in terms of the cultural factors in behavior. In penetrating beneath the external behavior of the delinquent boy it reveals the intimate interplay between his impulses and the effective stimuli of the environment. It shows how the cultural patterns, of his home, of his associates in the neighborhood, of the delinquent and criminal groups outside and especially inside correctional and penal institutions, define his wishes and attitudes and so control, almost in a deterministic fashion, his behavior. His account also discloses how certain changes in his social environment, by affording contact in an intimate and sympathetic way with the cultural patterns of normal society, redefine his impulses and direct his conduct into fields of socially approved behavior.

With materials available for a more adequate analysis of the rôle of cultural factors in conduct, the stage is set for fundamental studies in the interrelation and interaction of the constitutional and cultural factors in human behavior.

Finally, this study in conjunction with the study of *Delinquency Areas* points the way toward research into the processes of social treatment.

IV. Methodology and Social Values

Introduction

BY MORRIS JANOWITZ

ERNEST W. BURGESS from the start of his academic career was sensitive to the social context in which he did his research. He asked the question again and again, what is the purpose of sociological investigation. He recognized that sociology was fashioned by its methodology and by the values of the social scientist. He did not see the sociologist as philospher king, but rather that his special contribution derived from his sociological concepts and from his search for objectivity.

The search for objective knowledge was a legitimate goal; but in practice Burgess believed that the responsible sociologist contributed to social reform. In particular, as he launched his career he was attracted to the social survey. As he pointed out in his article "The Social Survey" (this volume, chap. 16), already written in 1916, it had the capacity to collect basic data required for social reform, and could also mobilize a community to face its problems. In other words, the nature of sociological methodology could not be separated from its impact on society. Thus a decade later, at the 1927 meeting of the Iowa Association of Economics and Sociologists, he delivered a paper entitled "Statistics and Case Studies as Methods of Sociological Research" (this volume, chap. 17). Burgess had a strong interest in the case study and did much to encourage his students to make use of case studies. In his view, there was no incompatibility between statistical analysis and case studies; in fact, both were required for sociological explanations and for the tasks of sociology. The case study method not only helped formulate hypotheses to be tested but supplied data in depth on human values and on the subjective aspects of social organization.

Values were an essential component of the subject matter of sociological research. They also supplied the context in which the results of sociology would be used. In "Social Planning and the Mores" (this volume, chap. 18) Burgess analyzed the value structures of the United States and the limitations these values place on the ultilization of sociological knowledge. This essay was an early and thoughtful contribution to the sociology of knowledge.

The question of values comes to involve the sociologist in controversial, value-laden issues and problems; and Burgess throughout his career was deeply involved in research which raised controversial issues. He felt strongly about these issues; his own values often challenged by social controversy and by the data he so painstakingly gathered in pursuit of their understanding. He was relentless in his belief that the sociologist should as a social scientist emancipate himself intellectually from the cultural values of his society. Challenges to this position troubled him. In "Values and Sociological Research" (this volume, chap. 19) he recognized the merit of Myrdal's suggestion that the use of explicit value premises might reveal hidden biases and help "to determine in a rational way the statement of problems and the definition of terms for theoretical analysis," by providing "a logical basis for practical and political conclusions."

He rejected unequivocally the notion that, by virtue of their expertise in the study of values, sociologists should "tell American society what values it should hold." However, he did not overlook the particular values to be held by the social researcher: "Is there no value that the social scientist holds? As a scientist, and particularly as a social scientist, he is irrevocably committed to one value, namely, freedom: freedom of thinking, freedom of teaching, freedom of research; in short, freedom to seek, to find, and to report the truth" (this volume, chap. 19).

Burgess was opposed to "passing resolutions," especially by research organizations, as a form of social action. As a sociologist he engaged in meaningful research on vital social topics. As a citizen he preferred to associate himself with reformist groups.

Because the value of freedom was of special concern to the intellectual community and to Burgess personally, he was actively involved in its defense. During the "McCarthy era," Burgess had been the object of investigation for his activism. He defended himself vigorously and with dignity. Characteristic of the man and his dedication to intellectual values and the scholarly approach to controversial issues, he urged, "The present commotion about McCarthyism should be raised above the present level of controversy. The situation should be studied objectively in terms of underlying conditions of American life and the emergence of previously submerged groups into participation in the political processes" ("Our Dynamic Society and Sociological Research," *Midwest Sociologist*, winter, 1955, p. 3). And in this same article, he spoke of the need for greater attention to "the Power Process" in terms of "social organization not as a static thing but in action" (ibid., p. 6). He left no doubt that research into "Social Inequality" was a matter of central concern on the agenda of sociology. For Ernest W. Burgess in his research, his teaching, and his public service, the pursuit of sociological knowledge—according to the scientific method—was compatible and enriched by active participation in the social process.

16

THE SOCIAL SURVEY:

A Field for Constructive Service by Departments of Sociology

THE SOCIAL SURVEY of a community is the scientific study of its conditions and needs for the purpose of presenting a constructive program for social advance. The following paper is written for those interested in the development of practical sociology in this country. Its purpose is twofold. It seeks to call attention to the possibilities within the social survey for service by departments of sociology. It attempts in addition to outline a general plan of organization by which the sociologist may best co-operate with the community. The type of relationship described below will be largely based on the experience in social surveys of the department of sociology in the University of Kansas under the leadership of Professor F. W. Blackmar.

To the sociologist there is little novel in the method of the social survey. Perhaps the absence of novelty has prevented an adequate realization of its importance. Indeed a case might well be made for the statement that the social survey was an invention of the sociologist. In every department of sociology in the country beginners in the science have been initiated into this method of community study. The success of the device was immediate and patent. The first-hand study of local conditions vitalized the work of the classroom. Students were convinced that social as well as natural phenomena were susceptible of scientific study. Affective reactions to "conditions as they are" crystallized in the social at-

Reprinted from the *American Journal of Sociology* 21 (1916) : 492–500.

titude which Patten terms "the emotional opposition to removable evils."

As an instrument of social measurement the social survey in the hands of the sociologist was until recently confined by the limitations of the classroom. Its technique was relatively simple. Its examination was more or less superficial. Its results were seldom utilized in social improvement. In short, the social survey in the college was little else than a laboratory toy, like the electric light before Edison, interesting for purposes of exhibition and training, but of slight practical value to the community. Social studies of permanent importance were made, not by departments of sociology, but by individuals, or by groups of social workers. Examples of these are Booth's *Life and Labour of the People of London*, Rowntree's *Poverty, A Study of Town Life* and Jane Addams' *Hull-House Maps and Papers*.

This statement of the origins of the survey is no reflection on the sociologist. The point may rather be well taken if his contribution has not been made. Is not the work of the social scientist, like that of the natural scientist in the case of the electric light, complete with the discovery of the method? Was not the brilliant Pittsburgh Survey but the work of a social Edison who reduced this discovery of the sociologist to human utilization?

The natural gratification of the sociologist in the transformation of his laboratory method into so efficient an instrument of social investigation should not prevent the perception of the future possibilities of service in connection with social survey. Indeed, the sociologist has not been indifferent to its recent practical development. In the University of Chicago and Columbia University as well as elsewhere the work in practical sociology has always been correlated with the investigation of city, state, and national problems. Other universities and colleges within the last three or four years have been experimenting with various types of service to the community through the social survey. The interest became so general that two years ago at the Minneapolis meeting of the American Sociological Society a committee was appointed to formulate a plan of organization for social surveys and social investigation. The illness and death of Professor C. R. Henderson, the chairman of the committee, delayed and then checked this movement toward a comparison of the methods and the forms of the social survey and a presentation of a definite plan of organization.

These two years, however, disclosed a growing appreciation of the value of the social survey. In at least two institutions, the University of Kansas and the University of Southern California, courses in the social survey have been introduced. Of greater significance have been the results of the participation of the sociologist in this method of social study as revealed in the differentiation of distinct forms of the survey. This development has been of two types: (1) surveys of the community by the sociologist upon his own initiative or at the request of the community; (2) surveys of the community in which the sociologist has been called upon to direct and organize the work.

The more common form of service to the community through the social survey by the sociologist has been of the first type. A community, or one or more organizations representing the community, has secured the expert service of the sociologist in making an inventory of its conditions and needs. This study may be general or partial. It may include all aspects of community life, or it may be limited to one or more divisions of the life of the community. The extension division of the University of Iowa is furnishing this type of service to the communities of the state. The department of sociology of the Ohio State University made a significant housing study at Circleville revealing conditions of overcrowding which rival if not surpass those of the worst districts in our largest cities. The social survey of Fargo, North Dakota, was made by a sociologist upon the request of a local organization. This form of the social survey is obviously valuable. The study of conditions by an expert makes possible sure and permanent progress upon the basis of an adequate and impartial examination of the situation. Comparison with conditions in other communities stimulates to social action. Last, but not least, is the present significance and future promise of this tendency of the community to turn to the social scientist for expert service.

This type of survey, however, presents a peril: satisfaction with a level of service which is lower than that which may be achieved. The sociologist should not fall short of the full measure of social opportunity presented. As an expert in social reconstruction he has performed but a part of his service in the analysis and the presentation of the needs of the community. His more difficult and more valuable service is his dynamic participation in the social movement of the community. Vital participation may be gauged not so much by the character of his findings as by the nature of his relation to the organic life of the community, that is, to social agencies, social activities, and public opinion. Which type of survey will better educate the public in regard to the social causes of undesirable conditions, will more effectively diffuse the knowledge of scientific methods of prevention and improvement, and will pave the way for united action of all forces in the community to promote a constructive program of social advance? The sociologist should guard against placing himself in the situation where the doing of the service that is insistently demanded may prevent the performance of the larger service which he should be equipped to render.

This larger service, I believe, is to be found in the second type of the survey. The distinctive characteristic of this form of social investigation is the study of local conditions and needs *by the community under expert direction.* The demand for the survey here as in the other type of the survey comes from the community. But the activity of the community does not cease here. The social expert who is selected to direct the study organizes the community for the work of investigation. This method of organization originated in the Belleville and in the Lawrence social surveys conducted under the direction of the department of sociology of the University of Kansas.

The first principle of this type of survey is that the community as a whole should be organized to promote the survey movement. If feasible, every civic, commercial, religious, and social organization should participate in the demand for the survey. In Belleville, a town of 2,300 persons, the local welfare society, representing practically all the civic interests in the community, initiated and promoted the survey movement. In Lawrence, eight organizations, namely, the Civic Study Club, the Federated Brotherhoods, the Federation of Women's Clubs, the Merchants' Association, the Ministers' Alliance, the Missionary Union, the Parent-Teacher's Association, the Social Service League, united in the request for the survey and elected representatives as members of the general social survey committee. This union of social agencies for the purpose of studying conditions is necessary if the survey is to be an organic expression of the social consciousness. A high degree of integration of organized public opinion is thus secured through the general committee representing all the voluntary organizations of the community.

The second principle of this type of the survey is that the study of conditions of life be made by the community under the direction of the expert in the technique of surveys. The sociologist is, or at any rate should be, specially trained to perform this service. He needs skill in two arts: the technical survey methods, and the technique of directing the organization of the community.

In the Kansas surveys the application of these principles took the following form. The general survey committee, composed of representatives of the organized community life, elected an executive committee to co-operate with the director of the survey, a sociologist, in the organization of the work of investigation. The function of the executive committee was twofold, in regard both to the raising of the finances and to the organization of the investigation. First, a method of raising funds to meet the necessary expenses of the survey was adopted and put in charge of a carefully selected finance committee. Secondly, the executive committee co-operated with the director of the survey in organizing the community. In the Kansas surveys the following divisions of the field were made: (1) topography and population; (2) community planning; (3) municipal administration; (4) trade, industry, and labor; (5) public health; (6) housing; (7) dependency; (8) delinquency; (9) recreation; (10) education; (11) churches and religion. Committees with a membership varying in size with the nature of the field of study were appointed to co-operate with the director and his staff of field workers.

As valuable as the organizing function of the director of the survey is his service in securing the co-operation of experts in the different special fields of investigation. The sociologist in his direction of the survey is able, not only to utilize the concrete practical knowledge of the local members of the committees of investigation, but also to bring to their assistance the special knowledge of experts in the university and in the departments of state. The director of the survey from his point of vantage in the university may offer the community the skilled service of different departments of the university: sociology, economics, political science, history, psychology, education, the extension division, etc. In addition, Kansas experience indicates that he may readily secure the invaluable co-operation of the state departments, such as the state board of health, the department of public instruction, the department of labor and industry. Thus, the social survey, if wisely organized, places at the service of the community both the expert knowledge of the university and the technical resources of the state.

Such, then, in substance is the outline of the organization of community self-study under expert direction. The distinctive advantages of this type of survey deserve further consideration.

The fundamental value of this type of survey lies in its organic relations to the community consciousness. The social survey of the community by the community signifies the development of teamwork. The sociologist as the director is in the position of the coach to the football team. The organization of local committees of investigation signifies a higher integration of the social consciousness. The psychological division of the community into the extremes of "boosters" and of "knockers" disappears before the constructive attitude involved in the scientific study of social problems. The social survey as related to social consciousness may well be described as a method of social introspection checked up by the statistical measurements and the comparative standards of the social expert. Experience shows that the following consequences arise from this type of the organic relation of the sociologist to the community. First, the study of the community by the community under expert direction secures the training of local workers. Secondly, this training of the active social workers of a community often involves on their part a complete change of attitude toward social problems. Concrete, practical experience in the use of scientific methods of investigation tends to rationalize the expression of the humanitarian interest. Thirdly, this participation and training of workers in the survey furnish a large and efficient group in the community ready and prepared to promote the program of constructive social advance proposed by the survey. On this last point the results of the Belleville and the Lawrence surveys speak for themselves. In Belleville the president of the local welfare society which conducted the survey was elected mayor upon a platform containing several of the most important recommendations of the survey. In Lawrence before the printing of the report three ordinances were enacted as direct results of the survey: one providing for the inspection and the supervision of the milk supply of the city, another establishing housing standards, and another creating a board and superintendent of public welfare.

A second advantage of this type of the survey is found in the nature of its stimulus to the sociologist and to the department of sociology. The sociologist as director of community self-study has opportunity for expression in the two arts in which he has specialized: first, in the use of impersonal tools of investigation, of statistics, and of interpretation, and, secondly, in the employment of the personal technique required for organizing co-operation and team-work.

The self-expression of the sociologist through the exercise of the "instinct of workmanship" in both organizing and directing community self-study brings out the possibilities of united action on the part of the several social sciences. A feature of the co-operation involved in this type of the survey fulfils one of the historic claims of the sociologist. The director of the social survey, by securing the co-operation of sociologist, political scientist, economist, historian, and psychologist, demonstrates the functional unity of social science. The problems of the community impinge squarely upon the sociologist, but their satisfactory solution demands the united action of all social scientists. Historically, it is fitting that the sociologist should participate in organizing concerted effort. It is also obvious that this union of activity is more readily secured where the sociologist is the director of community study than where his function is merely to report specific individual findings. The larger work of the sociologist, then, lies in the organization, not only of the community, but also of the expert service of the university and of the state.

There is still another advantage of this type of the survey to sociologists and departments of sociology. The stimulus of research vitalizes the work of the classroom. Society is the laboratory of the sociologist. The social survey provides a unique opportunity both for investigation and for social construction, both for the analysis of mental attitudes and for the study of the control of forces in securing improvement. To the advanced student the social survey affords severe and stimulating training in the technique of investigation and in the art of social action.

The third consideration in favor of this type of the survey inheres in the very nature of the participation of the sociologist in the social movement. Herein lies the solution of the problem of democracy and the expert. The method of community self-study under the direction of the specialist involves the co-operation of the group and the expert. The specialist must of necessity demonstrate his skill and his worth in the acid test of the concrete practical problem; the community realizes at first hand the superiority of the new over the old method. Community self-study under expert direction is democracy being at school to the social scientist. The social survey is to the community what the demonstration station is to the farmer.

The solution of the problem of democracy and the expert is, at best, of secondary importance to the function that the social survey may play in social progress. We have all been surprised and chagrined at the apparently slow onward movement of reform. The word "apparently" was used advisedly for the reason that we are prone to gaze on the superficial indications of change and to be unobservant of the deeper currents that shape our social life. Our reform movements of the past have too often been grounded upon the naïve idea that all that was needed was a simple substitution of the good "outs" for the bad "ins." Of course, no mere mechanical shift can have permanent value. What is necessary is an organic transformation of habits of sentiment, thought, and action of the American people. This change of heart and head cannot be efficiently effected upon a nation-wide scale; it must take place on a community basis. The hamlet, the village, the town, the neighborhood, the city are, from the standpoint of social psychology, the units for the achievement of democratic progress. The family is too small, the state and the nation are too large. In the community the problems of city planning, municipal housekeeping, public health, housing, delinquency, dependency, recreation, education, and social religion are to be worked out. The construction of the American life of the future is fundamentally a problem of the community. The social survey, then, of the type of community self-study under expert direction is the initial step toward the practical realization of efficient and socialized democracy.

A word, in conclusion, should be said in regard to the relation of the sociologist to agencies already in the field. By no implication should this paper be considered an argument for the monopolization of the social survey by departments of sociology. The department of surveys and exhibits of the Russell Sage Foundation has performed fine pioneer service in a series of effective surveys. No doubt, the leadership of the social survey movement will continue with this institution. Yet this one agency cannot hope to respond to all the calls for investigation and so must neglect the smaller cities and towns altogether. The university, on the contrary, with its specialists in all the varied aspects of community life constitutes an unorganized force of experts, a potential staff of social surveyors. The communities, too, are becoming more and more acutely aware of their social problems and are turning to departments of sociology for assistance in their solution. The task of the sociologist is twofold: to secure the co-operation of specialists in the university and of the departments of state and to organize the community for self-investigation under expert direction. For this reason the social survey is an inviting field for constructive service by departments of sociology.

STATISTICS AND CASE STUDIES AS METHODS OF SOCIOLOGICAL RESEARCH

THE ORGANIZATION three years ago of the Social Science Research Council gave a new impetus to research in the related fields of economics, political science, and sociology. The funds indispensable for the conduct of many fundamental studies, particularly those of a co-operative type, were now forthcoming in amounts that would have seemed staggering ten or even five years ago. One national foundation reported gifts[1] for co-operative programs of social science research in a few universities totalling in the aggregate several hundred thousand dollars. A year ago, the Social Science Research Council approved a program of research projects involving an expenditure of over $400,000 for 1926–27.[2]

With this assurance of funds adequate for the support of promising projects, attention in all the social sciences has naturally turned to the crucial question of the capacity to "make good" on a research program.

In fact, the Social Research Council itself has authorized the preparation of a case book on scientific methods in the social sciences. Professor Stuart Rice of the University of Pennsylvania and Professor R. M. MacIver, formerly of Toronto University and now of Barnard College, Columbia University, have been secured to compile and edit it.

The scope of this paper is not that of scientific methods in the

---

Reprinted from *Sociology and Social Research* 12 (1927) : 103–20. Paper read at the 1927 annual meeting of the Iowa Association of Economists and Sociologists.

field of all the social sciences, but is limited to sociology. In sociology, quite as much as in any social science, there is at present a searching inquiry into the nature and technique of research. This interest is perhaps greater than elsewhere because sociology is the latest comer in the family of the social sciences and is naturally self-conscious and not as yet entirely assured of status.

Both for those who view sociology with sympathetic criticism from within and for those who scrutinize the development of sociology with curious but not necessarily unfriendly eyes from without it may be helpful to recall the stages of progress in the thinking in the field of any, or indeed all, of the natural sciences.[3] There tends to be first a period of common sense observation influenced more or less by allegorical comparisons or analogies and by magical or romantic attempts at control. Next, in inquiring and thoughtful minds, there arises more critical observation, reflection, and speculation leading to the working out of basic conceptions and points of view from which are often derived principles of interpretation and even rules of action. This is the metaphysical or philosophical stage of thinking. Finally the method of natural science, of controlled observation and experimentation, is slowly and painstakingly applied to the description of the behavior of the phenomena.

Just as the magical stage of astronomy was astrology and of psychology was phrenology, both of which continue with us unto this day, so the magical and romantic stage of sociology was the elaboration of utopias. Among utopian sociologists must be classified Plato, with his ideal republic, Campanelli, with his city of the sun, Sir Thomas More, whose work christened this school of millennial thinking, as well as the later utopias of Butler, Morris, Bellamy, and Wells. Indeed, Mr. H. G. Wells, in a paper before the London Sociological Society, assigned as the real function of sociologists the devising of utopias.[4]

I would be the last to underestimate the prevalence at the present time of utopian sociology, and for that matter, of utopian social science. The thinking on public questions of the great masses of the people and also of the self-styled intelligentsia is still in the magical stage.

How else can be explained the abiding faith of the people in the omnipotence of political action to solve all economic, social, and civic problems? Dr. W. I. Thomas characterizes the ordering and forbidding technique of legislation as essentially magical in character.

> The oldest but most persistent form of social technique is that of "ordering-and-forbidding"—that is, meeting a crisis by an arbitrary act of will decreeing the disappearance of the undesirable or the appearance of the desirable phenomena, and using arbitrary physical action to enforce the decree. This method corresponds exactly to the magical phase of natural technique. A good instance of this in the social field is the typical legislative procedure of the day.[5]

The advocates of panaceas for social problems, social reformer and social revolutionist alike, belong to the various conflicting factions of the romantic utopian group.

The metaphysical stage of the development of the sciences is that of speculation. This is the period of armchair philosophy, of general observation, of cosmic theories, and of schools of thought. Psychology before the nineties was really the philosophy of the mind as is evident from the systematic works of Hume, Locke, Berkeley, Spencer, and Bain. Philosophy performs, it must be remembered, a necessary preliminary and indeed permanent function for natural science. It surveys the field, it plots the problems, and it formulates the concepts which are indispensable tools for research.

Auguste Comte, in publishing his work on *The Positive Philosophy*, claimed to have ushered in the scientific stage of sociology. Instead, his efforts mark the real beginning of the philosophical mode of systematic sociological thinking which continued in the voluminous writings of Herbert Spencer in England and Lester F. Ward in the United States and which still dominates the thinking and work of many contemporary sociologists.

The metaphysical period, while a necessary preparation for the scientific stage, seems in the perversity of nature destined to prevent, or at any rate to retard, its emergence. The most extreme illustration of this is found in the attitude of the medieval metaphysicians as recalled in an anecdote quoted by Dr. David Starr Jordan in a recent article:

In an essay attributed to Lord Bacon, the story is told of the effort on the part of a cult of priests to find out how many teeth a horse has. Appeal was made to the Fathers and to Aristotle without result. Finally, someone suggested looking at a horse. This was fiercely resented by the scholars. "Satan hath tempted this bold neophyte to declare unholy and unheard of ways of finding truth, contrary to all the teachings of the fathers." The disputants finally declared it to be "an everlasting mystery, because of a grievous dearth of historical and theological evidence thereof and so ordered the same writ down."[6]

We smile at this credulous reliance upon scholastic as over against empirical knowledge. Yet I have no doubt that a survey of the content of the volumes written by sociologists in the last quarter of a century would show that by far the larger part of them are the product of armchair philosophizing and the rehashing of the philosophizing of others rather than of the presentation and analysis of concrete materials. Many still prefer the dignity of the scholar who soars in the realm of theories to the humbler walk of the research student in contact with life.

In sociology, the beginning of the scientific period may be placed in 1906, the year marked by the publication of *Folkways* by William Graham Sumner. Here for the first time is a sociological work which bases generalizations upon concrete materials. His division of customs into *folkways* as convenient forms of group behavior, and *mores* as sanctioned modes of social conduct laid the foundation for an objective and a comparative study of culture.

Then, too, there is the monumental work, *The Polish Peasant in Europe and America* by Thomas and Znaniecki, which is an exhibit of the sociological study of a culture under conditions of transplantation from an old world to a new world environment.

With a growing realization, especially on the part of the younger sociologists, that the future of their science lay more in field research rather than in "book learning" has come a keener interest in the technique of investigation. Professor Franklin H. Giddings[7] for years has stressed the use of the statistical method while Professor Charles H. Cooley[8] has advocated the method of sympathetic introspection. Meanwhile the methods of statistics and of case study were being applied to the study of varied aspects of social life and at first almost entirely by others than sociologists.

Not even Professor Giddings was a more ardent advocate of the scientific value of statistics than was the founder of sociology, Auguste Comte. He held that mathematics was *par excellence* the method of science and indispensable to its development. Indeed, he was convinced, as many others have been, that the best method of determining how far a field of study has become scientific is by the extent to which its laws and generalizations have been given exact and precise quantitative expression. No one can dispute that in the physical sciences, astronomy, physics, chemistry, and biology, mathematical formulae have played a larger and a larger part. In recent years, psychology, which occupies a twilight zone between the physical and the social sciences, has been making heroic efforts to become more scientific, that is to say, statistical.

The prestige of statistics as *the one* scientific method has naturally often led in sociology and I suspect in psychology and the other social sciences, to a naïve and uncritical application of quantitative measurement to mental and social phenomena. This attitude of deference to statistics has taken two widely different manifestations. The first is that of reverence for all mass data, for all facts and all information presented in numerical fashion. The second is a worship of statistical technique in its most refined minutiae, as coefficient of correlation, standard deviation of error, and the higher mathematical formulae, often to the exclusion either of its applicability to the phenomena in question or its real bearing upon the hypothesis to be tested.

If the mere enumeration of data, no matter how precise, or if the most complicated and detailed higher calculation provide in themselves little or no contribution to science, of what use in sociology is statistics?

Personally, I have found helpful one of the definitions of statistics offered by Professor Arthur L. Bowley, namely, that "statistics is the science of the measurement of the social organism, regarded as a whole, in all its manifestations."[9] Perhaps I read into this definition meaning which the author of it did not intend nor imply when he spoke of the "social organism as a whole."

"A chief practical use of statistics is to show relative importance," continues Professor Bowley. "Statistics are almost always comparative. A statement of the number of paupers in the United Kingdom is valueless unless we know the total population. . . . In the case of most statistical estimates, it will be found that we need another for comparison before we can appreciate the meaning of the first."[10]

The value of statistics undoubtedly increases with the feasibility of comparisons. It is of little significance to know that 1,178,318 marriages were enumerated in the United States in 1924. But when this figure is compared with the number of unmarried persons of marriageable age, and with the number of divorces, its value is enhanced by every comparison. An isolated comparative fact, the knowledge that there were 28 divorces per 100,000 population in 1870 in the United States takes on larger meaning when the trend is disclosed showing a constant increase until the divorce rate in 1924 reached 152 per 100,000 population or over five times as great a ratio as 54 years ago.

Another valuable use of statistics is to show correlations between two variables, as for example, the divorce rate as compared with absence of children, or marriage and length of life. At the present time prediction in sociology and the social sciences rarely if ever follows the principles of causation disclosed in the physical sciences, namely, an invariable sequence of certain occurrence. Prediction in sociology at present, has certain definite limitations. We can predict that the divorce rate will continue to increase, but with the proviso, that the factors producing the increase continue to operate in the future as in the past without the check of counterbalancing factors. In many instances the theory of statistical probability in human behavior is contingent upon the customary. The fate of the textile industry is a case in point showing the havoc wrought by a change in fashion that was not predictable.

Professor Cooley, in a penetrating and illuminating article on methods of social research under the title, "The Roots of Social Knowledge," points out that prediction at present in social science depends upon the inertia and standardization of our modern economic and social life rather than upon the discovery of fundamental uniformities in human nature and society. He says:

Another impression which I take to be erroneous is that statistics is revealing uniformities or irregularities in social phenomena which indicate that these phenomena may in time prove to be subject to exact prediction in quite the same way as those of physics. It is true that statistics is revealing sequence, order, and a remarkable degree of predictability in certain social processes. By analysis of what has taken place during the past ten years, especially in the economic field, where the facts are largely material, it may be possible to forecast what will take place in the next five; and no one can say how far we may go in this direction. The whole basis of this, however, seems to be the prevalence of inertia and the rarity and slowness of the more originative processes. The greater part of human phenomena are so far routinized as to be more or less subject to calculation. Wherever men, under the impetus of habit and suggestion, are moving ahead in a mechanical manner, or where their intelligence is merely repeating what is essentially an old synthesis of motives—as, for example, in deciding whether to marry or not—exact methods are in place. The complex of human events can, to a great extent, be resolved into currents of tendency moving on definite lines at ascertainable speeds. If we can measure these lines and speeds it may be possible to predict their combined operation, much as the motion of a comet is predicted by calculating the resultant of the gravity, tangential momentum, and other forces acting upon it. The whole basis of prediction in such fields as that of the business cycles is the belief that the underlying motivation is essentially standardized or repetitive.

Probably no exact science could have foreseen the sudden rise of the automobile industry and the genius of Henry Ford, although now that this industry is developed and institutionalized we may perhaps calculate with some precision what it will bring forth in the near future.[11]

Moreover, even correlations, while suggesting relations of cause and effect leave unrevealed the process of causation. Several years ago in a paper presented before the American Sociological Society figures were quoted showing that married men lived longer than single men with the assumption of the favorable effect of marriage upon longevity. You at once ask if the correct explanation may not be that physical fitness involving greater expectation of life is favorable to marriage? Statistics in and of themselves give no answer. The explanation must be found, if at all, elsewhere. Indeed, in the discussion of the paper, the flippant question was raised whether married men really lived longer or that married life seemed longer. The implications of this jest, if followed up, strike deep into the basic assumption of the use and limitations of the statistical method. How can attitudes, the basic subject matter of human nature and society, be stated numerically? How can the so-called intangible facts of life, its qualitative aspects, be apprehended by so cruel an instrument as statistics? What figures will measure the degree of affection between husband and wife, or the nature and intensity of a father's pride in his children, or qualities of personality like charm, loyalty, and leadership?

Another way of stating this same point is to recognize that quantitative methods deal in the main with the cruder, more external aspects of human behavior, and that some other more sympathetic and discerning method is necessary to probe beneath the surface and to depict and analyze the inner life of the person.

The most serious deficiency of statistics for sociology as at present practised has yet to be mentioned. It is that the existing body of social statistics is based upon an atomistic rather than upon an organic conception of society.

By an atomistic conception of society is meant the notion that society is an aggregate of relatively independent individuals. In this sense society is thought of as a mere sum total of its component individuals. On the other hand, the organic conception of society, whatever else it implies, is, at least a recognition of the fact that society and its members alike are the product of social interaction. According to this explanation a gang is not the sum total of the individual boys who compose it but the organization of the boys into a new form of a group which at the same time creates a new type of boy, the gangster.

It is because to the sociologist society is an organization of persons rather than a collection of individuals that Bowley's definition of statistics as "the science of the measurement of the social organism as a whole" is so appropriate. In current statistical procedure, the unit of enumeration and measurement is almost always some atomistic rather than integral trait of the person. For example, current studies of the causes of desertion take such individual traits as unemployment, alcoholism, feeble-mindedness, wanderlust, and then tabulate the number of times that each is found to be a factor rather than make any effort to perceive the setting of each trait in the total personality.

Even if statistics rest upon the assumption that the individual and society may be divided into isolated units which can be counted, it does not follow that statistical data give us no knowledge of sociological value. Often statistics upon some superficial and external aspect of social life may measure the working of a fundamental process. Divorce, in our society, is an objective record that society approves the dissolution of the contract entered into a marriage. Yet divorces may be taken as an index, I admit a crude one, of the forces of family disintegration. A more adequate index of family disintegration is secured when desertion, "the poor man's divorce," is included in addition to divorce. Nevertheless, since both divorce and desertion are only two of the end results of the process of family disintegration, is there not some other objective fact which will more accurately reflect its actual workings? Our studies in city life in Chicago suggest that mobility, or change in the position and movement of the population, is perhaps the best objective correlate of social disorganization in general and of family disorganization in particular. Mr. Andrew W. Lind, who is making a study of indices of mobility, has surveyed changes in residence, transfers of children in and out of the schools, traffic counts of pedestrian, automobile, and passenger movement, and changes in land value. The conclusion at which we have tentatively arrived is that land values, especially when correlated with rents, probably provide the most satisfactory measure of the relative mobility of the population in the various parts of the city. Where mobility is highest, as in the central business district, family life is absent or most precarious, but where mobility is low, as in the suburbs, family life flourishes.

For statistics to be serviceable for the development of sociological science, they must always, whether in simple comparisons or in complex measurement of indices of social processes, refer to what Bowley terms "the social organism." In other words, statistics to have value for social science must measure some natural area or group. Social statistics in American cities on the basis of division into wards are notoriously unsatisfactory, because wards are arbitrarily determined, often gerrymandered with little or no regard for natural groupings by neighborhoods, nationalities, or trade areas. In St. Louis and in Chicago, the councils of social agencies have sponsored a division of the city into natural areas as a basis for usable social statistics.[12]

The case-study method was first introduced into social science as a handmaiden to statistics. LePlay's interest in monographic studies was primarily to secure data on family income and expenditure as a basis for the preparation of family budgets. Healy's adoption of the case method for the study of the individual delinquent grew out of his disappointment with earlier statistical findings secured from a superficial examination of cases.[13] He said, however, in summarizing his own statistical data derived from an intensive study of 1,000 cases of juvenile delinquency, that "statistics will never tell the whole story."[14]

In the period when the case-study was subordinated to statistics, it was open to the same sociological criticism as the latter. For the case-study, thought of primarily in terms of a questionnaire, was planned so as to secure data on points susceptible to enumeration and tabulation. The case to be studied was not conceived of as an organic whole, but as a sum of separable and independent units which could therefore be itemized, scheduled, and tabulated.

The first steps in the emancipation of the case-study from the domination of statistics was not taken by sociologists, but by journalists, by social workers, by psychiatrists, and by cultural anthropologists. The newspaper reporter quickly learned that while the public easily tires of dry statistics, its appetite is insatiable for dramatic cases. The social worker, while using a face sheet very convenient for statistical summaries, soon found the necessity in her work for recording something of the life history of the family and its progress under social treatment. Psychiatrists like William

Healy, turning their attention to the causation of juvenile delinquency, found the case study indispensable for disclosing processes and for giving insight into causation. Cultural anthropologists naturally tended to rely upon the monographic method for the description of the culture of primitive peoples.

Spencer was the first sociologist to make extensive use of case materials. From correspondents all over the world he collected a mass of ethnographic documents. He devoted his private fortune to the classification and publication of these materials.[15] Unfortunately, the philosophical cast of his mind predisposed him to pigeon-hole these cases under the categories of his sociological system, rather than to test hypotheses by cases. Spencer was notoriously guilty of amassing all favorable cases to prove a point in utter disregard of negative cases, as another sociologist took the pains to find out.

Perhaps the first disinterested arrangement of anthropological materials for sociological purposes is to be found in Sumner's *Folkways*. But the actual introduction of the case-study as a method of sociological field research was made by Thomas and Znaniecki in *The Polish Peasant in Europe and America*. Here for the first time are found personal documents as letters, statements, and autobiographies, as well as case records of social agencies with a fully developed scheme of socialized interpretation. The assumption throughout is the organic conception of an analysis of personal conduct and group behavior in its regular setting in a total cultural situation.

This organic or cultural explanation of human behavior has recently found a new formulation in the Gestalt or the configuration psychology.[16] Just as in perception any object is seen in its total setting as a part of a larger pattern, so any act of a person or group gets meaning in its configuration, or frame of reference, in the life experience of that person or group.

Thrasher, the author of *The Gang*, states this point in a recent article on "The Group Factor":

To study a delinquent as a mere individual, then, as if he could have developed in a social vacuum, is to get a very imperfect picture of him. The delinquent must be studied as a person (as an individual with status, or in his social relationships). His sentiments and attitudes, which may be of vital significance in any therapeutic program devised for him as well as in the diagnosis of his case, are most intimately related to the social complexes or configurations which have co-operated with other factors to create his personality. What will be the effect upon the delinquent boy of treatment which involves visits to the juvenile court, the detention home, or a correctional institution? In many gangs, the acquirement of such a record is a necessity for full standing in the group: it means added prestige and added incentive to delinquency; and the boy becomes a hero to be emulated in the eyes of his fellow gang boys. Yet this untoward effect is wholly unforeseen by those who inflict the punishment, that is, if the boy is not studied in his social setting. What is defined by the gang as devilish good sport and adventure, moreover, may be defined by the larger society as serious delinquency. There are two distinct social worlds here that must be considered if any real insight into the problem is to be achieved. The real meaning of the delinquent or his behavior, therefore, can only be understood in its *gestalt* or its social configuration.[17]

Sooner or later, the objection is sure to be raised: "Case studies are interesting and enlightening, true they give insights, they reveal motives and causes, they disclose processes, but are they scientific?" This question can perhaps best be answered in the words of Karl Pearson: "The man," he says, "who classifies facts of any kind whatever, who sees their mutual relations and describes their sequences, is applying the scientific method and is a man of science."[18] There is certainly nothing in this definition to exclude the case-study method from scientific procedure, provided that it involves classification, perception of relationships, and description of sequences.

But it is apparent that case-study as a method in sociology is still in its infancy. For the great majority of people, the account of a case has the status of an anecdote, of a story with human interest. The case record of a social agency represents a distinct advance over the anecdotal method, yet even here the disposition is to treat each case as individual and independent, and not as a specimen or as a type, which is essential for classification according to natural science procedure.

At the present time a group of sociologists under the impetus largely of Professor Thomas and Professor Park are at work accumulating personal documents, interpreting them, and raising questions of technique and the logic of the case-study method.

The sociological value of any case, it is soon discovered, depends first of all upon the grade of excellence of the document secured. The chief criterion of a good case document is that it be revealing, that it penetrate beneath the conventional mask each human being wears, and that it freely admit one into the inner recesses of the memories and wishes, fears and hopes, of the other person. This sharing of the innermost feelings and thoughts of another person is what is offered by the secret diary, the intimate autobiography, the personal letter, and the confidential interview.

But what is the technique of securing these revealing documents and may their authenticity and accuracy be verified?

My answer to these questions will probably not be completely satisfactory to all, or perhaps to any one.

The primary requisite of the seeker for personal documents is a sense for the dramatic in all human life, a sympathy broad enough to encompass the manifold diverse manifestations of human nature, even those that are commonly regarded as shocking or even outrageous. My own experience as well as my observation of the success and failure of students seems to show that the inhibitions to personal revelations are not generally so much in the subject as in the attitude of the inquirer. Both this dramatic sense and this sympathetic attitude indispensable for success in securing personal documents, naturally develop under favorable conditions of human association, but are also susceptible to special training for research work.

Our experience with personal documents has shown the great value of recording an interview in the language of the person interviewed.[19] This preserves the objectivity of the record. Otherwise the record is a translation into the language of the interviewer and thereby often quite unintentionally does violence to the original meaning. What an enormous improvement there would be in the case records of social agencies if all interviews were only entered in the language of the informant instead of the not infrequently misleading translation of the social worker.

It is even more difficult to give a conclusive answer to the question of the verifiability of the authenticity and accuracy of the autobiography, the interview, and other personal documents. One of course may trust to the experienced discrimination of the competent student of cases, as one relies upon the jeweler to distinguish almost at first glance the true from the spurious gem. Or reliance may be placed upon the testimony of Healy that contrary to his expectation he found only a negligible fraction of deception in interviews with thousands of juvenile delinquents he has examined. Or certain tests of the authenticity of a document may be devised, as for example, the test of its growing coherence and absence of contradiction with increasing detail. Or finally, an interesting if not conclusive argument can be made for the point that the authenticity of a document is to be measured by its fidelity in disclosing the person's conception of his rôle and that this is revealed quite as well in what he omits as in what he tells and in attempts at deception quite as much as in truth telling.

The logic of the case study as a method of natural science lies in the feasibility of classifying cases. This means that in analyzing a case it is treated as a specimen of a species. In society an individual case is a specimen of a species in a more intimate sense than in the biological world. Two dandelion plants are specimens of the dandelion species merely because of the kind of seed from which they grew, but two policemen are specimens of the police officer species because they participate in the code and the standards of a social pattern of what the policeman is or ought to be.

In treating an individual boys' gang as a specimen of boys' gangs in general, the assumption is that those traits are selected that characterize all boys' gangs. It is necessary, of course, to make comparisons, to study marginal and negative cases, and to arrive at classes and other groupings within these species.

It seems, then, that the possibilities are open to the case-study method to develop its technique in conformity with the requirements of science. The method of case study may eventually or may never win the exactness and precision of statistics but there can be no doubt that it will become increasingly standardized. It must be noted that the case study as a method is a distinctly different technique from that of statistics and with its own criteria of excellence.

In conclusion, it is probably sufficient to point out that the methods of statistics and of case study are not in conflict with each other; they are in fact mutually complementary. Statistical comparisons and correlations may often suggest leads for research by the case-study method, and documentary materials as they reveal social processes will inevitably point the way to more adequate statistical indices. If, however, statistics and case study are to yield their full contribution as tools of sociological research, they should be granted equal recognition and full opportunity for each to perfect its own technique. At the same time, the interaction of the two methods is certain to prove fruitful. From case studies light is now being thrown on the workings of social processes like mobility, formerly unseen or dimly perceived; the measurement of these processes opens up a new field of statistical effort.

SOCIAL PLANNING AND
THE MORES

SOCIOLOGISTS have been active in social planning. In increasing numbers they have been called into government service in Washington and elsewhere. They hold, or have held, important positions in agencies that directly or indirectly are concerned with the success or failure of the New Deal, as for example, the Consumers' Advisory Board, the Central Statistical Board, the Census Bureau, the Federal Relief Administration, the Agricultural Administrative Act, the Children's Bureau, the Bureau of Agricultural Economics and the Bureau of Labor Statistics.

Despite our natural gratification at the increasing participation of sociologists in the alphabetocracy at Washington, two rather disquieting questions may be raised:

First, are the sociologists in governmental service engaged upon research that is distinctly sociological?

Second, are sociologists making the full measure of contribution to the solution of problems of the depression and of recovery which an application of the distinctively sociological point of view and methods of research might be expected to insure?

Both these questions are to be answered in the negative. Sociologists are for the most part engaged upon research which other social scientists could perform as well or better. No demand has been made of sociology to mobilize and direct upon the considera-

Reprinted from *Publication of the American Sociological Society* 29, no. 3 (1935) : 1–18. Paper presented at the Twenty-Ninth Annual Meeting of the American Sociological Society, Chicago, 26–29 December 1934 (Chicago: H. G. Adair Printing Co., 1935).

tion of politics and programs of economic and social reconstruction its *distinctive* point of view and methods of research.

But what is the distinctive point of view of sociology? What special significance may it have for the successful achievement of the New Deal or of any similar program?

Sociology, as a separate discipline in the field of the social sciences, seems to have arisen to take account of a factor, or group of factors, which had been overlooked and neglected by economics and political science.

This forgotten factor has been given different names by students of society. William G. Sumner invented the terms " 'folkways' and 'mores.' " Anthropologists denominate this factor "culture." Historians use the phrase "historical backgrounds." Pareto stresses the study of "non-logical human action" as the task for sociological research.

Sumner, who was a political scientist and economist as well as sociologist, had no doubt of the signal significance of this factor. As early as 1881 he stated positively, and with characteristic emphasis, his conviction upon this point.

We are already in such a position with sociology that a person who has gained what we now possess of that science will bring to bear upon economic problems a sounder judgment and a more correct conception of all social relations than a person who may have read a library of the existing treatises on political economy. The essential elements of political economy are only corollaries or special cases of sociological principles.[1]

Sumner, in his epoch-making volume *Folkways*,[2] presents a mass of concrete material showing the role of custom and tradition in the behavior of primitive and historical peoples. He was particularly impressed by the controlling part played by certain customs which he called "the mores" in distinction from other customs which he termed "folkways."

Sumner defined "folkways" as the

Habits of the individual and customs of society which arise from efforts to satisfy needs. They become regulative for succeeding generations and take on the character of a social force. They can be modified, but only to a limited extent, by the purposeful efforts of men.[3]

Customs in the "mores," however, had a significance for a people which set them apart from the "folkways." Sumner defined "mores" as

the popular usages and traditions, when they include a judgment that they are conducive to societal welfare, and when they exert a coercion on the individual to conform to them, although they are not coordinated by any authority.[4]

Sumner ascribed to the mores the following characteristics:

1. The "mores" arise from experience and are maintained because they are believed to be essential to social welfare even when they run counter to natural human impulses and require (exact)? pain and sacrifice from the individual.

2. Although the "mores" arise out of past experience, they tend to resist the implications of present experiences, changing but slowly to meet the demands of technological change.

3. Significant events, as they occur, are interpreted not rationally and objectively but in the perspective of the mores. This explains why the same external event in the field of international relations has one interpretation in Washington, another in Berlin, a quite different one in Tokyo and a still variant meaning in Moscow. Our "mores" also explain why the American people are incapable of understanding what is now taking place in Germany, in Japan, and in the Soviet Union.[5]

4. The mores, changing but gradually under the impact of changed conditions of life, evolve along lines already present in the folkways and the mores.

5. Consequently, social programs of private or public bodies that run counter to the mores are foredoomed to partial or complete failure, while those that follow within their boundaries have promise of success.

This, in brief, is the thesis maintained by Sumner in *Folkways*. It may be called the theory of the cultural determinism of historical events. In essence it corresponds closely with Pareto's explanation of human behavior in terms of motivation by sentiment rather than by interest. Both Sumner and Pareto emphasize the non-logical character of much of human action. Both assert that the task of sociology in the division of labor between the social sciences is to isolate and define the mechanisms and processes of the non-rational aspects of the behavior of peoples. Only in this way may sociology make its contribution, complementary to that of economics and political science, to an understanding of human behavior.

This theory of cultural determinism appears to be the direct opposite of the many different formulations of the theory of economic determinism. At this point no attempt will be made either to reconcile these two points of view or to place them in a working relationship with each other. The point is that traditionally, economics and also political science, although to a lesser extent, have generally been conceived as sciences of man's activity as a rational animal, while sociology has essayed the more difficult task of formulating an inductive science of man as a creature of folkways and mores, imbued with sentiments, prejudices, and fixed ideas. This, perhaps, is the reason why the sociologist has not been called into consultation by practical men of affairs. He is concerned with what are thought to be the intangibles and imponderables in human behavior. But what if, in the last analysis, the success or failure of a given policy and program will turn upon the so-called intangibles and imponderables in the situation?

Sumner's definition of the "mores" and their role in human behavior may now be put to the test of an analysis of the American "ethos," or national character, in its relation to policies and programs of social planning.[6]

What may we take to be the dominant traits in the American national character?

The three outstanding conceptions in the mores which give form to the American national character appear to be individualism, democracy, and humanitarianism. These may be briefly described and analyzed in terms of their interplay in determining the run of attention, the peculiar formation of institutions, and the characteristic and accepted patterns of behavior of the American people.

Individualism may be defined as the belief in the individual as the fountain source of energy, initiative, and responsibility in society. As a consequence, the social and political order should impose the minimum of regulation and regimentation upon the individual and should encourage the maximum of effort and achievement from him.

Democracy may be defined as the faith of the American people in the social value of "government of the people, for the people, and by the people." As Sumner says:[7]

Democracy is in our American mores. It is a product of our physical and economic conditions. It is impossible to discuss or criticize it. It is glorified for popularity and is a subject of dithyrambic rhetoric. No one treats it with complete candor and sincerity. No one dares to analyze it as he would aristocracy or autocracy. He would get no hearing and would only incur abuse. This thing to be noted in all these cases is that the masses oppose a deaf ear to every argument against the mores.

In the United States grave defects in our democratic machinery of government can only be corrected by following the formula "the cure for the evils of democracy is more democracy."[8]

Humanitarianism may be defined as the impulse to do for others what you feel will be for their welfare. Its motivation should not be too closely inquired into. It may arise from altruistic sentiments. It may be the outcome of imagining one's self in the place of an unfortunate. It may result from a guilty conscience as penance for personal sins or public wrongs. It may be the expression of a wish to shine before the public as a philanthropist. Or it may be a combination of these and other motives.

Humanitarianism ranks with individualism and democracy as dominant articles of faith of the American people, although at times it seems to be in direct conflict with them.[9]

Individualism, democracy, and humanitarianism are all protected from criticism by what Sumner calls "pathos." He says:

Pathos is the glamor of sentiment which grows up around the pet notion of an age and people, and which protects it from criticism. . . . There is a pathos of democracy in the United States. . . . Humanitarianism is nourished by pathos and it stimulates pathos. The "poor" and the "laborers" are objects of pathos, on account of which these terms, in literature, refer to a conventional and unreal concept. Consequently there is no honest discussion of any topic which concerns the poor or laborers.[10]

"Rugged individualism" was a phrase dripping with pathos, until its unreality in a period of depression was facetiously exposed by the pun "ragged individualism."[11]

Sumner's theory of the mores and national character would imply that social, economic and political behavior in America would follow lines indicated by one or more of these dominant conceptions of individualism, democracy, and humanitarianism.

Pioneer conditions of American life set the stage for a hitherto unparalleled demonstration of the results achieved by giving full play to individual effort. The historian Turner has given an admirable analysis of the individualism of the American people as a product of the frontier. The exploitation of a continent released individual initiative and inventiveness; the great wastes entailed seemed as nothing in comparison with the tremendous natural resources of the country. The speculative spirit of the pioneer and of the prospector entered the mores. No limitations were placed upon individual success. Any boy, it was believed, even if born in a log cabin, had his chance to become a millionaire or president of the United States.

Individualism as a theory of society assumes that the greatest good of the greatest number is most likely to be achieved where each individual is given the maximum of freedom and responsibility.

This appeal to motives of individual success, according to its advocates, results in the development of aptitudes and in the attainment of standards of achievement and efficiency which benefit not only the individual but also society. The same justification is offered for the free play of the profit motive, for the institution of private property, and for the right of inheritance as necessary to stimulate individual effort and so promote the general welfare.

Included in the notion of the maximum freedom of behavior and of responsibility for the individual is the belief in his right to personal liberty. The corollary to this is the conception that "the least government is the best government." The popular antipathy to the policeman, the so-called lawlessness of the American people as reflected in our crime situation, the general resentment against regulations and regimentation are all expressions of the individualism that is still deeply ingrained in American mores and national character.

Democracy as the faith in the validity, if not in the infallibility of the public will as expressed at the ballot-box, has implications that must be considered with reference to any program of social planning.

Democracy glorifies the average man and discounts the man of exceptional ability. It assumes the capacity of the average man acting in the mass to make intelligent decisions on questions that affect his welfare and destiny. Democracy also assumes that the average man is able to discharge, more or less competently, any public office to which he may aspire.

The success of democracy in the town meeting of New England and its breakdown, especially in our larger cities, is well known to political scientists. Remedies have been proposed, some have been tried, but with only indifferent success. Primaries, the short ballot, direct election of senators, commission plan of city government, city managers—not any one of them has achieved the results claimed for them by their advocates.

The brilliant achievements of democracy in the United States have been not in the field of politics, but in industrial, civic, and social life. The organization of business enterprises, employers' associations, labor unions, boards of arbitration, represent significant achievements of democracy in industry. The shortcomings of political democracy have led to a development of voluntary civic agencies in American cities which almost completely parallel the political organization. In Chicago, for example, public-spirited citizens have organized a bureau of municipal efficiency, a citizens' association, a better government association, a crime commission, a Committee of Fifteen to investigate vice conditions, a juvenile protection association, a safety council, etc. These agencies, together with a multitude of philanthropic and social agencies are, in general, effectively organized and efficiently run. In this respect they are in marked contrast with the traditional inefficiency and incompetency of our more formal institutions.

Humanitarianism, as an article of the American faith, is often, but by no means always, in conformity with the principles of individualism and democracy.

The human sentiment to do what you believe to be good to others has supplied the main motivation to social reform and to the founding of social welfare institutions in the United States.

Social movements, enlisting the interest and support of socially-minded individuals, have arisen to cope with every social problem as it has emerged. The list is too long to enumerate, but it includes movements for public health, for progressive education, for better housing, for charities, for mental hygiene, for the care or the sterilization of the feeble-minded, for social settlements, for playgrounds and recreation, for the community center, for labor legislation, for visiting teachers, for social hygiene, against vice, for the Juvenile Court, for probation, for parole, against the saloon and for social surveys.

All of these social movements have had as leaders persons devoted to human welfare; the organizations fostered by these movements have in general maintained high standards of service. Yet the efforts of these hundred and one social movements, outside the field of public health, have not achieved the success to be expected from the devotion, energy and efficiency invested in them.

Voluntary agencies have, however, been more successful than our political institutions in their regimentation of the behavior of the public. The clients of welfare agencies, the majority of whom are foreigners, do not revolt against having their lives regulated, at least not until they become Americanized. It is a notorious fact that in every American community the law is not likely to be applied too rigorously against members of its best families who are regarded as pillars of society.

When the humanitarian observes the failure of voluntary effort to make people good, he tends to turn first to crusades and then to legislation to secure reform. This represents a union of the humanitarian and the democratic conceptions in the mores but is in conflict with laissez-faire or individualism. Despite bitter experience the American people still believe in making good by legislation. The failure of constitutional prohibition is a signal case of mass action in the United States, impelled by a union of humanitarian and democratic sentiments in the mores, which in its enforcement ran counter to sentiments of personal liberty ingrained in individualism which is also in the mores.

The "hypocrisy" attributed to Americans by Europeans flows naturally out of our humanitarian sentiments. We are readily disposed, because of our interest in the welfare of others, to impose upon them either our own standards of behavior, or standards of behavior higher than our own. Many persons quite sincerely voted "dry" for the sake of their weaker brother but continued to drink "wet." The Southern planter might have a virtuous feeling in aiding prohibition legislation to protect his Negro tenant with the serene consciousness that his own stock of liquors would not be curtailed. Social workers are often expected to enforce standards of housekeeping and conduct upon clients on relief which, under similar conditions, they would find difficult to observe in their own households.

What bearing, if any, does this discussion of the mores of individualism, democracy and humanitarianism have upon the New Deal and the programs of social planning now confronting the United States?

A few generalizations may tentatively be put forward to test the validity of the preceding analysis of American "mores" and national character.

1. Any program of social planning to be successful in the United States must follow a course in line with American traditions and habits of thinking. A program in violation of the dominant conceptions of the mores is certain sooner or later to result in failure.

2. Policies and programs of continental European nations,[12] have no lessons to give to the United States. The experiments now under way in Germany, Italy, and the Soviet Union are not and can not be understood by Americans. Therefore the success of any one of these programs would not be relevant to the Ameri-

can situation. The solutions of problems in the United States must be in terms of our own situation and in conformity with our mores.

3. Under the impulsion of the humanitarian ideal, the American people will, for the period of an emergency such as war or depression, tolerate and even demand social action of a type that they will be swift to repudiate as a matter of *permanent* national policy. It is important that the government and the party in power have an adequate realization of this primary fact.

4. Any proposal for a collective and controlled society, at any time in the near future, seems completely outside the picture of reality. Individualism and democracy are too deeply entrenched in the folkways and mores to sanction the regulation and regimentation necessary, even if these features in certain concrete instances might win approval through appeal to humanitarian sentiments as temporarily necessary for the public welfare.

Accepting for purposes of argument and for the moment these four generalizations, what application may be made to current programs of governmental planning?

1. The N. R. A., according to our Sumnerian analysis, would be quite evidently a case demanding a minimum of governmental regulation and a maximum of self-governing by industries. The codes of the different industries may be regarded as correcting a situation of anarchy naturally resulting from the Sherman Anti-Trust Law, which conspicuously failed to prevent the growth of large industrial units but which succeeded in preventing desirable trade agreements between competing enterprises.

2. The program of the Tennessee Valley Authority may be taken as a crucial case in long-time social planning. Its success or failure may exert a profound influence on the future course of social planning in the United States.

The mountaineers of the Tennessee Valley, individualists of the pioneer type, influenced hardly at all by the growth of our industrial and urban civilization, would seem to be the most unpromising subjects for social planning. This makes the experiment difficult, but all the more interesting and significant.

The project assumes that by a *tour de force* the industrial revolution which elsewhere in the United States required two or three generations will here be telescoped into four or five years and in that time mountaineers with their intense individualistic traditions and attitudes will become completely adjusted to the power age and modern technology.

It is only too apparent that if the customs, attitudes and reactions of the people are not as fully studied and taken into account as the geographic and economic situation, the Tennessee Valley project is likely to be a partial, if not a complete, failure.

3. The relief program of the federal and state governments is certain shortly to be put to the test. The humanitarian sentiments of the American people heartily approve, as an emergency measure, the expenditure of hundreds of millions of dollars annually for the support of those in distress. Until recently, the giving of relief was so colored with pathos that the public paid no attention to any criticism of its administration. In fact, there are certain signs, both in urban and rural districts, of a disposition to demand relief as a right and as an escape from work which for the unskilled wage earner provides no more, if as much, as relief.

Far more significant than the rising tide of public criticism against alleged waste and mismanagement of relief administration is the fact that relief-giving, as more than an emergency program, runs counter to the basic concepts of individualism and democracy. A solution is demanded that provides opportunity for work and for freedom from investigation and regimentation.

This brief discussion of these three governmental projects indicates the desirability of applying the test of public reaction to these and other proposals under consideration in the New Deal.

Certain objections to this line of thought must doubtless have occurred to the reader.

First of all, this paper has dealt only with the human or sociological aspects of the problem. Left entirely out of consideration is the factor of technological change. The present traditions and sentiments of the American developed in a pioneer situation; with the alleged break-down of an individualistic society will not sentiments of collectivism and of social control emerge favorable to the planning of a *collective* society?

This objection may be entirely valid. The economic situation has changed and is changing. It may also be conceded for the sake of argument that the rational way to meet these changes is through the establishment of a collectivistically planned society, even if its practicability has yet to be demonstrated. In short, economic determinism may be considered as pointing to a planned collectivistic society, while cultural determinism according to Sumner requires a policy and program developed tentatively, experimentally and always pragmatically in the process of the adjustment of the mores of individualism, democracy, and humanitarianism to changing life conditions.

The weight of anthropological and historical evidence would seem to support Sumner's position, namely, that the mores of a society change gradually and often irrationally, as in fashion, but in the long run in accordance with the trend of adjustment in the mores. The solution of the present crisis accordingly would appear to be either in a return to the old economic system or in a new program that takes shape within the trends now observable in the mores and in keeping with sentiments of individualism, democracy, and humanitarianism.

Any radical change in the national character of a people, that is, in their mores and institutions, can come, in the future as in the past, not by evolution, but by revolution. If a return to the old economic system brings failure, or if the New Deal or other similar program fails to stave off economic disaster, then as a final resort the American people, losing faith in their traditions and institutions, will have recourse to revolution. And in revolution, and only in revolution, will the new mores be forged that will make possible a planned collectivistic economic and social order. At present, there is no immediate prospect of a revolution. The faith of the overwhelming mass of the American people in this fifth year of the depression still seems to be as strong as ever in the efficacy of individualism, democracy and humanitarianism. The presidential election of 1932 and the Literary Digest poll of 1934 show that nearly one-third of the voters would like to return to the Old Deal, and a little over two-thirds of them prefer the New Deal. In the recent election the New Deal increased its majority in both houses of Congress. Those Americans who desire to experiment with the

European's programs of socialism, communism, and fascism are only a scattered handful composed mainly of intellectuals and of recent immigrants.

A second objection to the Sumnerian point of view is brought forward by those who believe it is possible "to put over" a collectivistic or any other program upon the American people as by the presential fiat, by cleverly devised propaganda, or by some sort of indirection. Secretary Ickes, recognizing certain difficulties with social planning, naively comments: "The 'engineering of human consent' to use a happy phrase of George Soule, is essential to social planning in a democracy."

This "happy phrase" "the engineering of human consent" seems to imply that the consent of the governed may somehow or other be obtained in much the same way that national advertising determines what cereals shall be eaten for breakfast, or what razors used for shaving, or what brands of tooth-paste purchased.

The facts are probably quite the contrary. Propaganda, although a highly developed art, has rigid limitations. Propaganda seems to have its greatest influence in the field of the folkways and in fashion. It has manifested increasing effects upon dress, food, manners but has diminishing influence upon politics and technology.

There is no doubt, however, of the widespread belief in the effectiveness of advertising and of what is popularly described as "bally-hoo" upon the attitudes and opinions of the public. The N. R. A. was introduced into business and industry with all the showmanship of P. T. Barnum and his circus. This education of the public upon which political parties spend so much time and money does frequently enable the parties to secure a mandate for all sorts of programs but it does not insure the effectiveness of the program because the full consequences of the program have not been adequately revealed.

Nor is this education of the public as effective as the political managers assume. For example, the Literary Digest polls in the last two presidential elections show very little shift in the distribution of voters from the pre-campaign period to the final returns on election day.

It is not the "consent" of the governed that is needed by the

New Deal or by any deal that is seeking to introduce systematic social planning in fields hitherto lacking in rational control. It is rather that each program should be worked out experimentally, pragmatically, and democratically to the end of securing not only a more desirable economy, but also a more desirable human living. In this surer but slower way programs of social planning may obtain a more than temporary public sanction.

A third point in objection, and an intriguing one, is that argument that education may effect a change in the mores without the necessity for a revolution. If it is impossible to educate, manipulate or coerce the *older* generation, the younger generation may be trained in the right way.[13] The Commission on the Social Studies in the Schools was set up by the American Historical Association with a grant from the Carnegie Foundation to outline a program of social science studies in the schools. The Commission fearlessly states its position on the function of education in creating the new social order.[14]

American society during the past hundred years has been moving from an individualistic and frontier economy to a collective and social economy; this trend has steadily gained in momentum, and is strikingly revealed in the contemporary decline of doctrines of laissez-faire and in the launching of programs of planning and control in local, state and national economy.

The emerging economy will involve the placing of restraints on individual enterprises, propensities, and acquisitive egoism in agriculture, industry, and labor and generally on the conception, ownership, management, and use of property, as the changing policies of government already indicate. . . .

The implications for education are clear and imperative: the efficient functioning of the emerging economy and the full utilization of its potentialities require profound changes in the attitudes and outlook of the American people, especially the rising generation—a complete and frank recognition that the old order is passing, and that knowledge of realities and capacity to cooperate are indispensable to the development and even the endurance of American society.

What the Commission on the Social Studies frankly and boldly proposes is that the schools shall deliberately propagandize the children of the next generation in the discarding of the old mores of individualism, democracy, and humanitarianism and indoctrinate them in the new mores of collectivism, social regimentation and social justice.

Waiving for the moment the question of the desirability of this program, there arises the problem of its feasibility. Attempts at indoctrination by the schools will make slow headway against the dominance in society of the present mores. Changes in the mores arise, as Sumner points out, not by the doctrinaire teachings of the intellectuals but out of discussion and reflection by the masses of the people over their day by day experience.

Attempts at present to manipulate the schools as agencies of propaganda for collectivism are certain to embroil our educational institutions in constant turmoil and confusion.

A fourth objection naturally arises from this discussion of the function of education in relation to the mores.

Are the American people to remain forever confined within the limitation of the mores? Must changes that are rational, that are required by economic trends always be circumscribed and hampered by sentiments and prejudices in the *mores* which are, in the nature of things, conservative, if not reactionary, and not subject to appeal by reason?

This was a problem which caused Sumner concern. Although he did not come directly to grips with it, he did by implication indicate a working conception of the relation of education to the mores. He says:

> It is by criticism that the person is protected against credulity, emotion, and fallacy. . . . An educated man ought to be beyond the reach of suggestions from advertisements, newspapers, speeches, and stories. . . . In short, individuality and personality of character are opposites of suggestibility. . . . A highly trained judgment is required to correct or select one's own ideas and to resist fixed ideas. The supreme criticism is criticism of one's self.[15]

To Sumner the chief task of education is not to *indoctrinate* individuals but to train them in the power of criticism. Since the folkways and mores arise and are maintained in suggestion, the training of its members to be critical will be the greatest protection of society against the irrationality of the mores.

Instead of recommending that the schools indoctrinate students for a new social order, the Commission on Social Studies might have proposed that a prime function of education is to develop powers of criticism and self-criticism in the members of society. As John Dewey, an outstanding advocate of a new social order, states: "the first step, as far as subject-matter and method are concerned, is to make sure of an educational system that informs students about the present state of society in a way that enables them to understand the conditions and forces at work."[16] The analysis and criticism of the present system and of all proposed substitute systems should be disinterested and impartial, with conclusions to be arrived at by students and not imposed upon them by teachers.

There remains a fifth objection that has so far been side-stepped. Is the rationality and desirability of a collective society to be assumed?

The Commission on the Social Studies asserts that "in the United States, as in other countries, the age of individualism and laissez-faire in economy and government is closing and that a new age of collectivism is emerging."[17] This conclusion can not be accepted as a statement of fact but merely as an expression of opinion in a report of a Commission which four of its prominent members refused to sign. There is no consensus of economists upon the probabilities of success of a planned collectivistic society. Certainly the present stage of experiments in collectivism in Italy and the Soviet Union do not warrant any final conclusion upon their prospects of ultimate success. Indeed, the results so far achieved in planned economy and in social regimentation in these countries have already had the effect of causing a reaction in the United States against any similar experimentation in this country.

These attitudes, while emotional rather than rational, are partly determined by and partly reinforced by the traditional conceptions in our mores of individualism and democracy. In fact, this American cultural complex against collectivism and regimentation may make possible in the United States economic and social planning of a kind entirely different from that now in progress on the European continent.

Three conditions seem necessary for the success of an American type of social planning.

The first of these is that social planning proceed within the traditional framework of a free society in which the values of individualism and democracy are preserved, nurtured, and extended. The voluntary association of the different groups in our population, consumers as well as producers, with only the necessary minimum of governmental supervision and regulation should be encouraged. Proposals for social and economic security of the individual are to be examined for their value in insuring the welfare of the individual in a free society.

The second prerequisite for the success of an American type of social planning is a complete and thoroughgoing restatement of the conceptions of individualism, democracy, and humanitarianism, a restatement with reference not to the pioneer period but to the realities of an urban and technical civilization.

The third condition for the success of social planning in America is to secure participation of specialists and technicians in the undertaking, but in their proper functioning.[18]

The barrage of attack upon the "brain trust" in Washington brings acutely to the fore the thread-worn topic of how a democracy, with its glorification of the average man, can manage to secure the benefits of the services of the man of special ability who tends to be distrusted by the mass of the people.

At once ludicrous and tragic is the unwarranted alarm sincerely felt by business man and worker alike as they witness the growing aggregation of professors at Washington.

This reaction of the public needs to be taken seriously and not lightly. In the first place, the function of the specialist in government service should be clearly defined. Once this function is recognized and established as a consultative and research service rather than a task of administration and of decision-making, a large part of the difficulty will disappear.

There will, however, remain a more subtle and difficult problem. The popular feeling of distrust of the specialist is largely due to his abstract treatment of human situations. To the average man the expert and the reformer are alike in their disposition to formulate and champion welfare programs without sufficiently taking into account the feelings, attitudes, and wishes of the human beings involved.

The feelings, attitudes, and wishes of people are part of the situation and should also be considered. It is, as we have seen, the sociologist who by training and interest is fitted to deal with the human factors in the situation, that is, with human nature, traditions and customs.

The social scientist attempts too often to deal with human nature as the natural scientist deals with physical nature, namely, as if it were a mechanical thing to be shaped arbitrarily into this or that form as conditions require. But human nature and the customs and traditions of a people are living organisms, susceptible to change, it is true, but change in the nature of growth, which is as much influenced by their already established tendencies as by the conditions of the external environment.[19]

It is important, therefore, that programs of social planning should take account not only of technological or material change but also of our immaterial culture, our customs and our institutions. When the public is assured that all factors in the situation, including those of human nature, are adequately being considered and our traditional American values are being safeguarded, much of the distrust of the expert will be eliminated.

In conclusion it is freely conceded that Sumner's analysis of the role of the mores in social change was largely derived from his study of the static societies of primitive peoples where change took place slowly if at all. Modern societies are not static, but dynamic, technological changes occur rapidly, bringing in their wake numerous social and economic consequences. The question must therefore be considered to what extent and with what modifications Sumner's explanations apply to the more rapid changes in a dynamic sociey.

Sumner, no doubt, perceived in the so-called phenomena of "cultural lag" the inertia of the mores to change.

On the other hand, fashion, propaganda, and social movements characteristic of modern society introduce new factors into the social equation, factors which Sumner did not adequately reckon with. Since Sumner, new devices of communication and transportation, the motion picture, the radio, and the automobile have profoundly altered the social relationships which condition, if indeed they do not constitute, society.

These agencies, much more than economic inventions, have destroyed the pre-existing social order, but it does not follow that they have destroyed individualism and democracy. In fact, the radio, the motion picture, the automobile and the press in the process of creating a new social order are the *very* instrumentalities through which modern democracy can adequately function and the new individualism be realized.

These new devices of communication, essential for the adaptation of democracy and individualism to modern life conditions can be, and have been, perverted for propaganda in the interests of regimentation and dictatorship. Freedom from censorship and from control, whether by the government or by private commercial interests, should be guaranteed not only to the press, but also to the radio and the cinema.

It is perhaps also through these new instrumentalities of communication that the sentiment of humanitarianism can be deflated of its romantic fallacies and brought fruitfully to bear upon the realities of life. Here the sociologist may also be of assistance by substituting realistic description and interpretation of human life for the prevailing sentimental stereotypes.

In conclusion, certain points already made may be briefly summed up as follows:

America, again in the twentieth century, as in the eighteenth, one hundred and fifty years ago, has the opportunity under new conditions of life to work out a democratic solution of the crucial problems which now face all the nations of the world. We are favored with abundant natural resources. We have reached an unparalleled technological development. Our national temperament and character are favorable to a democratic solution to our economic and human problems. To the successful accomplishment of this task the services of all the social sciences, history, sociology and education, as well as economics and political science, may well be dedicated.

19

VALUES AND SOCIOLOGICAL RESEARCH

THE ESSENTIAL DATA for sociological research are values. Albion W. Small was one of the first sociologists to formulate this proposition explicitly. In his words "The history of mankind is the evolution of human values."

Man is the evaluating animal. No other animal has values. Very little of human behavior is, strictly speaking, biological. It is almost all social behavior or conduct. Conduct is a response to the group definitions of behavior as approved or disapproved, right or wrong, good or bad, proper or improper, beautiful or ugly, holy or sinful, sacred or secular, moral or expedient.

Both groups and persons have values. The values of the group are primary since all of us are born into a world of values. Those of the person are therefore derivative. The study of values is essential to understanding the motivations of human action. Values, as W. I. Thomas stated, are "the definitions of the situation" made by the groups of which persons are members.

Every group has its characteristic values, its own definitions of the situation. The old time American family professed the values of authority, duty and permanence. The modern family in this country stresses the values of companionship, personality development and the happiness of its members.

With whatever aspects of human behavior the sociologist deals

Reprinted from *Social Problems* 2, no. 1 (1954) : 16–20, with permission of The Society for the Study of Social Problems. Excerpt from the Presidential Address read at the annual meeting of the Society for the Study of Social Problems, Berkeley, California, 29 August–1 September 1953.

he sooner or later is confronted by values, values in transition, the conflict of values, the redefinition of values and the emergence of new values. Gunnar Myrdal in his study of the Negro in this country found that the values of the American Creed were the central fact influencing changes in attitudes and behavior.

Methods of Research

If the study of values is the central subject of investigation by the sociologist, what is to be his method of research?

Various research techniques are relevant to the study of values. But *which* is the most *appropriate* method? The personal document undoubtedly is the most revealing of values. It may be written by the person himself, be obtained by an interview, or be a recording of a talk. On the basis of intensive interviews, a questionnaire may later be constructed to obtain representative findings that can be statistically analyzed.

The significance of the personal document as a research instrument can hardly be overestimated. It is to the sociologist what the microscope is to the biologist. It makes visible and therefore subject to observation and analysis what otherwise cannot be perceived.

Can Values Be Studied Scientifically?

Two objections have been raised against the possibility of making a scientific study of values. One is that values are mutable. They are ever shifting with changes in the social situation. Furthermore, the study of a value and the dissemination of the research findings often may lead to a change in values. The fact, however, that values may change because of research makes their study all the more imperative and highlights the need for their continuous study.

The second objection refers to the personal and social equation of the research worker. How can a sociologist who has his personal system of values study objectively the values of our own or any society? Some have proposed that he should recognize this limitation and frankly and fully confess his value system when reporting his research findings.

This proposal runs counter to the traditional position that the sociologist, like the cultural anthropologist, should as a social scientist emancipate himself intellectually from the cultural values of his society. As Robert E. Park once said, he should acquire if possible the objectivity of the botanist who studies the potato bug without sentiment or aversion to it. So also a sociologist, as a social scientist, should achieve and receive the same recognition for objectivity. If he is not objective, he is no social scientist. Why need he confess his lack of objectivity? His injection of his own values into his research will be glaringly evident to his peers.

Myrdal's use of explicit value premises in sociological research concerning the Negro problem in America does, however, have merit. He states the advantages of this procedure as follows:

The use of explicit value premises serves three main purposes: 1. to purge as far as possible the scientific investigation of distorting biases which usually are the result of hidden biases; 2. to determine in a rational way the statement of problems and the definition of terms for the theoretical analysis; 3. to lay a logical basis for practical and political conclusions. (*An American Dilemma* [New York, 1944], p. lvi)

Value premises should be selected by the criterion of relevance and significance to the culture under study. Alternative sets of value premises would be most appropriate. (Ibid., p. 1045)

The Role of the Sociologist in Changing Values

If the sociologist studies values, how they originate, develop, and change, should he not be preeminently the one to tell American society what values it should hold? Some sociologists have taken this position, fortunately more in the past than at present. The role of the sociologist is not that of a prophet. The sociologist, however, may if he desires, clarify the issues on the current conflict of changes in values. Take as an illustration the shift in our society from a high valuation on the insitutional to a greater appreciation of the companionship factors holding the family together. Institutional factors are the mores, religion, and law which in the past sanctioned decision-making by the husband, obedience of wife and children, and duty to remain married. The companionship factors uniting family members are equality and mutuality in decisions, love and affection, and the personality development of family members. The sociologist may point out that the institutional values were related to the *rural* situation of one hundred years ago and that the companionship values arise in the *urban* environment with the decline of the family as an economic unit of production. He may also call attention to the fact that many family difficulties which end in the divorce courts are the result of the conflict of these institutional and companionship values. He may present evidence of the trend now in process from the institutional to the companionship family. The true role of the sociologist is to identify, define, and analyze values and relate them to the situations to which they are a response.

Academic Freedom and the Social Scientist

But is there no value that the social scientist holds? As a scientist, and particularly as a social scientist, he is irrevocably committed to one value, namely, freedom: freedom of thinking, freedom of teaching, freedom of research; in short, freedom to seek, to find, and to report the truth.

We are living in a time when these academic freedoms are imperilled. We cannot but be alarmed at bold and brazen attempts to bully university professors, to misinform the public, and to create public hysteria. There are the big lie, the smear, the hit-and-run tactics of Senator McCarthy. There are the unAmerican activities of the House Committee on UnAmerican Activities. There are the star-chamber tactics of Senator Jenner and his senatorial investigating committee on Internal Security that has specialized in intimidating professors, research workers, and students in our colleges and universities.

Social scientists as individuals in their organized societies must stand uncompromisingly for academic freedom. Our teaching and our research must always be held above suspicion of being influenced by any interest group—religious, political, or economic.

In the present crisis the impulse is strong in all of us to do something about it. And in our American culture, doing something is passing a resolution. To this kind of action I am emphatically and unalterably opposed. In the first place it is ineffective. Probably no newspaper would print a report of the resolution. Perhaps a paper might publish it as tending to prove that sociologists are tinged with red.

The *main* reason for my opposition to passing resolutions is that such action is not in accordance with the role of the sociologist. The sociologist should defend academic freedom in a way that expresses his capabilities as a sociologist.

But what contribution can the sociologist make to national security and to the buttressing of academic freedom that no one else can do as well as he? The answer should be self-evident: by research on the values at stake in the current controversy and by the study of the methods now being used to silence professors, to demoralize government workers, to intimidate clergymen, and to throttle newspaper men.

Two great values are at the center of the present controversy. These are freedom and security. Those who are spearheading the attack on freedom of the mind profess to believe that this is necessary to safeguard the internal security of this country. We who are defenders of freedom of thought, of teaching, and of research maintain that freedom of all scientists to investigate and to report their findings is the best guarantee of national security.

Evidence is now available from the experience of fascist, communist, and democratic governments on the relation to national security of thought control on the one hand and freedom of thinking on the other. Research should be undertaken to show whether free expression or suppression of thinking, teaching, and research better promotes national security and defense.

The second project I would suggest for research is an investigation of the methods employed by these investigating committees to determine the loyalty of American citizens. From Martin Dies through Senator McCarthy to Representative Velde and Senator Jenner the method is monotonously the same: guilt by association. This method originated with Mrs. Elizabeth Dilling in her book, *The Red Net Work*. With her own classification of organizations as "red" she included in this volume men and women as devoted to their country, to scientific research, and to human welfare as Jane Addams, Newton D. Baker, Franz Boas, John Dewey, Albert Einstein, Harry Emerson Fosdick, Felix Frankfurter, Sigmund Freud, Mahatma Gandhi, Robert M. Hutchins, Julia Lathrop, Charles E. Merriam, Wesley Mitchell, Lewis Mumford, Reinhold Niebuhr, William F. Ogburn, Robert E. Park, Roscoe Pound, Edward A. Ross, John R. Ryan, Rex G. Tugwell and Thorstein Veblen. So distinguished was the group stigmatized by Mrs. Dilling as "red" that it was regarded as an honor to be cited by her.

Most of the organizations listed by Mrs. Dilling and many others were officially designated as communist-fronts by Attorney General Clark in his 1946 list of "subversive" organizations. In preparing this list, the Attorney General gave none of these organizations a hearing. After the list was released he denied a hearing to organizations which asked to present rebuttal evidence. The preparation and issuance of a list in such a manner was a flagrantly unAmerican procedure.

In his recent appearance before the Committee on UnAmerican Activities Bishop Oxnam pointed out that affiliation with these organizations as a test of loyalty was retroactive, not only before the time they were listed by the Attorney General as subversive but before some of them actually became communist-controlled.

Because of the way in which the list was prepared and the undiscriminating fashion in which it is being used I suggest a study of this list of so-called "subversive" organizations. The study should include (1) a history of each organization, (2) the evidence of infiltration and control by Communists at different periods, (3) the purpose of the organization and how far its activity was or was not in the interests of the United States, (4) the way in which the organization was or was not manipulated to serve Communist purposes, (5) evidence of any activity on the part of the organization to overthrow by violence the United States government, and (6) any evidence about the organization that would lead a loyal American to believe or suspect that it was Communist-controlled at the time of joining it.

These are only two of several research projects that might be undertaken. Others will occur to you. They represent, however, the type of action by sociologists that might make an impact on the public. They are examples of effective rather than futile action.

Conclusion

Summarizing the points made in this paper:

Values are the central subject matter of sociology. The nature of personal and social values and of their modification in response to changes in the situation may best be made in the preliminary stages of research by obtaining personal documents and through the case-study method. There are difficulties in studying values but these can be overcome by recognizing their mutability and by being objective in studying them. Research on values, however, does not qualify the sociologist to be the dictator of values to a society. His role is limited to presenting his findings, analyzing the issues, pointing out trends, and indicating the probable consequences of different courses of action. One value, however, the sociologist as social scientist must defend courageously and vigorously. This value is freedom of thinking, teaching, and research. In defending it, however, he should not take futile action, like passing resolutions, but employ the most powerful weapon at his command. This weapon is not a secret one. It is research upon the issue in controversy and on the methods now being used to stifle and destroy our cherished American values of freedom of speech, of association, of religion, and of research.

Notes

Chapter 2

1. "British Conurbations in 1921," *Sociological Review*, XIV (April, 1922), 111–12.

2. See E. H. Shideler, *The Retail Business Organization as an Index of Community Organization* (in preparation).

3. For a study of this cultural area of city life see Nels Anderson, *The Hobo*, Chicago, 1923.

4. Weber, *The Growth of Cities*, p. 442.

5. Adapted from W. B. Monro, *Municipal Government and Administration*, II, 377.

6. *Report of the Chicago Subway and Traction Commission*, p. 81, and the *Report on a Physical Plan for a Unified Transportation System*, p. 391.

7. Data compiled by automobile industries.

8. Statistics of mailing division, Chicago Post-office.

9. Determined from *Census Estimates for Intercensual Years*.

10. From statistics furnished by Mr. R. Johnson, traffic supervisor, Illinois Bell Telephone Company.

11. From 1912–23, land values per front foot increased in Bridgeport from $600 to $1,250; in Division-Ashland-Milwaukee district, from $2,000 to $4,500; in "Back of the Yards," from $1,000 to $3,000; in Englewood, from $2,500 to $8,000; in Wilson Avenue, from $1,000 to $6,000; but decreased in the Loop from $20,000 to $16,500.

12. Nels Anderson, *The Slum: An Area of Deterioration in the Growth of the City*; Ernest R. Mowrer, *Family Disorganization in Chicago*; Walter C. Reckless, *The Natural History of Vice Areas in Chicago*; E. H. Shideler, *The Retail Business Organization as an Index of Business Organization*; F. M. Thrasher, *One Thousand Boys' Gangs in Chicago; a Study of Their Organization and Habitat*; H. W. Zorbaugh, *The Lower North Side; a Study in Community Organization*.

Chapter 3

1. A distinction made by Professor Robert E. Park.
2. See this volume, chap. 1.
3. See Ernest W. Burgess, ed., *The City: Papers and Proceedings of the American Sociological Association, Twentieth Annual Meeting*, p. 163.
4. One of the committees of the Chicago Council of Social Agencies has a sub-committee which is studying this problem in connection with the subject of uniform districts for social agencies. Several departments of the city government are interested in considering the possibilities of uniform administrative districts.
5. See this volume, chap. 2.

Chapter 4

1. See Louis Wirth, *The Ghetto: A Study in Isolation* (Chicago, 1928), Chapters III and IV.
2. T. J. Woofter, Jr., *Negro Problems in Cities* (New York, 1918), p. 37.
3. For a more detailed analysis of the processes of urban growth, see E. W. Burgess, "The Growth of the City" [this volume, chap. 2].
4. From a manuscript, "The Study of the Negro Family in Chicago."
5. Monroe N. Work, "Negro Real Estate Holders of Chicago" (Master's thesis, University of Chicago), p. 7.
6. *The New Negro* (New York, 1925), pp. 309–10.
7. Carter G. Woodson, *A Century of Negro Migration*, p. 41.
8. Woofter, in *Negro Problems in Cities*, Chapter V, gives a classification of Negro neighborhoods as follows: migrant neighborhoods, large central colonies, middle class neighborhoods, and home-owning neighborhoods.
9. "In analyzing responsibility for depreciation, it is difficult to determine to just what extent the Negroes are there because of prior depreciation, and to what extent present depreciation is due to their presence. At present the fact stands out that Negro occupancy is an unmistakable symptom of depreciation—an indication that the value of property has fallen to their economic level, as well as an aid to depreciation in its last stages." *The Negro in Chicago*, 1922, pp. 204–5.
10. R. E. Moore, *History of Bethel A. M. E. Church, Chicago* (Chicago, 1915), pp. 39–44.
11. *Op. cit.* pp. 78–80.
12. *The Negro in Chicago*, pp. 342–44.

Chapter 5

1. *The City*, p. 97.
2. W. I. Thomas, *The Polish Peasant in Europe and America*.

3. Ernest R. Mowrer, *Family Disorganization* [1928].

4. *Ibid.*, p. 25.

5. R. E. Park and E. W. Burgess, *Introduction to the Science of Sociology*, p. 55.

6. *American Journal of Sociology*, September 1925.

7. *The Journal of Abnormal Psychology and Social Psychology*, XIX, No. 3 (October-December 1924), 230–35.

8. *Human Nature and the Social Order*, p. 152.

9. *Social Organization*, p. 28. See also Ellsworth Faris, "The Nature of Human Nature," *Proceedings of the American Sociological Society*, XX.

Chapter 7

1. Due to the fact that most of our schedules were anonymous, we were not able to contact very many of the subjects for subsequent study.

2. These were eleven "agreement" questions.

3. For computing this coefficient the distribution of ratings was split into two groups so as to include the ratings of "happy" and "very happy" in one group and all other ratings in another. The adjustment scores were split into two groups at the median of the distribution.

4. As would be expected we found that wide differences in educational achievement were associated with low adjustment scores.

Chapter 8

1. Ernest R. Mowrer, *The Family*, Chicago, University of Chicago Press, 1932, pp. 11–19.

2. *The Doctrine and Discipline of Divorce, Restored to the good of both sexes from the bondage of Canon Law and other Mistakes*, London, 1643.

3. Divorce rate for 1937 estimated by S. A. Stouffer and Lyle M. Spencer in article "Recent Increases in Marriage and Divorce," *American Journal of Sociology*, 44, January 1939, p. 552.

4. From *Recent Social Trends in the United States, Report of the President's Research Committee on Social Trends*, by permission of the publishers, McGraw-Hill Book Company, Inc.

5. F. Stuart Chapin, *Cultural Change*, New York, Century, 1928, Chapter 10, "The Cultural Lag in the Family."

6. See L. K. Frank in *Recent Social Trends*, New York, McGraw-Hill Book Co., Inc., Chapter 15, "Childhood and Youth," pp. 751–800; and Florence L. Goodenough and John E. Anderson, *Experimental Child Study*, New York, 1931, D. Appleton-Century Co., Chapter 1, "Historical Beginnings."

7. Best known of these are the Family Counsel, Philadelphia, Mrs. Mudd, director, and the Institute of Family Relations, Los Angeles, Paul Popenoe, director. A list of 32 family consultation centers is given in the *Journal of Social Hygiene*, No. 22, 1936, pp. 34–36. See also Ralph P.

Bridgman, "Guidance for Marriage and Family Life," *Annals of the American Academy of Political and Social Science*, No. 160, March 1932, pp. 144–164; and Mary S. Fisher, "The Development of Marriage and Family Counselling in the United States," *Parent Education*, 3, April 1 and May 15, 1933, pp. 3–9.

8. New York, The Macmillan Co., 1933.

9. Willard Waller, *The Family, a Dynamic Interpretation*, New York, Cordon, 1938, Part II, "Courtship and Interaction," pp. 171–302.

10. See Ira S. Wile, Editor, *The Sexual Life of the Unmarried Adult*, Vanguard Press, New York, 1934; Dorothy Dunbar Bromley, *Youth and Sex*, New York, Harper and Brothers, 1938.

11. "Personality," *Encyclopedia of the Social Sciences*, New York, The Macmillan Co., 1930–35, Vol. 12, p. 86.

Chapter 9

1. Otto Pollak, *Social Adjustment in Old Age*, Social Science Research Council Bulletin 29 (New York, 1948), Ch. 6.

2. William H. Harlan, *Isolation and Conduct in Later Life: A Study of Four Hundred Sixty-Four Chicagoans of Ages Sixty to Ninety-five*, unpublished Ph.D. dissertation, Chicago: University of Chicago Libraries, 1950.

3. Ruth Albrecht, *The Social Roles of Old People*, unpublished Ph.D. dissertation, Chicago: University of Chicago Libraries, 1951.

4. National Conference on Aging, Washington, D.C., 1950, *Some Facts About Aging Population*, Washington: Federal Security Agency, 1950; *ibid., Man and His Years*, Raleigh: Health Publications Institute, 1951; and Ruth Shonle Cavan, Ernest W. Burgess, Robert J. Havighurst, and Herbert Goldhamer, *Personal Adjustment in Old Age*, Chicago: Science Research Associates, 1949.

5. Willard Waller, *The Family: A Dynamic Interpretation* (New York: Cordon Co., 1938), pp. 369–70 and 376–77.

6. Ernest W. Burgess and Paul Wallin, *Engagement and Marriage*, Philadelphia: J. B. Lippincott Co., [1953].

Chapter 10

1. Robert C. Angell, *The Family Encounters the Depression* (New York: Scribner, 1936); Ruth S. Cavan and Katharine H. Ranck, *The Family and the Depression* (Chicago: University of Chicago Press, 1938).

2. Pitirim Sorokin, *Social and Cultural Dynamics* (New York: Harper, 1937), Vol. 4, p. 776.

3. Carle C. Zimmerman, *The Family and Civilization* (New York: Harper, 1947), p. 796.

4. Pitirim Sorokin, *The Crisis of Our Age* (New York: Dutton, 1941),

p. 203; Carle C. Zimmerman and Merle E. Frampton, *Family and Society* (New York: D. Van Nostrand, 1935), pp. 129–30.

5. Joseph Abrahams and Lloyd W. McCorkle, "Group Psychotherapy of Military Offenders," *American Journal of Sociology* 51 (1945) : 455–64.

Chapter 11

1. For an excellent survey of theories of criminality see Bernaldo de Quiros, *Modern Theories of Criminality* (Boston, 1911).

2. P. Näcke, "Lombroso und die Kriminal-Anthropologie von Heute," in *Zeitschrift für Kriminal-Anthropologie* (1897), p. 19.

3. Lombroso in the later editions of *L'Uomo delinquente* concedes the rôle of social factors without, however, quite relinquishing the position that "all criminals are born criminals."

4. Gabriel Tarde, *Penal Philosophy* (Boston, 1912), pp. 218–65.

5. *Ibid.*, pp. 331–42.

6. William A. Bonger, *Criminality and Economic Conditions* (Boston, 1916).

7. Quoted in Bernaldo de Quiros, *op. cit.* pp. 20, 22–23. See also Enrico Ferri, *Criminal Sociology* (Boston, 1917), pp. 125–94.

8. William Healy, *The Individual Delinquent* (Boston, 1915), pp. 15–17.

9. *Ibid.*, pp. 22–26.

10. Cooley, *Human Nature and the Social Order* (New York, 1902), and *Social Organization* (New York, 1909).

11. *The Judge Baker Foundation Studies* by William Healy and Augusta F. Bronner, now published in part, show distinct progress in the recognition of the personal and social factors in delinquency.

12. Robert E. Park and Ernest W. Burgess, *Introduction to the Science of Sociology* (Chicago, 1921), p. 55.

13. For the cases in this paper the writer is indebted to Mr. James Bredin, Miss Mary Dixon, Mrs. Lorraine Green, Mr. Charles S. Johnson, Miss Hazel E. Schmidt, and others. These cases were written in simple, narrative style. The art of sociological case-writing has yet to develop. The argument for precision of analysis in case study has been convincingly and concretely put by Mrs. Ada E. Sheffield in a paper read at the Milwaukee meeting of the National Conference of Social Work and published in the *Survey* of November 12, 1921, under the title "Clue Aspects in Social Case Work." An excellent model for sociologists of analytical description is offered in two case studies of delinquent girls in a paper "Some Problems in Delinquency—Where do They Belong," read by Dr. Jessie Taft at the Pittsburgh meeting of the American Sociological Society and published in the sixteenth volume of its *Papers and Proceedings*, pp. 186–96. See also the *Judge Baker Foundation Studies*.

14. *Report of Cook County Juvenile Court*, 1916.

15. William James made the distinction between objective and intro-spective types in his contrast between "tough-minded" and "tender-minded" persons. Compare also the extroverted and introverted types of personality differentiated by the psychoanalysts.

16. "Personality Traits: Their Classification and Measurement," *Journal of Abnormal Psychology and Social Psychology*, XVI (1921), 7.

17. See Park and Burgess, *Introduction to the Science of Sociology*.

Chapter 13

1. "Concerning Parole in Illinois," The Journal of Criminal Law and Criminology, 26, 1935, p. 515.

Chapter 14

1. Sheldon and Eleanor T. Glueck, *Unraveling Juvenile Delinquency*, New York, The Commonwealth Fund, 1950, p. 196.

2. William Healy and Augusta F. Bronner, *New Light on Delinquency and Its Treatment*, New Haven, Yale University Press, 1936, pp. 121–131.

3. Franz Alexander and William Healy, *Roots of Crime*, New York, Knopf, 1935.

4. Glueck, *op. cit.*, p. 261.

5. *Ibid.*, p. 263.

6. *Ibid.*, p. 264.

7. *Ibid.*, p. 269.

8. *Ibid.*, pp. 162–163.

Chapter 15

1. Delinquency areas are those having rates above the median rate in the series. See *Delinquency Areas*, p. 208.

2. *Delinquents and Criminals, Their Making and Unmaking*, p. 251.

3. *Ibid.*, pp. 290–99.

4. *The Individual Delinquent*, p. 230.

5. *Survey Graphic*, LXIII (February 1, 1930), 506.

6. The report of the librarian of the Illinois State Penitentiary at Joliet gives an average of sixteen books per capita a year for the inmate popula-tion. See A. A. Bruce, A. J. Harno, E. W. Burgess, and J. Landesco, *The Workings of the Indeterminate Sentence Law and the Parole System in Illinois*, p. 160.

Chapter 17

1. Laura Spelman Rockefeller Memorial, *Annual Reports*.

2. Social Science Research Council, *Annual Report of the Chairman*, p. 9.

3. *See* Harriet Martineau, *The Positive Philosophy of August Comte* (London, 1893), for Comte's well-known theory of the historical stages in

the development of the sciences. For more realistic accounts of the origin and progress of natural science method, see also Lucien Lévy-Bruhl, *Primitive Mentality* (New York, 1923); Lynn Thorndike, *A History of Magic and Experimental Science during the First Thirteen Centuries of our Era* (New York, 1923); W. I. Thomas and F. Znaniecki, *The Polish Peasant in Europe and America*, Vol. I (1918), pp. 1–86; and Robert E. Park and E. W. Burgess, *Introduction to the Science of Sociology* (1921), Chapter I, "Sociology and the Social Sciences."

4. The creation of Utopias and their exhaustive criticism is the proper and distinctive method of sociology."—*Sociological Papers* (1906), p. 367.

5. *The Polish Peasant in Europe and America*, p. 3.

6. *Scientific Monthly*, XXIV (February, 1927), 146.

7. The Concepts and Methods of Sociology," *American Journal of Sociology*, X (1904–05), pp. 161–176, and "The Service of Statistics to Sociology," *Quarterly Publications of the American Statistical Association*, XIV (1914), 21–29.

8. *Social Organization*, p. 7, and "The Roots of Social Knowledge," *American Journal of Sociology*, XXXII (1926–27), 59–79. *See also* Ellsworth Faris, "The Nature of Human Nature," *Proceedings of the American Sociological Society*, XX (1925), 15–29.

9. *Elements of Statistics* (5th edition, 1926), p. 7.

10. *Ibid.*, pp. 9–10.

11. *American Journal of Sociology*, XXXII (1926–27), 74–75.

12. *See* Blanche Renard, "Uniform Districting in a Large City for Social and Civic Purposes"; E. W. Burgess, "The Natural Area as the Unit for Social Work in the Large City"; and Helen I. Clarke, "Uniform Area Plan for Chicago City-Wide Agencies," *Proceedings of the National Conference of Social Work*, 1926, pp. 500–514.

13. W. Healy, *The Individual Delinquent*, pp. 15–18; 23–26.

14. *Ibid.*, p. 131.

15. *Descriptive Sociology* (London, 1873–1925).

16. See H. Helson, "The Psychology of Gestalt," *American Journal of Psychology*, XXXVI, 342–70, 494–526; XXXVII, 25–62, 789–823, as well as writings of W. Köhler and K. Koffka.

17. *Welfare Magazine*, XVIII (1927), 143.

18. Quoted by Charles E. Gehlke in a paper, "The Use and Limitations of Statistics in Sociological Research," *Proceedings of the American Sociological Society*, XXI (1927), 141.

19. *See* Clifford R. Shaw, "The Case Study Method," *Proceedings of the American Sociological Society*, XXI (1927).

Chapter 18

1. Sumner, "Sociology," in *War and Other Essays*.

2. With his growing interest in sociology Sumner set for himself the task of the preparation of a monumental work "The Science of Society."

His aim was "to describe and analyze" social, economic, and political phenomena in their orientation within the framework of the customs and philosophy, not only of primitive, but of modern peoples as well. The completion of this task was not encompassed by Sumner but has at last been achieved by the devoted efforts of his friend and disciple, Albert G. Keller. Fortunately, however, Sumner did decide to publish as a preliminary volume his treatise on "Folkways," which may be considered as a statement of his methodology for the larger work.

3. *Folkways*, p. iv.

4. *Ibid*, p. iii.

5. Similarly, the new mores and the fixed findings of the Mexican dialectic prevent Bolshevists in Russia from arriving at any objective understanding of events taking place in the outside capitalistic world.

6. It is true that Sumner spoke of the European *ethos* and denied to the countries of Western Europe an *ethos* or a group character, that is a totality of characteristic traits by which a group is individualized and differentiated from others. He recognized for the Orient a Hindu *ethos*, a Japanese *ethos*, and a Chinese *ethos*. He even refers to the Russian *ethos*. Had his studies of modern European peoples been as intensive as of primitive and Oriental cultures, he doubtless would have conceded to each of them an *ethos* or distinctive group character within the common inheritance of Western society.

7. *Folkways*, pp. 76–77.

8. Frederick Howe.

9. Sumner includes with humanitarianism many tendencies which at first do not seem to be associated with it:

> The philosophical drift in the mores of our time is towards state regulation, militarism, imperialism, towards petting and flattering the poor and laboring classes, and in favor of whatever is altruistic and humanitarian. What man of us ever gets out of his adopted attitude, for or against these now ruling tendencies, so that he forms judgments, not by his ruling interest or conviction, but by the supposed impact of demogogic data on an empty brain? We have no grounds for confidence in these ruling tendencies of our time. They are only the present phases in the endless shifting of our philosophical generalizations, and it is only proposed, by the application of social policy, to subject society to another set of arbitrary interferences, dictated by a new set of dogmatic prepossessions that would only be a continuation of old methods and errors. (*Folkways*, p. 98.)

10. *Folkways*, pp. 180–81.

11. Sumner, as a thoroughgoing individualist never refers to the pathos of protection against criticism of individualism.

12. With the possible exception of Scandinavian countries.

13. This theory was advanced by Plato. See *Ideal Republic*.

14. *Conclusions and Recommendations of the Commission*, pp. 33–35.

15. *Folkways*, p. 24.

16. Pamphlet on "Education and the Social Order," p. 2.

17. Conclusions and Recommendations: Report of the Commission on the Social Studies, p. 16.

18. In England and in Sweden the utilization of the expert in government is of long standing and appropriate patterns have been worked out. England has royal commissions and Sweden has social boards which make investigations and present reports of fact finding bearing upon matters of legislation. The experience of both England and Sweden with their mores of individualism and democracy similar to ours contains much that may be helpful to us as we proceed in social planning.

19. C. H. Cooley has presented an illuminating account of "the tentative process." See *Social Progress*. Chapter I.

Biographical Sketch

BY NANCY GOLDMAN

ERNEST WATSON BURGESS was born on 16 May 1886 in Tilbury, Ontario, Canada, and he died on 27 December 1966 in Chicago. During these eighty years he was an incredibly busy and productive sociologist combining a strong commitment to classroom teaching with a heavy research agenda. In addition, he assumed extensive professional responsibilities as editor of various professional publications and as an elected officer in many organizations as well as serving as a consultant to numerous public and private agencies. He carried on a voluminous correspondence with his students, colleagues, and professionals in other fields and was active in Chicago's civic and reform endeavors.

Burgess was the son of Mary Ann Jane Wilson, descendant of a prosperous Canadian farmer, and Edmund James Burgess, of English parentage, who served as Anglican minister and teacher in Canada and the United States. He had a sister, Roberta, who was less than two years his senior and who remained his confidante throughout his bachelor life.

In 1888, Burgess's family moved to Whitehall, Michigan, and in 1905, to Kingfisher, Oklahoma. He received his A.B. at the small Kingfisher College in 1908 and enrolled that fall in the Department of Sociology at the University of Chicago. Julius Temple Howe, one of his professors at Kingfisher, had studied sociology at Chicago. He made it possible for Burgess, who was obviously intelligent and strongly motivated, to be interviewed by Albion W. Small, chairman of the Department of Sociology at the University of Chicago, and as a result, Burgess obtained a fellowship.

Burgess was a student on the Chicago campus while the "big four"—W. I. Thomas, George Vincent, Charles Henderson, and Albion Small—were active, and from them he received his training, which sought to fuse theoretical concerns with empirical research. He became George Vincent's research assistant, made an outstanding academic record, and was elected president of the Student Sociological Club. He was active as well in the Cosmopolitan Club, an early academic interracial group.

During the academic year 1912–13, Burgess was an instructor in sociology at Toledo University. After the completion of his Ph.D. degree in 1913, he served as assistant professor of sociology at the University of Kansas, 1913–15, and at Ohio State University, 1915–16. During these years he was actively engaged in social survey work. In 1916 he returned to the University of Chicago as assistant professor of sociology and remained at Chicago until his retirement in 1952. He was promoted to associate professor in 1921 and to Professor in 1927. He served as chairman of the department from 1946 until 1951. Even after his retirement, he was for a number of years an active professor emeritus on the Chicago campus, engaged in research and writing.

When Burgess arrived at the University of Chicago in 1916, he took over Charles Henderson's courses on the community and on urban sociology. He was assigned an office close to Robert E. Park in Harper Library, and although Park was more than twenty years his senior, they became close colleagues. They taught a course on introductory sociology, and out of this enterprise they prepared the source book *Introduction to the Science of Sociology*, which was published in 1921 and became the standard treatise and textbook of the "Chicago School" of sociology. In 1925, together with Roderick F. McKenzie, Park and Burgess published the important collection of essays entitled *The City*, which contained Burgess's exposition of the zonal hypothesis of urban growth and his overview of the tasks of local community research. Burgess's interest broadened, and he taught courses on the family, criminology, and social pathology. These courses reflect his vigorous research efforts on the family, community, and social deviance, especially on criminal behavior.

The allocation of an annual grant of $25,000 to the Division of Social Science by the Laura Spelman Rockefeller Foundation matched by local funds supplied an important source of support for Burgess's work. He reached out in many directions for interdisciplinary stimulation and for access to empirical data. In the early 1920s the University of Chicago established the Local Community Research Committee to pursue both historical and sociological research on Chicago local communities; Ernest Burgess served as an active member of this committee, which grew into the Chicago Community Inventory under Philip M. Hauser. When the Chicago Area Project was organized in the 1930s as a pioneer community action program, he was one of the prime movers. His interest led him to seek work with criminologists, welfare and family service agencies, municipal authorities, and a host of other professional associations. He had close contacts with the U. S. Census since he was involved in the early efforts in small area reporting. Ernest Burgess enjoyed these contacts, and they were indispensable in the collection of essential data. At the same time he was supervising and encouraging a large number of graduate students preparing monographs for the "University of Chicago Sociological Series," which became an important element of the heritage of the period of the 1920s and 1930s.

From 1921 to 1930 Burgess held the office of secretary-treasurer and managing editor of the American Sociological Society and thereby had the responsibility for editing its proceedings. In 1934 he was elected president of the society. He served as editor of the *American Journal of Sociology* from 1936 to 1940, and of *Marriage and Family Living* from 1939 to 1950. He was director of the Behavior Research Fund from 1931 to 1939 and in this capacity edited and published a series of research monographs on delinquency and child development. Burgess was also deeply involved in the affairs of the Social Science Research Council during the period in which it served as an important intellectual focal point in the social sciences. First, he was a member of its research committee and a chairman of its key Problems and Policy Committee, next vice-chairman of the council, and then chairman in 1945–46. In 1950, he was elected vice-president of the American

Association for the Advancement of Science. Burgess was both a founding member and president of a variety of professional associations. He was elected president of the Social Research Association in 1942; the National Conference on Family Relations, 1942; the Gerontological Society, 1952; and the Society for the Study of Social Issues, 1953.

Burgess was an organizer of the first White House Conference on Family and Youth and of the first such conference on aging. During World War II, he was a member of various government committees and participated in preparations for postwar reconversion plans. His civic involvement in Chicago was extensive, and he became a member of the Mayor's Committee for Senior Citizens, the Chicago Crime Commission, and the Citizens Association of Chicago. Burgess was a product of the period when University of Chicago professors were members of downtown clubs; he joined the City Club and took part in its extensive discussions of civic reform, a continuous topic in the Chicago metropolitan area.

After his retirement, his interest focused on family research and problems of old age. With Donald Bogue, he was associated with the Family Research Center, later named the Community and Family Research Center.

Ernest Burgess was deeply interested in the problems of social change in Soviet Russia. He studied the language and culture of Russia and visited the country three times in the 1930s. He sought to make use of Soviet materials in his course work long before "comparative sociology" became fashionable. In 1954, he was questioned by the Jenner Committee of the U. S. Senate about his contacts with the Soviet Union. Everett Hughes reported that "Professor Burgess was sternly accused by Senator Jenner who queried him, 'Professor Burgess, is it not true that in 1927 you joined an organization known as the Friends of Soviet Russia?' Burgess replied, 'Oh no sir, that was not in 1927. It was in 1925, and you haven't got the name quite right.' " Burgess was a stickler for facts and not easily intimidated or moved from his convictions.

Leonard S. Cottrell, Jr., at a memorial service for Burgess, assessed his contribution in these words:

Professor Burgess was not a systematic theoretician but an eclectic par excellence. He had no great interest in the elaboration of broad, neatly articulated conceptual systems, but made use of parts of available theories or constructed limited conceptualizations of his own. To some, this meant that Burgess was naïve, atheoretical, and a raw empiricist. They are badly mistaken. He was far from naïve and knew very well what he was doing theory-wise.

Just as in theory so in method, Professor Burgess was pragmatic and eclectic. During the late 1920s and early 1930s, much time was devoted to debating the relative merits of case study and statistical methods for acquiring valid sociological knowledge. Professor Burgess was an astute and skilful user of case-study procedures for collecting and analyzing data on social behavior, an art which unfortunately has languished to the detriment of our discipline. He published several important papers on the subject. However, he had no difficulty in shifting readily to quantitative methods and becoming proficient in the use of those that were relevant to his needs. In his use of different types of methodology, he was by no means a superficial dilettante. He was constantly working toward command of the methods he found promising by taking courses, tutoring, and self-study. In the days of the Park and Burgess Research Seminar, Professor Park would sometimes hurl Jovian thunderbolts at the folly of the statisticians or the misguided Freudians. Professor Burgess, sitting beside him, would nod solemn approval, twinkling the while at those of us who knew of his assiduous study of those forbidden mysteries.

A description of Professor Burgess' scientific orientation would be incomplete if it failed to take note of his strong interest in the application of research findings to the practical problems of society. He was strongly committed to the necessity for freedom of inquiry and the independent pursuit of knowledge wherever the scientist's interest led him; but he was no dweller in the ivory tower. He had a responsible concern for the welfare and development of his fellow human beings. Moreover, he believed and indeed demonstrated in his own work that scientifically sound research could be done in the arena of real life. This was peculiarly characteristic of his research on marriage and the family.

Bibliography of Ernest W. Burgess

"Juvenile Delinquency in a Small City." *Journal of Criminal Law and Criminology* 6 (1916) : 724–28.

"The Social Survey: A Field for Constructive Service by Departments of Sociology." *American Journal of Sociology* 21 (1916) : 492–500.

Columbus Pool Rooms. Columbus, Ohio: Central Philanthropic Council, 1916.

The Function of Socialization in Social Evolution. Chicago: University of Chicago Press, 1916.

Lawrence Social Survey. With F. W. Blackmar. Topeka, Kans.: Kansas State Printing Plant, 1917.

Introduction to the Science of Sociology. With Robert E. Park. Chicago: University of Chicago Press, 1921.

"The Study of the Delinquent as a Person." *American Journal of Sociology* 28 (1923) : 657–80.

"The Pre-adolescent Girl of the Immigrant Type and Her Home." *Religious Education* 18 (1923) : 350–61.

"The Trend of Sociological Research." *Journal of Applied Sociology* 8 (1924) : 131–40.

"Can Neighborhood Work Have a Scientific Basis?" *Proceedings of the National Conference on Social Work.* Fifty-first Annual Session. Chicago: University of Chicago Press, 1924. Pp. 406–11.

The City. With Robert E. Park and Roderick D. McKenzie. Chicago: The University of Chicago Press, 1925.

"The Family as a Unit of Interacting Personalities." *The Family* 7 (1926) : 3–9.

"Topical Summaries of Current Literature: The Family." *American Journal of Sociology* 32 (1926) : 104–15.

"The Natural Area as the Unit for Social Work in the Large City." *Pro-*

ceedings of the National Conference on Social Work. Fifty-third Annual Session. Chicago: University of Chicago Press, 1926. Pp. 504–10.

The City: Papers and Proceedings of the American Sociological Association. Twentieth Annual Meeting. Edited by Ernest W. Burgess. Chicago: University of Chicago Press, 1926.

"The Romantic Impulse and Family Disorganization." *Survey* 57 (1926): 290–94.

"The Contribution of Sociology to Family Social Work." *The Family* 8 (1927): 191–93.

"Statistics and Case Research as Methods of Sociological Research." *Sociology and Social Research* 12 (1927): 103–20.

"The Determination of Gradients in the Growth of the City." In *The Progress of Sociology: Papers and Proceedings of the American Sociological Association.* Twenty-first Annual Meeting. Chicago: University of Chicago Press, 1927. Pp. 178–84.

The Urban Community: Selected Papers From the Proceedings of the American Sociological Association, 1925. Chicago: University of Chicago Press, 1927.

"Who is Grown Up?" *Survey* 60 (1928): 17.

"The Changing American Family." *Religious Education* 23 (1928): 408–15.

"Factors Making for Success or Failure on Parole." *Journal of Criminal Law and Criminology* 19, part 2 (1928): 239–306. Reprinted in *Parole and the Indeterminate Sentence.* Chicago: Parole Board of Illinois, 1928. Pp. 205–49.

"What Social Case Records Should Contain to be Useful for Sociological Interpretation." *Social Forces* 6 (1928): 524–32.

"The Family and the Person." *Publication of the American Sociological Society* 22 (1928): 133–43.

"Family Tradition and Personality Development." In *Proceedings of the National Conference of Social Work.* Fifty-fifth Annual Session. Chicago: University of Chicago Press, 1928. Pp. 322–30.

"Residential Segregation in American Cities." *The Annals of the American Academy* 140 (1928): 105–15.

"The Use of Census Data in Local Community Studies." In *Proceedings of the National Conference of Social Work.* Fifty-fifth Annual Session. Chicago: University of Chicago Press, 1928. Pp. 634–37.

"Is Prediction Feasible in Social Work? An Inquiry Based upon a Sociological Study of Parole Records." *Social Forces* 7 (1929): 533–45.

"The Family and the Person." In *Personality and the Social Group*, edited by Ernest W. Burgess. Chicago: University of Chicago Press, 1929. Pp. 121–33.

"Cultural Approach to the Study of Personality." *Mental Hygiene* 14 (1930) : 307–25.

"Communication." *American Journal of Sociology* 34 (1928) : 117–29; 34 (1929) : 1072–80; 35 (1930) : 991–1001.

"The New Community and Its Future." *Annals of the American Academy* 149 (1930) : 157–64.

"The Value of Sociological Community Studies for the Work of Social Agencies." *Social Forces* 8 (1930) : 481–91.

"Discussion." In *The Jack-Roller: A Delinquent Boy's Own Story*, by Clifford R. Shaw. Chicago: University of Chicago Press, 1930. Pp. 184–97.

Social Backgrounds of Chicago's Local Communities. With Vivien Marie Palmer. Local Community Research Committee, University of Chicago, 1930.

Census Data of the City of Chicago. Edited by Ernest W. Burgess and Charles Newcomb. Chicago: The University of Chicago Press, 1931.

"Editor's Preface." In *Children's Behavior Problems*, by Luton Ackerson. Chicago: University of Chicago Press, 1931.

"Frank Wilson Blackmar, Pioneer Sociologist." *Sociology and Social Research* 16 (1932) : 322–25.

"Comment" on "Relation of Felonies to Environmental Factors in Indianapolis." *Social Forces* 10 (1932) : 511–12.

"Editor's Foreword." In *Behavior Mechanisms in Monkeys*, by Heinrich Klüver. Chicago: University of Chicago Press, 1933.

Census Data of the City of Chicago, 1930. Edited by Ernest W. Burgess and Charles Newcomb. Chicago: The University of Chicago Press, 1933.

The Adolescent in the Family: A Study of Personality Development in the Home Environment. Report of the Subcommittee on the Function of Home Activities in the Education of the Child. White House Conference on Child Health and Protection. New York: Appleton Century Co., 1934.

"Licensed Gambling?" *Journal of Criminal Law and Criminology* 26 (1935) : 307–8.

"Social Planning and the Mores." In *Papers and Proceedings of the American Sociological Association*. Twenty-ninth Annual Meeting. Chicago: H. G. Adair Printing Company, 1935.

"The Prediction of Adjustment in Marriage." With Leonard S. Cottrell, Jr. *American Sociological Review* (1936) : 737–51.

"Chaos in Parole Statistics." *Journal of Criminal Law and Criminology* 27 (1936) : 471–72.

"Protecting the Public by Parole and Parole Prediction." *Journal of Criminal Law and Criminology* 27 (1936) : 491–502.

"Development of Criminological Research in the Soviet Union." With Nathan Berman. *American Sociological Review* 2 (1937) : 213–22.

"Chicago Area Project." With Joseph D. Lohman. *National Probation Association Yearbook* (1937), pp. 8–28.

"Introduction." With Paul S. Schroeder, M.D. In *The Family and the Depression*, edited by Ruth S. Cavan and Katherine H. Ranck. Chicago: University of Chicago Press, 1938.

"Personality Traits of the Brothers." In *Brothers in Crime*, by Clifford R. Shaw. Chicago: University of Chicago Press, 1938. Pp. 326–35.

"Predictive Factors in the Success or Failure of Marriage." *Marriage and Family Living* 1 (1939) : 1–3.

"The Influence of Sigmund Freud upon Sociology in the United States." *American Journal of Sociology* 45 (1939) : 356–74.

"Three Pioneers in the Field of Sex." *Marriage and Family Living* 1 (1939) : 76.

Predicting Success or Failure in Marriage. With Leonard S. Cottrell, Jr. New York: Prentice-Hall, Inc., 1939.

"Symposium on Social Breakdown: A Plan for Measurement and Control —A Sociologist's Point of View." *The Family* 21 (1941) : 296–98.

"An Experiment in the Standardization of the Case Study Method." *Sociometry*, 1941, pp. 329–48.

"George Edgar Vincent: 1864–1941." *American Journal of Sociology* 46 (1941) : 887.

"Memorandum on the Problems of Prediction in the Defense Program." In *The Prediction of Personal Adjustment*, by Paul Horst. New York: Social Science Research Council, 1941. Pp. 159–78.

"Rejoinder to 'The Prediction of Personal Adjustment: A Symposium.'" *American Journal of Sociology* 48 (1942) : 84–86.

The Selection of Cases for Small Social Science Studies. With T. C. McCormick. New York: Social Science Research Council, 1942.

"The Effect of War on the American Family." *American Journal of Sociology* 48 (1942) : 343–52.

"Analysis." In *The American Family: The Problems of Family Relations*

Facing American Youth. Washington D.C.: National Education Association, 1942.

"Educative Effects of the Urban Environment." In *Environment and Education*, by Ernest W. Burgess, W. Lloyd Warner, Franz Alexander, and Margaret Mead. Chicago: University of Chicago Press, 1942.

"Harold Holzer: Abstract of a Longer Life History." With Frederick Elkin. *Journal of Abnormal and Social Psychology* 38 (1943): sup. 48–86.

"Comment." *American Journal of Sociology* 49 (43): 147–48.

"Homogamy in Social Characteristics." With Paul Wallin. *American Journal of Sociology* 49 (1943): 109–24.

"Marriage Counseling in a Changing Society." *Marriage and Family Living* 5 (1943): 8–10.

"Delinquency or Recreation." *National Probation Association Yearbook* (1943), pp. 138–48.

"What the Family Faces in the Light of 1,000 Couples." In *What The American Family Faces*, edited by L. F. Wood and J. E. Mullen. Chicago: The Eugene Hughes Publishing Co. 1943. Pp. 5–11.

"Predicting Adjustment in Marriage from Adjustment in Engagement." With Paul Wallin. *American Journal of Sociology* 49 (1944): 324–30.

"Personal Appearance and Neuroticism as Related to Age at Marriage." With Paul Wallin. *Human Biology* 16 (1944): 15–22.

"In Memoriam: Robert E. Park." *American Journal of Sociology* 49 (1944): 478.

"Postwar Problem of the Family." *Marriage and Family Living* 6 (1944): 47–50.

"Homagamy in Personality Characteristics." With Paul Wallin. *Journal of Abnormal and Social Psychology* 39 (1944): 475–81.

"Contribution of Robert E. Park to Sociology." *Sociology and Social Research* 29 (1945): 255–61.

"Sociological Research Methods." *American Journal of Sociology* 50 (1945): 474–82.

"Family Allowances for Children." With Harvey J. Locke. *Marriage and Family Living* 7 (1945): 12.

"Unemployment and the Family." *Marriage and Family Living* 7 (1945): 87 ff.

"Research." *Marriage and Family Living* 8 (1946): 64–65.

"The Family and Sociological Theory." *Social Forces* 26 (1947): 1–6.

"Family and Sociological Research." *Social Forces* 26 (1947): 14–23.

"Wise Choice of a Mate." In *Successful Marriage*, edited by Ernest W. Burgess and Morris Fishbein. New York: Doubleday and Co., 1947. Pp. 17–31.

"William I. Thomas as a Teacher." *Sociology and Social Research* 32 (1948) : 760–64.

"Discussion of 'The Present Status and Future Orientation of Research on the Family.'" *American Sociological Review* 13 (1948) : 129–32.

"The Family in a Changing Society." *American Journal of Sociology* 53 (1948) : 417–22.

A Selected Bibliography of Sociological Family Research. With A. J. Reiss. Salt Lake City, Utah: University of Utah, 1948.

"The Value and Limitations of Marriage Prediction Tests." *Marriage and Family Living* 12 (1950) : 54–55.

"Predictive Methods and Family Stability." *Annals of the American Academy* 272 (1950) : 47–52.

The American Veteran Back Home. By Ernest W. Burgess and others. New York: Longmans, Green, Inc., 1951.

"Family Living in the Later Decades." *Annals of the American Academy* 279 (1952) : 106–14.

"Selected Bibliography in Marriage and the Family." *Marriage and Family Living* 14 (1952) : 274–75.

"Comment on Lowrie's Dating Theories and Student Responses." *American Sociological Review* 16 (1951) : 843–44; 17 (1952) : 365.

"Louis Wirth, 1897–1952." *American Sociological Review* 17 (1952) : 499.

"The Aims of the Society for the Study of Social Problems." *Social Problems* 1 (1953) : 2–3.

"Social Factors in the Etiology and Prevention of Mental Disorders." *Social Problems* 1 (1953) : 53–56.

The Family: From Institution to Companionship. With H. J. Locke. New York: American Book Co., 1953.

Engagement and Marriage. With Paul Wallin. New York: J. B. Lippincott Co. 1953.

"Social Relations, Activities and Personal Adjustment." *American Journal of Sociology* 59 (1954) : 352–60.

"Economic, Cultural, and Social Factors in Family Breakdown." *American Journal of Orthopsychiatry* 24 (1954) : 462–70.

"Values and Sociological Research." *Social Problems* 2 (1954) : 16–20.

"Can Potential Delinquents be Identified Scientifically?" In *Twenty Fourth Annual Governor's Conference on Youth and Community Service.* Springfield, Illinois: Illinois Youth Commission, 1955. Pp. 33–39.

"Our Dynamic Society and Sociological Research." *Midwest Sociologist* (1955) : 3–7.

"Charles Spurgeon Johnson: Social Scientist, Editor, and Educational Statesman." With Elmer A. Carter and Clarence H. Faust. *Phylon* 17 (1955) : 317–25.

"Seven Significant Changes in Sociology." *Sociology and Social Research* 40 (1956) : 385–86.

"Trends in the Psychological and the Sociological Study of the Family." *Transactions of the Third World Congress of Sociology* 4 (1956) : 14–23.

"The Older Generation and the Family." In *The New Frontiers of Aging*, edited by Wilma Donahue and Clark Tibbitts. Ann Arbor: University of Michigan Press, 1957. Pp. 158–71.

"A Study of the Development of the Child in the Family." In *Studies of the Family II*, edited by Nels Anderson. Göltingen: Vandenhoeck and Ruprecht, 1957. Pp. 17–45.

Aging in Western Societies. Edited by Ernest W. Burgess. Chicago: University of Chicago Press, 1960.

Retirement Villages. Edited by Ernest W. Burgess. Ann Arbor: Division of Gerontology, University of Michigan, 1961.

"Social Problems and Social Processes." In *Human Behavior and Social Processes*, edited by Arnold Rose. Boston: Houghton Mifflin Co., 1962. Pp. 381–400.

Contributions to Urban Sociology. Edited by Ernest W. Burgess and Donald J. Bogue. Chicago: University of Chicago Press, 1964.